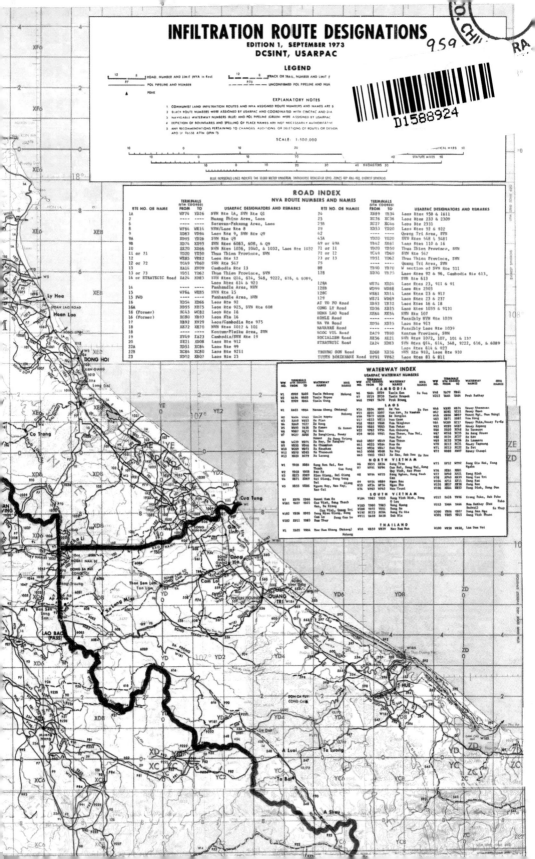

BREAK IN THE CHAIN:
INTELLIGENCE IGNORED

BREAK IN THE CHAIN: INTELLIGENCE IGNORED

Military Intelligence in Vietnam and Why the Easter Offensive
Should Have Turned out Differently

W. R. (BOB) BAKER

CASEMATE

Philadelphia & Oxford

Published in the United States of America and Great Britain in 2021 by
CASEMATE PUBLISHERS
1950 Lawrence Road, Havertown, PA 19083, USA
and
The Old Music Hall, 106–108 Cowley Road, Oxford OX4 1JE, UK

Hardback Edition: ISBN 978-1-61200-991-9
Digital Edition: ISBN 978-1-61200-992-6

A CIP record for this book is available from the British Library

Printed and bound in the United States of America by Sheridan

Typeset by Lapiz Digital Services.

For a complete list of Casemate titles, please contact:

CASEMATE PUBLISHERS (US)
Telephone (610) 853-9131
Fax (610) 853-9146
Email: casemate@casematepublishers.com
www.casematepublishers.com

CASEMATE PUBLISHERS (UK)
Telephone (01865) 241249
Email: casemate-uk@casematepublishers.co.uk
www.casematepublishers.co.uk

Contents

Dedication

It is probable that Bruce Crosby and Gary Westcott at Firebase (FB) Sarge were the first US soldiers killed at the commencement of the Easter Offensive on March 30, 1972. To them both, and all the other servicemen who lost their lives during that oft-neglected chapter of the Vietnam War, this book is dedicated.

It is written also for the 571st Military Intelligence Detachment, 525 Military Intelligence Group. During the tumultuous days of the North Vietnamese invasion, six infantry divisions (with one forming in southern I Corps), three composite artillery divisions, a naval sapper regiment, four independent infantry regiments, and two armored regiments come pouring out of Laos and the Demilitarized Zone (DMZ) into I Corps. Intelligence and support troops of the 571st never once lost sight of nor departed from the mission to provide accurate and timely intelligence to halt the enemy advance.

And to my wife Libbie, who supported me throughout the years it took to write this book and listened to my complaints and small victories, I can only offer my undying love and thanks for your love and for all the years we've had together and all the years to come. And to my children and grandchildren, who have given me joy and their support.

Acknowledgements

I would like to thank the following:

Command historians Lori Stewart at the US Army Intelligence School, Ft. Huachuca, Arizona, and Robert Vanderpool of the Seventh Air Force, Korea, for their kind assistance. Thanks also go to the Center for Naval Analysis (CNA), in particular through Robin Smith's efforts, for finding and allowing me to cite from their May 1974 analysis of the Easter Offensive of 1972, and to the Central Intelligence Agency (CIA), who found four reports from the period, two of which were heavily redacted, despite being over 45 years old.

Dr. William C. Spracher (COL, USA, ret.) has been generous with his time and his promptings have been appreciated. This book has its beginnings as another article for the *American Intelligence Journal*, which Bill (as its editor) would have been happy to receive before it was decided that a book would be able to contain much more of this topic.

Bob Dillon, an IBM employee who worked in Thailand during the war, spent time and effort in explaining *Igloo White* and the role of Nakhon Phanom (NKP) in this program and reviewed this part of the book.

G. Duane Whitman, for his internet site and his recalling of the 407th Radio Research Detachment's operations along the DMZ and his reminder that the first two Americans killed during the Easter Offensive of 1972 were intel types.

Dr. James Willbanks (LTC, USA, ret.), author of many books, including *The Battle of An Loc,* who was wounded at An Loc and was also the chief historian at the US Army Command and General Staff College (USACGSC). He was always free to answer my questions, and his responses were most appreciated. Likewise, Thomas McKenna (LTC, USA, ret.), author of *Kontum: The Battle to Save South Vietnam*, shared his experiences in II Corps. He wrote me, "I encourage you to write a book on this subject. The people, like you, who have first-hand knowledge of what happened, need to write about it so it will be preserved for, and hopefully heeded by, future generations."

The US Army's Center for Military History's Marie Forte found the write-up for the 525 Military Intelligence Group's Meritorious Unit Citation—her efforts are appreciated.

Robert Wells (the S-1 for Team 155) for his insights into the workings of Team 155 and his personal recollections.

Michael Bigelow, US Army Intelligence and Security Command (INSCOM) command historian, for searching for intelligence records that might be available.

My sincere thanks for being able to find a document rapidly goes to Rebekka Bernotat and Genoa Stanford the US Army Armor Center at Ft. Benning, Georgia. Their perseverance is both laudable and appreciated.

Rich Botkin, author of *Ride the Thunder*, who became a friend who always answered my enquiries and is a great humanitarian that few know about.

Gil Hansen, former executive officer (XO) of the USS *Buchanan* (DDG-14), for his narratives on supporting Captain John Ripley and Major James E. Smock at the Dong Ha Bridge, as well as his ship's actions in the region. Likewise, Dean Myers for his assistance in allowing me access to the *Buchanan's* website and other insights.

Richard Baker and Marlea Leljedal at the Army War College guided me through their processes and responded to each and every query that I had the very next day.

Colonel Gerald Turley, USMC, and Robert Destatte, who were both gracious enough to answer questions. Also to Robert for sharing his graphics with me, as well.

Lewis Sorley for his clarifications and assistance, especially *The Abrams Tapes*.

Kevin Morrow attempted to find "old" material from Vietnam in the inner recesses of government archives.

Norman Fulkerson, author of *An American Knight*, was always available to answer questions about his book on Captain Ripley.

The Remnant and Michael Matt for publishing my Christmas 1971 reflection.

Lyman Reid of the National Archives at College Park, MD, for assistance in obtaining documentation in researching this book.

Art B. Cook (formerly 1LT, USA) who piloted the Huey used by our detachment to Quang Tri, rescuing stranded soldiers in the process, for answering a few questions by email.

The Vietnam Center and Archives for their extensive collections.

The US Geological Survey for their efficient and courteous handling of my various map requests.

To Ellen Cousins, a preeminent researcher who was able to find many items I had given up trying to find myself.

To my old European Defense Analysis Center (EUDAC) friends: Terry Rain, Larry Demers, Mike Scharfbillig, Vince Cattera, Barney Davis, Guido Michetti II, and Mike Quirk. We kept mutual friendships for almost 40 years, friendships that first started in Germany in a joint-service assignment. Thanks to the internet, we have kept in touch and mourned those of us who have passed away. Their encouragement, help, and assistance in the preparation of this book is most appreciated.

My thanks to the Vietnam Veterans for Factual History (VVFH) for their assistance and encouragement. I am a member and I am honored to know many who are also proud of our military service in Vietnam and others who also appreciate what we were trying to do there.

Author's Note

The terms Viet Cong (VC) and North Vietnamese Army (NVA) are used throughout this text rather than the more proper National Liberation Front (NLF) and People's Army of Vietnam (PAVN). This choice was made because of the general readership's greater familiarity with the former terms than the latter ones and they are terms that have always been used by me and others.

Introduction

Not sure what to expect, I processed into the 525th Military Intelligence Group (MIG) and was asked where I wanted to go. I could stay in Saigon (with its Olympic-size pool, bowling alley, clubs, and theater), head to the Mekong Delta, or go north to I Corps. Thinking it was somehow a trap or joke of some kind, because the Army never gave options for anything, I chose to go north. The clerk thought I was crazy. Little did I know that I would soon see the enemy in huge numbers. In fact, two NVA infantry divisions (joining a third that had entered three weeks earlier), three composite artillery divisions, a naval sapper regiment, four independent infantry regiments, and two armored regiments came pouring out of Laos and the DMZ and into I Corps at the inception of the Easter Offensive of 1972. Four more NVA divisions would join them soon enough.

This is both a personal story and a professional story. It involves a cast of thousands, yet is also centered on a very few. It is also a story about one intelligence outfit in particular—the 571st Military Intelligence Detachment, 525th Military Intelligence Group. This story also ends with asking questions that may never be answered, for the dead may have been sacrificed by incompetency, egos, or political expediency.

Intelligence is sometimes said to be a contradiction in terms, especially by those who do not do the work. During the Easter Offensive of 1972, it was and it wasn't. At first, the situation looked dire. Others had no idea what was occurring and, as a consequence, showed their incompetence and unpreparedness, despite the warnings. Incredibly, the very senior US leadership was absent, and there were so many who had no idea what was taking place in the far north of South Vietnam for days afterwards, both in-country and at home.

Not all intelligence activity took a holiday, however. In March 1972, there began a flow of indicators that something was amiss. Political VC activity was increasing, and an NVA division, accompanied by two NVA regiments, moved into position west and northwest of Hue. NVA reconnaissance became more active, and desertion within the Army of the Republic of Vietnam (ARVN, pronounced "Arvin") seemed on the increase. All these and more were duly reported, but all had fallen on deaf ears.

The reasons for this inaction are many. The annual Tet holiday, where generals, in-country and at-home, had been warning that enemy actions were expected, came and went meekly by. The all-knowing press took them to task for being wrong.

The Easter holiday was coming and the generals and even the US ambassador had plans elsewhere. But perhaps the greatest reason was that the alarm was being spread by a unit that ran agents (Human Intelligence/HUMINT) throughout the I Corps area. On the whole scale of intelligence, this type of information was always rated last, in favor of intelligence that has been heard (SIGINT) or seen (PHOTINT and TIC), Knowing this, and because the intelligence was of such vital importance, an Intelligence Summary (INTSUM) was created that went to all units daily in I Corps (which became the First Regional Assistance Command/FRAC), Military Assistance Command, Vietnam (MACV), Seventh Air Force, the Navy—including the SEALs, via the Naval Intelligence Operations (NILO)—Central Intelligence Agency (CIA), Defense Intelligence Agency (DIA), etc. Not only was it critical at every level of command to be made aware of what was occurring, but we thought that sending it Ops Immediate (OO in message format—a faster and more critical degree of message urgency) would also almost demand action.

Strikingly similar to the Easter Offensive of 1972 were World War II's Operation *Market Garden* in September 1944 and the Battle of the Bulge a few months later. In both, intelligence was in-hand for the Allies, but the generals thought they knew better. "Ike's intelligence chief, as well as Bradley's, had handfuls of dust that they threw in each other's eyes"[1] leading up to the Battle of the Bulge, and so too with Field Marshal Bernard Montgomery and General Frederick Browning during *Market Garden*.

Though 28 years had transpired since those events, history would soon repeat itself yet again, in terms of intelligence ignored. A look at all the various US intelligence activity occurring before and during the first few weeks of the Easter Offensive of 1972 ultimately begs the question, "What happened?"

PART I

FROM ARMY BRAT TO VIETNAM

CHAPTER I

From Army Brat to Basic Training

Growing up as an Army brat had its own challenges and rewards. My father was an enlisted man during a time when making rank was very slow and often political. He was a combat engineer for most of his career. Ultimately, my mother gave birth to seven of us, four boys and three girls. As the oldest, I had to quickly mature and often take care of my siblings. There were and are times that only a military family can truly appreciate. Making an end-of-month paycheck stretch until the next month was very difficult, especially as the family grew in number. Moving every couple of years, new schools, new friends, new environments, all combined to make life pleasant, terrible, or somewhere in-between.

My earliest recollection of the Army was of 1958 at Patrick Air Force Base (AFB), Florida. We had moved there from Toledo, Ohio, and the two places were as different as night is from day. Though not very well known, the Army once controlled Cape Canaveral, until the National Aeronautics and Space Administration (NASA) took it over, and Army soldiers with dependents lived on the air force base. I could see the end of the airstrip from our quarters. I also remember a few launches at Cape Canaveral where the missile went up a few thousand feet and then plunged back down into the water. This happened close to an area where we could park waiting for my father at the end of his day. I also remember being at the beach, across the causeway from the housing area, seeing missiles flying southward, gaining altitude to reach space. We even went through a hurricane. In spare moments, we caught snakes and various insects behind our quadruplex. Ironically, a married sister of mine and her Air Force husband lived in the same quarters area 25 years later.

From Florida, we went to Huntsville, Alabama, where my father was non-commissioned officer (NCO) in-charge of the Test Lab. On the way, I remember stopping for lunch at a hamburger place. It was my first introduction to how different the races were treated. Seeing signs delineating "Negro" and "White" over the bathrooms and water fountains, I remember asking my mom what "Negro" meant and why there were different signs. I never saw anything of the sort in any military facility and my mom explained what this all meant. She made it clear that this was wrong and needed to be changed. Housing on military bases and schools were desegregated and I never encountered this overt prejudice again, thankfully.

After Alabama, it was on to Kaiserslautern, Germany, until the Berlin Wall went up on my birthday on a Sunday in 1961. I remember my father (and others) being called in to work and returning with an M14 rifle, which was kept by the door with his web gear for a week or so, something that had never occurred before. We left for the United States a few months afterwards (minus my father), heading for New York City via Bremerhaven on the troopship SS *General Patch*. Of course, the ship ran into a mid-Atlantic storm. As the oldest of the children, I was always sent to the dining room on the opposite side of the ship to get crackers and lemons. I was allowed to traverse some engineering spaces in the middle of the ship, so I wouldn't have to take the long way around. I vividly remember the seasickness and waves that seemed a lot taller than the ship itself.

Staying in the proximity of my father's parents in Albuquerque, New Mexico, for almost two years was generally boring, as I remember, except for spectacular sunsets, getting lost walking home after the first day of school, Boy Scouts, and having to dance with a girl for the first time in 6th grade. Then to Aberdeen Proving Grounds, Maryland. This was a time, during my middle school years, that forged some of my favorite memories. The local high school was a regional school for 7th–12th grades, and, to my eyes, it was a huge building. I remember choking on a speech I had to give to the entire school and our 8th grade trip to Washington, DC. We lived close to the Chesapeake and I remember going fishing with a friend in a rowboat. This school was also where I heard, over the school's public address system, that President John F. Kennedy had been assassinated.

I had to cycle past the outdoor tank museum to my first job—boxing groceries at the post commissary. Because it was an Army proving ground, there were a lot more weapons to see. I remember an Armed Forces Day demonstration in which a Cobra gunship came screaming in behind the grandstands and let loose its miniguns for the crowd. I used the bicycle to see my first girlfriend. At this time, new groups from England were also making the headlines (The Beatles, Rolling Stones, etc.) and they heavily influenced our hairstyles.

We then went westward again to Fitzsimmons Army Medical Center in Denver (Aurora), Colorado, for a couple of years. It was at the high school, which was only one year old, where I learned to like reading. Other memories are of the wrestling team, squashing into a Nash Metropolitan (with beer in the trunk), competing with soldiers to work at the post commissary, and fast cars.

My last two years of high school were spent dodging tornadoes in Salina, Kansas. The old Shilling AFB had become a city airport, with most of the buildings and housing area transferred to the Army. As it became a sub-post of Ft. Riley, the post housing called Shilling Manor became a "Home of the Waiting Wives." Servicemen of all the US Armed Services (officer and enlisted) bound for Vietnam could drop off their families at this post until their tour was completed. It was a challenge to keep teenagers occupied and out of trouble, but it seemed to work—everyone in the same boat, as it were. Though families were safe, not everyone could escape "The Visit" that brought an officer and a chaplain to the door—it could be a very sad place. A nearby Army family and the family of a US Navy pilot come immediately to mind when I think of this, especially every Memorial Day.

There was no choice but to learn to drive a car before my father left for Vietnam the first time in 1967 (1970 for the second time). I also took on volunteering to coach football, baseball, and basketball for the younger kids of the post. The Army must have seen some merit of employing teenagers, as they paid us after the first year.

As I neared high-school graduation, I remember former students returning from Vietnam speaking to the class. This usually included displaying their wounds, if they had any. For teenagers from the post, the impact was deeper than they would publicly admit. The realization that their fathers might return with such a wound, or worse, had an unspoken effect on us all. Most of us also expected to be in one of the services. Almost all of us knew that college would have to wait, and we were raised to believe that country came first and we had an obligation to serve, if called—Jane Fonda and college kids burning their draft cards were not really the "true" America to us. Unfortunately, the TV branded everyone of a certain age as being a hippie and antiwar, but it wasn't so.

My youngest sister was born in the civilian hospital in Salina in 1967; her twin sister didn't survive but an hour. As the oldest of seven, I had to inform my mother (and my siblings) about the twin and make arrangements to have my father return from Vietnam. My father was able to stay at Schilling afterwards for a couple of years until he again returned to Vietnam in 1970.

A short time later, after I moved back to Albuquerque, I received a letter to take an Armed Forces physical, courtesy of the local draft board. Knowing that this meant that I was potentially going to be drafted, the Selective Service Lottery of July 1, 1970, held my rapt attention. Watching each number being picked on television until my birthday was chosen—a rather low number of 58—it was felt that anyone who had a number less than 100 was certainly going to be chosen. So, I decided to enter the Army for three years with a choice of Military Occupational Specialty (MOS), instead of two years and no choice of anything, if drafted.

Entering the Army upset my grandfather—he had tried to have his son and me enter the US Navy, as he was a retired Navy captain. For years growing up, my grandfather asked me to read Navy books and he would talk glowingly about naval service. He would never mention the Navy again after I enlisted.

I remember how an Army master sergeant had taken an interest in my career choice at the recruiting center. I had the distinct impression that he guided me into intelligence, not only based on my general aptitude (GT) score, but also because my father was in Vietnam at that time, perhaps because he saw something in me that I didn't—I'll never know for sure. He could tell I was an Army brat from all the posts I had lived at; all residences were required to be listed on one of the forms.

I vividly remember going through another type of physical after enlisting, I guess to make sure there were no changes in your health since the first medical. We were nearly done and still in our skivvies, with a number on a string around our necks, when we were all lined up in a long-walled room. Suddenly, a door to my left slammed open and two US Marines entered. A Gunnery Sergeant (gunny) proceeded to troop the line, periodically pointing to some of us, saying, "You!" When he had passed us all, he turned and shouted, "All those who I pointed to, take a step forward. Welcome to the United States Marine Corps!" Those who were picked (not me) were nothing short of being stupefied. The corporal who had accompanied the gunny through the door had written each number on a clipboard, which he called out. They all left, stage right.

It was now off to basic training at Ft. Ord, California. Unfortunately, after a week, Ft. Ord became full and the Army, in its wisdom, literally sent the whole barracks of soldiers cross-country to Ft. Jackson, South Carolina. We had left sunny California and, of course, it was raining in South Carolina when we arrived at 0200 (2 am). We were put on a bus from the airport to the post, and it was after 3am when we finally arrived. Instead of moving us inside (which would have made sense, especially since there were so many drunken trainees), the drill sergeant—extremely tired and irritated as he was—asked us, "Where are your raincoats?" Almost every one of us had packed our duffle bags with the heavier and bulkier items on the bottom—guess where the raincoat was? "Didn't anyone tell you stupid bastards to wear a raincoat when it's raining? Put 'em on!" the drill sergeant commanded. Of course, we had to comply. We were already wet and all our dry clothes became soaked as we emptied our duffle bags onto the pavement. After everyone was properly dressed, we marched into a building about 50 yards away. We all had similar thoughts, "Welcome to the Army … it's going to be a long few months."

Basic training was an interesting experience, and I have a collection of disparate memories:

- There were guys who had lived in the backwoods of the South, and had never had immunization shots before, who would pass out when they received them.
- I became an expert with an M16 rifle; it helped that I had shot .22 rifles in the basement of my high-school shooting range. A draftee in a neighboring company actually wanted out of the Army so bad that he pointed his M16 at his foot and fired it.
- The gas chamber, where we had to take off our gas masks until the drill sergeant told us to put them on again. They pumped in tear gas into a small one-room hut, which made everyone vomit before he gave us the order to put them back on.

- Cadence calls, which kept the formation in-step with each other, offended the post commander's wife because they usually were profane. Drill sergeants were supposed to stop using them, but they "never got the word."
- A "comfort caddy" drove between the companies, coincidently after each payday. Strictly against so many rules, prostitutes could quickly sell their wares and would never stay in one place very long.
- Pugil sticks and the "Spirit of the Bayonet" were occasional parts of a curriculum designed to teach self-defense without using a rifle. Two opponents were selected or volunteered and put on protective clothing and a helmet and give a pugil stick consisting of two pads of material on both ends of a stick. Bayonet training was being scorned by outside military groups as too violent and the Army didn't seem to want to tell these same people that it was necessary for a soldier's self-protection.
- Two guys waited to jump in the "rack" (bed) with each other just as the drill sergeant entered the barracks—they wanted out of the Army and they were quickly accommodated.
- There was a detail of guys who stoked coal for the entire barracks to be able to have hot water in the morning. The water was usually warm, at best.
- Patrolling was an interesting experience. We were all called upon to lead a patrol during the day and at night, trying to evade the machine guns that fired BBs at us from concealed locations, which included trees.
- We were always on the lookout for our company's executive officer (XO; a new 2nd lieutenant), who always found a reason to put any trainee into the "dying cockroach" position. Laying on your back and then arching it until you were told to stop was a torture which the 2nd lieutenant seemed to enjoy. Our drill sergeant never had us do it. Whenever we saw the butter-bar (a term for a 2nd lieutenant) coming towards us, we immediately went another way to avoid him.

Finally, there was our "campout," technically called a bivouac, which deserves a little more explanation. After completing our daily training at the rifle range, we marched to a place where we would bivouac for the night. En route it started to snow (it hadn't snowed in Ft. Jackson in years, we were told). We set up the tents, dug a small trench around each of them for drainage, ate C-rations, and proceeded to freeze our tails off. Asking for volunteers for the night's guard duty, one of the drill sergeants said that the guards would be able to sleep in the heated tent. I knew enough never to volunteer, but I was freezing, and I raised my hand and moved inside. Awakened for the 0300 (3 am) shift, it was bitterly cold, and I was stuck out in the middle of nowhere where I couldn't see anything but trees and snow. I knew my General Orders and that there would be a drill sergeant checking on all the guards, but my teeth were rattling. Sure enough, about a half-hour later, I heard footsteps crunching the snow headed for me.

"Halt, who goes there?" I challenged. The footsteps kept coming, so I repeated myself, though louder this time (saying to myself that this was getting to be asinine). The idiot still kept coming, to which I said, "You stupid son-of-a-bitch, I said halt!" Just for emphasis, I let the bolt of my M16 go forward, which chambered a live round! (Why in heaven's name they gave us live rounds, I'll never know.) The drill sergeant stopped dead in his tracks and we went through the rest of the drill. Afterward, he told me it was a good thing I did what I did. To which I replied that I was glad he stopped, too. He asked me if I would have actually fired at him. I replied that I would probably have fired over his head first. He gave me a quizzical look and he left me to shiver for the rest of my guard tour.

Another instructive incident was being thrown off a rifle range, not a good thing by any means. We had gone through most of our M16 training, so much so that it was almost routine to be alone in a foxhole with the target located downrange from us. You had to wait for the range officer/NCO to give his okay to fire your weapon and it was said like this: "Ready on the right. Ready on the left. Ready on the firing line. Commence …." The very next word was "firing." Everyone knew the magic word, everyone was sighted on their individual target, and everyone was waiting for this word. Everyone except me. I squeezed off a round, then it dawned on me that no one else had fired. I froze, hoping and praying that the smoke coming from the barrel of my M16 would quickly disappear. Uh … nope. I hadn't been called so many obscenities ever before—emanating from the loudspeaker for all to hear! My platoon sergeant slid into the foxhole next to me and told me what a "dumb shit" I was. I agreed with him, and he had me remove the magazine of my weapon, eject the automatically inserted round, take out the magazine, and check it to make sure it was empty. The range officer/NCO hadn't let up on his tirade during this whole time on the loudspeaker, so everyone could hear about my lack of family pedigree, etc. Luckily, this wasn't the qualifying round for scoring, but I spent the rest of the day on the range picking up shell casings and being intermittently dressed down for being a "dumb shit," which I agree, I was. (I did later qualify as an expert on the M16.)

One last basic training event occurred a few days before graduation. A few soldiers from the 82nd Airborne at Ft. Bragg, North Carolina, came over to talk with us about joining the airborne. The $50 in jump pay added to $134.40 in base pay just wasn't going to hack it for me. An airborne corporal asked if I was just chicken, to which I replied that it was just plain stupid to jump out of a perfectly good airplane. I guess no one had ever told him that before because he was speechless. Our drill sergeant had alerted us to their idea of applying pressure to join. He was a great guy and didn't have "wall sessions" (where drill sergeants, to impress a point he was making, would throw you against a wall—of course, it wouldn't be done in front of anyone else) with his trainees. We all felt lucky to have had him as our drill sergeant.

CHAPTER 2

US Army Intelligence School

The whole process of entering a career in the intelligence field gave one a sense of exclusivity. The extra testing, the multiple and periodic warnings to everyone about not bringing disgrace to our uniform and our branch, all gave us a sense of elitism and responsibility. It didn't hurt that our class advisor was a US Marine Corps (USMC) Gunnery Sergeant, just in case some "positive reinforcement" was necessary.

Outside of the purely intelligence workplaces, the rest of the Army could care less about who you were or what your job was—your rank automatically established your intelligence, abilities, and qualifications, and whether you had to do the work that no one else wanted to do (as the well-known expression has it, "shit rolls downhill"). It was not unusual to be told as a group, however, that we were the "best and the brightest" and we tried to live up to the expression. I would notice later that everyone had enlisted for a type of intelligence (combat intelligence, agent, area specialist, etc.), the few draftees that one encountered undoubtedly had at least some college experience, and there were no branch transfers either (i.e., changing from another field, such as infantry, into intelligence) until the war in Vietnam ended and the "Volunteer Army" began (and things were never to be the same again).

I was in the first intelligence class to go through Ft. Huachuca, Arizona, since the Intelligence Center and School moved from Ft. Holabird, Maryland. The class seemed to be delayed a week or two as those of us who were present moved wall lockers, foot lockers, desks, and all sorts of furniture into the World War II-era barracks, which only differed from the ones at Ft. Jackson in that the boilers weren't coal-fired. I knew generally what the course was going to attempt to teach us and I found time to read about tactics and strategy. Works by Sun Tzu, Patton, B. H. Liddell Hart, and others all became part of my personal readings. Some I had read before beginning 10th grade, as I had a course in English in which all I had to do was to read books (approved, of course) and compose book reports. How units moved, envelopments, military crests, and a host of other terms and examples became absorbed and understood. Some of these examples were also taught in our intelligence analysis classes. Ft. Huachuca was, at least at the time, among the most boring places in the world for most of us. Lots of sand and desert expanses made life dull and dreary—books helped to pass the time.

There were all sorts of intelligence classes and instructors at the school. Having experienced interrogators and other intelligence types talk about what they did in the field helped everyone to understand the breadth of the overall intelligence field. We also had a USMC captain as an instructor, who tended to be very blunt and to the point, far more than the other instructors. He gained our undying respect and admiration when he "locked the heels" (put them at attention and gave them a good chewing out) of a few Army Special Forces soldiers who started to push others around during a morning break; this was our first introduction to the mutual dislike of the two military branches. We also noted that we were being trained alongside others who were there for the same course or other specialized training, such as four or five Marines, a SEAL team, and Army Special Forces soldiers. In fact, the day the SEALs arrived we had a rare morning formation in which the company commanding officer welcomed them to the Intelligence School. The (no neck) SEALs had a great laugh when the company commander's voice broke a few times as he attempted to project his voice. As I was fairly close to them in the formation, I heard them chuckle when one of them noticed a company commander's Ranger tab on his uniform, but without any Vietnam service. The Marines who shared our barracks were good guys. With so many of them around, it seemed, we became a fairly united group of guys. There was one thing, though—we had no idea why they insisted on ironing their "covers" (caps). It remained a subject of good-natured ribbing for the entire time we were together.

As for the course, we learned a variety of things in class: creating topical files; the intelligence cycle; the types of intelligence reports; and basic ways to look at the battlefield (for example, if enemy artillery had moved or was moving forward, it is a good indicator of a forthcoming attack), to name but a few. Our Marine captain instructor, assisted by our class adviser, taught us about the more practical aspects of the war in Vietnam and what we might need to know. For instance, we learned how to determine how far out an artillery shell came from by measuring its angle and impact point—a SHELLREP. By using multiple and recent crater ellipses and taking a bearing with a compass, we could use a small-scale map to triangulate the bearings to the artillery firing point. It seemed apparent that the Intelligence School had, at some time in the near past, shifted gears and returned to teaching conventional warfare. I was most grateful to our USMC instructors for the practical and unconventional warfare aspects and, as I was to have thrust upon me, conventional warfare intelligence had applications in what was to come.

Most important, however, there were two main things that drove the Intelligence (alternately also known as an Order of Battle or OB) Analyst class: a perfect knowledge in reading a Universal Transverse Mercator (UTM) map and scoring well in "The Barn." Map reading was considered so important that classes at night were offered. Every symbol, every measurement, how to convert the UTMs to geographic coordinates, where an enemy artillery position might likely be positioned—everything was drummed into our heads. Everyone went to the night classes. Frankly, there wasn't much else to do.

"The Barn" was held up more or less as the graduation exercise. Maps of East and West Germany walled a large room. Everyone was assigned to a 3- or 4-person team. The scenario was that the Soviet forces had begun to invade West Germany from East Germany and we were the G-2 (intelligence) section of a US division opposite the Fulda Gap. We were to compile Essential Elements of Information (EEIs) and Other Intelligence Requirements (OIRs) for the commander. In what became individual team requests for certain information, we would take a pre-measured strip of paper to one of the referees and would be quizzed as to why we needed this particular item of information. The requests had to be timely, make sense, and had to be something appropriate to the current OB and tactical situation. This game had been played often enough that if you asked the right questions, there were pre-printed answers given in return. The questions and answers became the points scored for each team, which were also posted on a chalk board for all to see.

US Army Field Manual 30-5, *Combat Intelligence*, served as our guide for this all-day class final that brought together everything that we had learned. Towards the end of this long, but very eventful class, I convinced my team to go along with me in asking for particular types of weather information from the referees. I submitted a slip of paper for specific and certain weather information. The referee, not recognizing what I was angling for, asked the reason for this information and I deliberately hemmed and hawed. He started to get angry and asked once more, to which I replied that this type of information was specifically needed for the commander if he wished to use tactical nuclear weapons. That did it; the eruption was loud and profane! A hush immediately fell across the class as the referees joined in asking if I had lost my "fucking mind?" I replied that this information was necessary for the Collection Plan (a compilation of information needed and sources tasked) and should be available for the commander, especially given the number of Soviet divisions attempting to pour through the Fulda Gap. They were speechless and the Army major running this event said that no one had ever asked this before in the history of The Barn. Telling me to return to my team, I first asked if I wasn't right to ask for this information—very grudgingly, they agreed it was. This single question all but concluded The Barn exercise for our class.

Today, what was a 96B Military Occupational Specialty (MOS) is now a 35F MOS. The training time is double (at 16 weeks and three days) what it was when I went through Ft. Huachuca's first course in 1971. The Barn has been replaced with a nine-day program simulating a threat environment using the Distributed Common Ground System-Army (DCGS-A). I'll admit to not being enamored with the sound of any "wired" Army intelligence system, because I can imagine being often second-guessed and inundated by many others with emails. And what if there is no power or communications available and a battery runs out? Having experienced and been part of many different types of intelligence, so much depends on the sources, types, and analysis of the intelligence received to make any kind of deductions.

I also remember a classmate who tried to beat "the odds." It was well known that this classmate had applied for Vietnam many times since he arrived; each time his request was rejected, and he would quickly put in another application. I remember well when our gunny read off all the names and assignments during our last day of class. After reading five or so names, he said it would be easier just to read off the names of everyone who *wasn't* going to Vietnam. Only about four people had their names announced and our class "volunteer" was not among them. I remember looking over at him and seeing the proverbial light bulb go on in his head when he realized he was going to Vietnam with the rest of us. He went red-faced, then pale, and started to fidget almost uncontrollably. The entire class watched and started to laugh and the gunny asked those nearby why everyone was laughing. Someone told him and I remember the gunny turning away so we couldn't see him laughing, too. (I was later told by my classmates in Vietnam that our "volunteer" was working in the NCO club at the MACV Annex.)

Having scored first in the course, I was asked to stay at the school, with an increase in rank. I initially accepted, but after a week I had second thoughts. We were trained for combat operations and I would have no such experience by staying at Ft. Huachuca. I also missed "the guys" and how we "belonged" together. It took another week to change my orders again, but everyone understood my rationale and wished me luck.

CHAPTER 3

On to Vietnam

If you wish for peace, understand war—particularly the guerrilla and subversive forms of war.

—B. H. LIDDELL HART

I flew to Albuquerque, New Mexico, to see a friend of mine from high school and we ended up taking a tent with us in his VW Bug to Salina, Kansas, where my family was. Knowing that I would probably have to drive jeeps and other vehicles in Vietnam, I learned to drive the VW Bug, which had a stick-shift. In an odd twist of fate, my father was on his 30-day leave returning from his second tour to Vietnam as I was headed for my only excursion in August 1971. We got to Salina and found my parents had recently departed and their next duty station was to be at Ft. Bliss, Texas. I had no idea where they were spending their leave, so I called Ft. Bliss every couple of days to see if they were there yet. We didn't catch up with each other at Ft. Bliss, until three days before the end of my 30-day leave.

At the Replacement Center in the Oakland Army Depot in Oakland, California, they actually tried to put soldiers on KP (kitchen police) the first day there at 0400. *What'll they do if we don't show up at 0400? Send us to Vietnam?*—I slept in instead. After a couple of days of listening for your name to be called twice daily, I was finally given a date and time to leave. Those who were called moved into what looked like a converted commissary storage facility that had a lot of bunk beds, pinball machines, free food, TVs, radios, and phones. The building was locked until our departure a couple of days later—I guess they didn't trust us.

Finally, the day arrived and we waited for the buses to take us to Travis AFB. It was during this time that an unexpected event occurred. All of us were dressed in combat fatigues and most of us were sitting on the floor with our duffle bags, not saying a word, with faces that showed the realization of what our forthcoming airplane ride meant, when someone brought out his cassette player and played the song, "I Feel like I'm Fixin' to Die Rag," by Country Joe and the Fish. The senior NCOs who only recently joined us in waiting for the buses were not amused, but they were greatly outnumbered, so they didn't say a word.

After an unscheduled stop from Travis to Alaska for gas (where a soldier actually went "over the hill"—Absent Without Leave (AWOL)—in combat fatigues, no less), and a planned fuel stop in Japan, we arrived in Bien Hoa, Republic of Vietnam. When the chartered civilian aircraft stopped near the gate and everyone deplaned, I distinctly remember reaching the door of the plane when the heat, humidity, and smell stopped me dead in my tracks. By the time I walked down the flight of steps to the tarmac, I felt certain that every mosquito in the country had bitten me and I was slapping myself silly trying to kill as many as I could (and I was losing).

From Bien Hoa Air Base, we were bussed to the 90th Replacement Battalion in Long Binh, where a sign hung over the gate stating that the life expectancy of a 2nd lieutenant was delineated in an unremembered but very short number of days, hours, and minutes. After a day of processing and the night sleeping outside on a board (if you had seen the size of the rats in the rafters of the barracks, you'd understand why), I was assigned to Headquarters (HQ), 525th Military Intelligence Group, located at the MACV Annex.

The Annex was a startling, remarkable sight. Its Olympic-size swimming pool, little library next to it, a movie theater, bowling alley, and officer and NCO clubs were all entirely unexpected and seemed almost embarrassing to find in a war zone. I quickly made another discovery. I was about two weeks behind the rest of the class in arriving in Vietnam, so they were all settled in before I got there. I found that all but two persons of my intelligence analyst class who were sent to Vietnam were assigned to our group HQ and the MACV HQ (sometimes called Pentagon East). A couple of classmates were assigned to the MACV Tank (where various intelligence functions were accomplished), which proved to be a stroke of luck that I was able to take advantage of later.

I never could get used to the hooch maids just walking into the bathrooms as they pleased. I appreciated that they were local hires and cleaning the restrooms was their job, but I had to get close-into a urinal more than once and it was certainly something I never got used to.

After processing into the group, I was actually *asked* where I wanted to go! At first, I thought they were kidding because this was just never done. In reply, I inquired where the action was currently occurring. I was told that down south in the Delta and up north in I Corps were probably the two most active areas. I chose the latter, figuring that the mosquitoes and humidity would be worse in any watery area. I soon found out that wherever you were temperatures were almost always in the 90s Fahrenheit, at least, during the day and there was 100 percent humidity, so it didn't really matter where you were in Vietnam (except for monsoons—they occurred at different times in South Vietnam).

The assignment clerk (after asking me repeatedly if I was sure I didn't want to stay in the HQ) and my classmates just couldn't understand my decision. I explained that as long as I had to be there, I actually wanted to do something. They all thought

I was crazy, but somehow "suffering" by the poolside just didn't quite seem right. I laughingly told the clerk that I wanted to earn my $65 in Hostile Fire Pay. The other person who didn't stay in the Saigon area, my best friend in Intel School, Chris Petrakis (who would repeatedly play music by The Who every chance he could), was assigned to the 11th Cavalry, I was told. I could never track him down there or afterwards.

The next day, I was aboard a C-123 headed northbound for Da Nang, also known as Rocket City. I stayed strapped in against the plane's side as someone became airsick—the twin-engine aircraft seemed very susceptible to air turbulence. Trying a little "mind over matter," I wondered if my decision to go north was the right one, as I somehow held down the gag reflex.

By the end of the year (1971), there were 158,000 US soldiers in Vietnam. President Nixon announced 70,000 more troops would be removed by May 1, 1972. This number tumbled during the Easter Offensive to only 24,000 at the end of 1972. As 525th MI Group was one of the very last units to leave Vietnam in 1973 and though "drops" (early departures from the usual one-year tour) continued, some structure had to be maintained to continue functioning as an intelligence unit for US and South Vietnamese forces.

CHAPTER 4

My New Home

I wasn't sure what to really expect when I arrived at the 1st Battalion (Provisional), 525th MI Group in Da Nang. It took a few days to come to grips with how and what the battalion and its detachments were doing and what the daily routine consisted of.

Since I was the only intelligence analyst assigned to the battalion, I worked for the battalion S-3 (Operations), Major David M. Fisher and Sergeant 1st Class David Anderson, the Non-Commissioned Officer in Charge (NCOIC). In another office were others who were also part of the S-3: SGT Robert Rosenblatt, SGT Roger Crittenden, and a 2nd lieutenant from Louisiana, who was also a West Point graduate. Lieutenant Colonel Robert W. Wells commanded our unit and our XO was known as "Man Mountain" on account of his size, to say nothing about how he sweated profusely, despite having the only air-conditioned office in the unit (not including the communications equipment).

On the practical side, I was told to keep one of my dog tags in its rubber cover and thread it through the laces of one of my boots, in case there was no other way of being identified if hit. I was issued a gas mask, an M16, a bandolier of ammo, and a flak jacket, all of which stayed with me everywhere I went, including staying within arm's reach from my rack—this was definitely not Saigon.

To reinforce this new reality, I was in Da Nang three days when I was first shot at, this time while driving a jeep headed for Da Nang Airbase. It is a chilling experience when you're not sure where you are and you can't see where the person shooting at you is located. At least two armed soldiers were always required to be in a jeep for protection and all we knew was that whoever was trying to kill us was behind us and to our right flank, somewhere. (The VC were very open-minded when it came to recruiting anyone, of any gender and/or age.) People around us were scattering in many different directions and my compatriot said he couldn't see the sniper. He yelled, "Let's get the fuck outta' here!" I was only too happy to accept his recommendation and shouted in response, "Hold on," as I ducked down in the seat, up-shifted, and hit the gas. Our return trip was a few hours later when darkness had already fallen. As we were unsure what to expect along the normal (and faster) route, we took side streets that probably had never seen a jeep (or Americans) before. It took some time, but we returned without further incident. However, we vowed never to return deliberately through some of those streets at night again. Afterward, in talking with others about this incident, I was informed that the NVA and the VC would shoot wounded soldiers and they did not usually take US enlisted soldiers or junior officers prisoner. The implication was clear: fight and keep on fighting was the only choice, or as they said in Vietnam, *danh cho den cuoi cung* ("fight to the end"). This was further confirmed in the forthcoming Easter Offensive.

The aforementioned incident took place near where the West German hospital ship MV *Helgoland* was normally docked. This ship often served as a bellwether for VC activity—when the ship weighed anchor and put to sea, everyone rightly expected VC rockets or local attacks in the city. Moreover, there was an open bazaar area next to the ship where the Vietnamese sold food, clothes, and other things. It was also a place where "Proud Mary" was usually found. Proud Mary received her name by the Americans because she was a middle-aged, Montagnard woman who often ran around naked. She was ignored by the Vietnamese and Americans because she acted like she needed proper mental care, as if running around naked wasn't already a clue. Of course, there were also the older mama sans who, when they had the urge to evacuate their bowels, would drop their drawers along the roadway and do their business, too.

Twice that I remember, members of our unit had to run for gas masks, as the smell of tear gas slowly crept everywhere. The smell brought one immediately back to basic training, so everyone knew what to expect—that's why they rushed to wherever they had placed their gas mask, hopefully before they started retching. Though we were all issued a gas mask, no one carried it because it was too bulky. The culprit of both instances was the Quan Canh (QC; South Vietnamese Military Police), who had a compound not far away, and were probably breaking up some local demonstrations.

Hearing Da Nang Air Base being hit with 122mm rockets for the first (but definitely not the last) time about a week or so after I arrived was an interesting experience. The base of the rocket made a great ash tray and validated Da Nang's reputation for being called Rocket City. The 122s were not always limited to the airfield, though. As time went by, I slept through most these attacks unless they got close. During these occasions, I would jump up completely awake, grab my M16, and head for the door.

All of our unit's intelligence-types were agents or area specialists, except for me—the only intelligence/OB analyst assigned to the entire battalion. All the intel types were either career or had enlisted for their career field. Our battalion ran Unilateral (UNILAT) agents and Bilateral (BILAT) agent nets with South Vietnamese Unit 101. Colonel Hoang Ngoc Lung (J-2, intelligence, chief of the South Vietnamese Joint General Staff) specifically wrote that they were "supported devotedly by the 525th MI Group in funds, resources, and technical advice ...."[1] Making distribution of the agent reports that we received daily, I soon asked why some things were not given to ARVN? I was told that though they were our allies, it was well-known that the VC had infiltrated most, if not all, of ARVN, including their intelligence apparatus. Special Forces and Congressional Medal of Honor awardee Master Sergeant Roy Benavidez relates a time in 1965 when, as an advisor to ARVN's 25th Infantry Division, it seemed obvious that an ARVN S-2, who had been to the United States a number of times for training, had set him up for an ambush, though this was never officially proven.[2]

A few soldiers in our battalion were also Defense Against Methods of Entry (DAME) and Defense Against Sound Entry (DASE) qualified. Our counterintelligence (CI) agents (wearing civilian clothes) filled our S-2 office and were the only ones who drove the two Land Rovers. In total, there were about five or six officers (including the CO and XO) and six or seven enlisted intel-types, with about eight to ten others (signal, S-1, S-4 and motor stables) normally stationed in Da Nang.

We had a cover designation of the 30th Communications Detachment, with "30 CD" stenciled in white on the bumper of our jeeps and our deuce-and-a-half truck. We were supposedly keeping our true unit secret from the Vietnamese, but we had only one antenna on-site and, if that wasn't odd enough, if you looked underneath the hood of our vehicles, you'd find our true organization also stenciled in white! There were at least a couple of jeeps stolen from our unit while I was there, so it's easy to imagine that everyone knew who we were. Anyone driving past curfew had to be at least a buck sergeant (another way to say a three-stripe sergeant), so I immediately became an "acting jack" (a temporary sergeant, without being paid as such, of course).

Our unit, soon to change its designation and become the 571st Military Intelligence Detachment of the 525th MI Group, had a UH-1H Iroquois (Huey) "Slick" (no weapons hanging on the outside of the helicopter) assigned to us for about three weeks each month from the 358th Aviation Detachment in Vung Tau. (If I had better eyes, I might have been piloting a Huey, too—it was my first career choice.) Occasionally, when one of the door gunners came down sick, I would fill-in as a door gunner, always sitting on my flak jacket—priority protection first! The Huey was used to transport personnel, small equipment, and classified material (aka, *ass and trash* missions) to/from our detachments/teams in Quang Tri, Hue, Tam Ky, Chu Lai, and Quang Ngai (and sometimes elsewhere). I can still remember flying to Quang Tri and being caught unaware as a flight of two Cobra gunships came up from behind and screamed by on either side of us. I remember asking what the hell was that through my microphone—they were really hauling!

Our Huey was normally tied down on Da Nang Airfield and would refuel at an Army refueling pad at XXIV Corps, which later became FRAC. Not knowing that the fuel port on the Huey is on the right side, where I was door gunner that day, I was instructed to fill it up. Jumping onto the pad, there were pumps that looked like the ones used for cars back home, but with much longer hoses. The crew thought it was funny that I couldn't find where to insert the hose as I began pressing the rear of the Huey everywhere for about five minutes (which seemed exceedingly long when you're embarrassed).

We then headed for the red clay of Chu Lai afterwards and I remember this mission because the clouds were so low that we flew at a maximum altitude of only a couple of hundred feet, to and fro over the South China Sea. I don't remember if it was this mission or not, but once someone shot a few rounds at us from the very white coastal beach—luckily, they didn't hit anyone. The pilot swung into the general area where the presumed VC shot at us, but we were unable to draw any further fire. Things like that do get your attention, though.

I also remember a few trips to Da Nang Airfield, especially one in particular. We were in a jeep at one end of the airfield (where the mortuary was) when a couple of US Air Force (USAF) F-4 Phantoms decided to express their view of inter-service cooperation by flying overhead with their afterburners on (which they normally did at takeoff). Perhaps it was just me, but they seemed lower than normal in lifting up off the runway. It took some time for our hearing to be restored and we were actually a little singed by the flames of their engines.

When I arrived in Da Nang, I had my first haircut at the airbase. As a fellow soldier waited and kept my weapon, I sat in a regular barber's chair while an elderly barber cut my hair. After he was finished, he cranked the chair back and had me turn over while he gave a massage with his hands in a "praying" position. Finished with that, he cranked the chair back and proceeded to grab my head and twist it quickly to either side. It was great! Though I had never had that done before, I remember mentioning to my fellow soldier that the Vietnamese barber could have easily broken my neck if he had wanted to.

When I first arrived at the unit, there was often a poker game going on a couple nights a week. I remember in one of my first games I won almost an entire paycheck from one of the communications guys; I worked hard to return the money to him after hearing his woeful tale of how he had to send money back home to his wife and kids, etc. The funny thing was that these card games virtually ended a month or so later.

Nobody moved much when monsoons hit. On October 23, 1971, Typhoon Hester struck and was regarded as one of the most destructive storms to hit Vietnam since 1944. It hit the coast of Vietnam near Hue with winds reaching 105mph. There were buckets and buckets of water falling everywhere, the Han River crested over its banks, and the temperature change was seemingly dramatic enough that we wore field jackets; though the real temperature was probably in the 70s, it felt much colder. In these conditions, C-rations and Sundries Packs (SP) containing chocolate, cigarettes, and toilet paper were used up rather quickly.

As Christmas neared, we were fortunate enough to see the Bob Hope Christmas Show on December 21, 1971 on Freedom Hill. We knew Mr. Hope had been discussing the Vietnam situation in other countries recently, but we were all a little surprised when he launched into an angry and profane defense of his actions. After his remarks, he regained his composure and asked us (we were all in ponchos as it had been lightly raining for days) if we really thought any of his previous remarks would be broadcast on TV?

Andrew Finlayson, a retired USMC officer who served in Vietnam twice, observed the repeated failures of ceasefires. "The enemy routinely disregarded these 'truces' and 'ceasefires,' but that did not deter our political leaders from instituting them time and again. One would have thought the lesson of the Tet truce of 1968 would have been enough for these politicians to forego such lunacies, but that was not the case."[3] It was relatively quiet during the Christmas 1971 ceasefire, though the VC violated it, yet again—perhaps it should have signaled a warning of what was to come. It was busy for me, though. I had "The Guard" on Christmas Eve over our tiny installation. I was in charge of *everything* until morning. It was my job to check the Vietnamese guards every so often (not keeping a set schedule that might be noticed by prying eyes) and perform radio checks with Saigon (which never heard us) and a few others (including the CIA compound a few blocks away—they never would respond). It was more challenging this night, however. All the men decided to drown their longings for home through the bottle. The booze flowed freely and complicated my job immensely. They weren't rowdy so much as they were crying in their beer and lapping it up in large quantities. I had to keep a watchful eye on them all and resist their entreaties to have "just one," which surely would have become two or more. Quite a few men were getting sick and had to be guided to their racks. The confusion continued into the wee hours when the professional drinkers finally called it a night and hobbled to their beds. Hangovers awaited most of them. My vigilance continued, but I knew if the VC decided to assault our facility, I only had my M16 and a bandolier to stave off their advances and I seriously doubted how long our Vietnamese guards would last with only their M1 carbines for protection. If "Charley" (the VC) didn't know where the Americans were by now, they only had to listen for the snoring—it was so loud that our dog mascot left our compound. The night ended without incident, however, although the sounds of war were heard a few times in the distance.

Sometime during the beginning of 1972, I don't remember exactly when, we were all given a surprise, the kind of surprise only the Army seemed to be capable of—everyone had to re-qualify on the weapons! Though most of us had taken and returned fire, it seems "someone" (as the mysterious Army source was nicely referred to) mandated it, so it had to be done. Taking our individual M16s, .38 revolvers and .45 semi-automatics, shotguns, AK-47s, SKS rifles, and anything else we had available, we loaded up a couple of jeeps and headed just outside Da Nang. We shot up a lot of "enemy" trees, as we had made up our minds not to return until the hundreds of rounds we came with were all used up.

While we were able to confirm that the .45s never seemed to shoot straight, we also noticed Vietnamese villagers walking up a path that angled towards our location. I vividly remember a young man, wearing white, about our age, who stopped to talk. He wasn't made jumpy by the weapons going off in the hands of the 10 or so of us "re-qualifiers," and he asked for a handout. He had lost a leg below the one of his knees and he said that he used to be a Vietnamese Marine. All of us chipped in and wished him well. We all agreed with the idiom, "There, but for the grace of God ...." We left shortly afterwards, somewhat somberly, having given this peculiar and idiotic Army requirement its just due.

Another time, I remember "off-roading" with a jeep with another soldier. We almost tipped the jeep over a few times, as we had only about a half-hour to kill, but we found it a fun vehicle to drive.

The China Beach Post Exchange (PX) was located on the other side of the Han River from us. In order to get there, we had to cross a long bridge, where kids would also gather at both ends. The reason for their gathering was to attempt to steal what they could from your person or from your jeep or truck, as you were compelled to slow way down upon entering the bridge. The kids were well adept at stealing watches in one fell swoop by grabbing the dial and quickly twisting the watch off. Of course, our prime concern was our weapons, but it was odd having to swat the kids away from reaching into the jeep. Many soldiers lost watches, and any other things not tied down, to the urchins who saw easy marks. This especially applied to larger items that soldiers sometimes bought at the South Korean-run PX at China Beach, such as sound equipment and cameras.

Another time, MAJ Fisher and I drove miles outside of Da Nang to a rather well-built, large house in a French style. I waited outside as the major conversed in Vietnamese with a man inside. About 15 minutes later, a few kids came by and asked for the usual—cigarettes, candy, etc. More and more children arrived until I was surrounded by 25–30 kids, ranging in age from 7 to 14 or so. I grabbed my M16, holding it above my head, as I started to make numerous 360-degree spins as the kids tried to take what they could from my pockets. My concern was also for personal safety—kids were known to have tossed grenades and also to have used guns against American troops. Yelling for support and watching the kids as best I could, I was about to fire a few rounds in the air when the major and his contact dispersed the children. Being afraid of children was so unnatural a feeling, especially since I came from a large family, that this incident still bothers me today when I think of it.

The XXIV Corps (later FRAC) HQ and the 95th Evacuation Hospital (95th Evac) were also located across the Han River. The latter brings to mind an incident that was unusual for our unit and which took time finally to be resolved. As the Army was drawing down, units were being sent back home or their colors cased, which also left some personnel who hadn't completed the minimum time in-country necessary to be able to leave. The 1st Sergeant (1SG) we had when I first arrived returned to the United States when he hit his Date Eligible for Return from Overseas (DEROS) and another 1SG took his place. This man was infantry and he immediately put the whole outfit on edge (we were slackers in his mind). Things soon hit boiling point about two weeks later, when he had our motor vehicle NCO reassigned. It was well-known that this NCO drank after hours in the solitude of his room, but he was always at work on-time, our vehicles always worked, and no one thought anything of it. Unfortunately, he fell one night and had to be taken to the 95th Evac. He never returned and it wasn't until the new 1SG became fairly inebriated one night himself that he boasted that he had gotten rid of the NCO because he was black!

The word spread like wildfire and the next evening, quite by accident, the entire unit was involved in a water fight. It was oddly surreal. For at least an hour, fire cans, pots, cups, and any container that could hold water was used to splash the opposing team, which changed every few minutes. Then, in a scene I vividly remember, the new 1SG was forced to walk between the opposing sides to his room. No one said a word—the stillness was eerie. The water war quickly resumed but ended shortly afterwards as the urgency and resolve evaporated.

The 525th MI Group Inspector General (IG) came to visit a week or so later. What the new 1SG didn't know was that I was also the Equal Opportunity NCO for our unit and I related what I knew and had personally heard from the 1SG. I was but one of more than 10 people who complained. The IG was also a former XO of our unit and he knew all of us well, and we knew and respected him. As a result, a new 1SG came to our unit a very short time afterwards.

I also remember laughingly mentioning to the IG that I had received a letter to report for induction for the draft. I showed him my draft notice. Since we knew each other, we had a good laugh. He wrote something down on his pad of paper, took my notice, and said he would take care of it. Being the smartass, as I sometimes am, I said I'd be glad to go and report stateside if it would help clear things up.

Military groups are usually very "tight"—sharing the same ups and downs with each other draws units together. I remember an incident where, for some reason I can't recall, one of "our people" was taken under arrest by the Military Police (MPs) in Saigon. The injustice of what the MPs had done galvanized our unit. As our Huey was up from Vung Tau, we estimated that we could cram many of us into the Huey and break our compatriot out of the hoosegow (jail). Someone in the *headshed* (command group) got wind of the plot and squashed our raid. As I remember, our compatriot did return, but this incident is an example of how cohesive a unit can be and how much like a family it becomes.

Occasionally, a few of us would listen to "Hanoi Hannah" on the radio. She was pathetic, as was the music she played. I can't possibly imagine anyone ever taking what she said as true, much less anyone actually trying to switch sides. Ridiculous isn't too strong a word to describe her radio program.

The half-dozen or so helicopter missions I completed had a practical side in addition to being a substitute door gunner. I remembered GEN Patton's dictum to, "Get up in the lines and see what's going on [because] you can't know what the hell they're up to unless you go up and see it with your own eyes." As previously noted, a major part of our intelligence training was map reading. Actually seeing the terrain features helped to bring home what the maps of the areas were displaying. Sometimes the features didn't seem to match up, especially villages, defiles, and sometimes trails, but it was easy then to add changes to our own maps. To see with your own eyes potential avenues of approach, possible military crests, and prospective interdiction points complemented our maps, giving us a certain "feel" of the area, a one-man *Intelligence Preparation of the Battlefield*.

The updated maps, and being able to visualize some of these areas, proved to be invaluable when the Easter Offensive of 1972 broke out in I Corps. Our intelligence detachment was able to provide virtually the only intelligence available for the first two weeks of the offensive, which began on March 30, 1972, due to the weather's low ceiling that pervaded most of the upper two provinces (Quang Tri and Thua Thien). As the only intelligence analyst assigned to the 571st, I was ordered not to fill-in for the door gunners after the NVA poured over the DMZ and stormed into South Vietnam from Laos.

Other trips by jeep, such as going to Phu Bai via the Hai Van Pass, also had an ancillary effect of getting a "feel" for the terrain, too. In this case though, you could plainly hear the weapons and mortars, instead of the whop, whop, whop of the Huey's blades making hearing other sounds difficult, if not impossible. ARVN had positions at various places along the Pass to protect convoys and other vehicles running through. As we sped by (going as fast as we could, uphill and downhill), we heard weapons being fired at us as we came off the bottom of the pass where the QL-1 road flattened out and straightened in a northerly direction. MAJ Fisher always drove and I always rode shotgun, so I kept focused looking backward, but I could never see where any of it was coming from, so we kept the pedal to the metal. Seeing the general layout of some of the major cities and towns in provinces also helped me to provide specific references and information during the Easter Offensive.

At first, my primary responsibility was to make sure that the agent reports we received by teletype (RTT) were distributed to various US organizations. We also had liaison with South Korean and Republic of China units before they departed I Corps. Amazingly, there was no "context" to what was being reported. The area specialists at the various detachments wrote the Intelligence Information Reports (IIRs) in the established manner, but we, at the battalion, seemed to simply pass them along. After a short while, I asked if we couldn't get our own maps of I Corps; now that the South Vietnamese had taken over military responsibility, it became Military

Region-1 (MR-1) with US support coming from FRAC/XXIV Corps. Maps would allow us to keep track of Main Force and Local Force VC and NVA unit movements and help locate any items of special interest, such as arms caches. The 1:50,000 scale UTM maps took a lot of wall space, grease pencils, and rolls of acetate.

Using 5×8 cards (since this era was well before computers were commonly used), I began creating unit, personnel, and equipment files on every VC and NVA unit that were mentioned in anything, including our secret IIRs (agent reports). Luckily, I had kept the intel/OB "bibles," Field Manual (FM) 30-5 *Combat Intelligence* and FM 21-26 *Military Symbols,* with me from Intel School, which helped me to make an initial start in compiling items of potential future interest. (Little did I know how valuable these would soon become.) Unit and subject files (e.g., commanders, activities, etc.) sometimes grew into quite large folders.

We also tracked atrocities committed by the VC and NVA. For instance, NVA troops would take wounded Special Forces soldiers and cut them open while alive, or sometimes burn them with a flamethrower, to induce other Special Forces soldiers to rescue—these were the types of detail found in the reports.[4] For years, reports about the VC using young villagers as manual laborers or as constant blood donors for their wounded, and sexually abusing the females, were common.[5] I never remember running across any report of the VC doing anything non-violently. I maintained separate files on VC acts of terrorism, which included kidnappings and assassinations, and a separate file on their atrocities. These files made clear how sadistic and cruel most of the VC were to US personnel, soldiers of ARVN and Vietnam Marine Corps (VNMC), and the civilian populace (including women, children, and infants).

The maps developed into something of a showpiece for visitors from many different units and organizations, before and especially during the Easter Offensive. Our command element was also able to take advantage of the maps when briefing others. In addition to fixing current positions of enemy units, I could now track and display unit movements, VC infiltration routes, sighting of the infamous "Salt and Pepper" propaganda team (see below), etc. Personnel from our teams throughout I Corps coming through Da Nang—permanently leaving, going, or returning from Rest and Recuperation (R&R) or just assigned to the 571st—were briefed on what their agent reports added to the overall situation. I was able to ask, for example, for more coverage of certain areas and what might be expected in all of their reporting area and listen to the problems they were experiencing or things that they needed (such as ready reference material of units in their area).

As time and capability grew, so did a better understanding of what was going on in I Corps. (Though it no longer officially existed as an American command, "I Corps" remained the normal way this area was referred to by almost everyone; it was now officially a South Vietnamese area, however). Other sources of intelligence—for example, the XXIV Corps Periodic Intelligence Report (PERINTREP), 1st Military Intelligence Aerial and Reconnaissance (MIBARS) reports, etc.—assisted us in assessing whatever activity was developing, though with the US withdrawals our intelligence sources seemed to be drying up rapidly. After a few months, it was evident that XXIV Corps information was extremely limited. It was rare that any useful information was gleaned from their reports, which usually only consisted of the same old locations for enemy units generated on what looked like an early computer using a very small-sized font. To confirm my suspicions, I once compared two of their PERINTREPs and found they were exactly the same. There was no "paralysis through analysis" there. MIBARs reports were usually very short, but always useful. I'll admit that I couldn't believe that the NVA were so busy in South Vietnam at first, but their reporting was welcome until they left country in early 1972.

The VC, though they continued to infiltrate into Da Nang and elsewhere in I Corps, had seen better days. They had lost so many people through the years after Tet 1968 that the NVA had now almost entirely manned or augmented personnel in most VC Main Force units. The VC still managed to scare the local populace, however, so one paid attention to the locals when they talked of "*beaucoup VC*."

Vietnamization's impact on the VC was sometimes expressed in captured documents bemoaning the fact that there were so many "white hamlets," places where there were no VC cadres present. There was an attendant increase of countrywide VC activity during the Easter Offensive, which was to be expected. "There's also a massive change in the physical location of the VCI [Viet Cong Infrastructure] with respect to the population. They're now largely outside the populated areas. They were largely inside the populated areas," stated MR-2 commander John Paul Vann during a Commander's Weekly Intelligence Estimate Update (WIEU) on March 25, 1972.[6] There remained incidents of terrorism, such as "Honda boys or cowboys" throwing grenades or Molotov cocktails at jeeps and trucks, etc. Infiltration information was usually passed along locally to the 196th Light Infantry Brigade that still remained in-country to protect Da Nang's port facilities. Likewise, this and other "special" information was also passed to the Naval Intelligence Liaison Office (NILO, who were also a direct link to the SEALS) and to the Special Forces (SF).

One such particular item of special interest was the "Salt and Pepper" VC propaganda platoon that usually operated to the west of Chu Lai (former home of the 23rd Infantry Americal Division). Believed to be a white and a black deserter, I would immediately call the Special Forces folks to let them know I had "something special for them" (the insinuation was clear) and they always showed up about half-an-hour later. They were already saddled up and their Hueys ready to go when their intel guy returned with the pertinent information. This notification occurred about three or four times while I was there. The sighting information was also immediately transmitted to Saigon. Interestingly, the two deserters were also mentioned in information received by a Mobile Advisory Team (MAT) officer in Quang Ngai in March 1970.[7] A mobile VC Prisoner of War (POW) camp was also identified in the area. It was believed that the traitors and the camp would have been known to each.

As we often came across weapon cache information, I remember an instance when we went with an Americal platoon to confirm a cache location, inventory its contents, and destroy it. Though the information seemed good, however, there was nothing at the location or its vicinity. The 571st MI Detachment was fortunate on a number of occasions to be able to provide timely and accurate developed tactical information which led to the destruction of SAM sites, arms caches, enemy locations, and the infiltration of NVA and VC units.

We also had a key role in *Brightlight* reporting—sightings and other information on POWs, other military, and civilian personnel. I remember many such reports during my tour. Upon receipt of any such indications, everyone worked hard to ensure that the information was expedited via FLASH (the highest and most immediate priority message) that could interrupt all other message traffic and by personal message delivery, to everyone, especially the Joint Personnel Recovery Command (JPRC), MACV, XXIV Corps/FRAC and nearby units throughout I Corps. Looking at the 525th Staff Duty Officer (SDO) logs for February–April 1972, there were 13 instances of *Brightlight* reports sent to the group HQ in Saigon from all the detachments of the 525th MI Group, including one that discusses a VC POW Camp in Vinh Binh Province (Mekong Delta).

The ever-present search for any indications of anything (sightings and equipment) from China was also great. We had a person who could speak a couple of Chinese dialects, and he spent most of his time in Hue, which had a large ethnic Chinese population. Little known to many, Theodore Gostas, a US Army captain assigned to the 135th MI Battalion (a 525th MI Group-subordinate unit), was captured during Tet 1968 in Hue, where he was assigned. Taken through North Vietnam by his captors, he spent time in China before being sent to the "Hanoi Hilton" prison in Hanoi. He suffered torture and other physical and mental deprivations in the five years of his confinement, four-and-a-half years of which were in isolation.

There were also a few times in which our agents reported information on US military and other Western civilians under control of VC or NVA units. These reports were sent electronically with the codeword *Brightlight* and were sent under FLASH priority, overriding any other traffic, to a couple of different units in and out of Vietnam.

Our agents would sometimes use beacons to mark a special location, such as weapon caches. These were small devices (~1½ feet) that sent tones that could be received around 20 miles away. Their employment required careful coordination because their battery life was measured in days after emplacement.

Usually, the information we received was often somewhat dated, but occasionally we would have intelligence that might be actionable. Waiting for normal information processing and then targeting to occur might take far too long to be of much tactical value. As Special Forces had an on-call capability, I knew that if I had a lucrative target they would be able to get the it neutralized. They were great to work with and were able to take credit for the destruction of some targets we fed them, which was okay be me (I distinctly remember a surface-to-air missile (SAM) site becoming "inactive" as a result of this coordination). Likewise, I was able to feed targets (especially the more "remote" ones) to my classmates in Saigon who worked different desk areas. Some targets were eradicated by Arc Light (B-52) strikes based on our information. I use the word "eradicated" advisedly—the totality of an Arc Light strike is devastatingly complete. I remember one such strike in particular, on a SAM site in Laos—it was rare when we received information from inside this country. I knew my friend in Saigon would be able to get the information over to the right people and, sure enough, about a week later I received word that "it was taken care of."

The CIA had a compound close to the US Consulate and MACV compounds in Da Nang. Though we were required to make daily evening radio contact with them, they never answered anyone the entire time I was there. No one thought they were very discrete either, with their silver Huey flying around to various places (I remember flying door gunner once in our Huey parked next to their shiny silver Huey in Hue) and their Bushmaster aircraft (which only they possessed) parked on Da Nang Airfield. I remember having to deliver something to their compound once, shortly after I first arrived in Da Nang. Headed towards the MACV compound, I stopped and asked an old Vietnamese gentleman if he knew where such-and-such street was, to which he replied in halting English, "Oh, CIA. Turn here ...." It was hilarious! Who was kidding whom?

Information on the VC was especially wanted by a group of South Vietnamese agents known as the "White Mice." While there was apparently another group of MPs who were known by this appellation, this was a different group—the Military Security Service (MSS)—who wore civilian clothes and had a little white mouse pin on their lapels. They were greatly feared by the locals, and were reputed to be very corrupt, as well. They had the legal right to shoot any Vietnamese anywhere, at any time, and answer to no one. I met one such person at a local restaurant in Da Nang once while I was there. The service was unusually prompt and the owner extremely attentive. We ate well, though we weren't told until later what animal the meat came from. We also drank well, a drink I don't remember at all, except for its effectiveness.

Once, I was able to experience what our CI section (our S-2) did, when I accompanied them on a stake-out of a suspected VC operative late one night in Da Nang. Agents in two of the three vehicles conducted the actual surveillance.

I accompanied MAJ Fisher, who might have been needed for his linguistic skills, in a jeep at the corner of the street. It was two hours of sheer boredom, which I was told was not at all unusual, before it was called off.

Towards the end of 1971, our unit had a distinguished visitor who was forever talked about by all who attended his farewell speech. Major General (MG), and soon to become Lieutenant General (LTG), James F. Hollingsworth often seemed to make headlines with the press as deputy commander of MR-1. Just like his friend, General Creighton Abrams—the MACV commander—both had served under General George S. Patton in World War II. Patton and Hollingsworth also seemed to enjoy putting themselves in harm's way, both on the battlefield and in the press, where they often freely expressed themselves in politically incorrect terms. Likewise, both carried ivory-handled pistols. Apparently, it was eventually decided that MG Hollingsworth should probably be closer to Saigon, so he was promoted to take control of MR-III.

Before he left to assume his new command, MG Hollingsworth made the rounds to say goodbye to all American units that remained in I Corps. Standing at parade rest, we listened to the general tell us what he would like to do personally to the draft dodgers back home—it was fortunate that the press was not present to hear the general's desires personally to castrate them all, which would certainly have gotten him into even more trouble. Everyone's eyes widened as we looked guardedly at each other. The speech was polished off by one of the most memorable lines I've ever heard personally: "I don't know what you do here, but you're doing a damn good job." If one person had made a sound, we would have all collapsed laughing! Having said that, MG Hollingsworth was one of those rare leaders that you wanted around when the bullets started flying and he was famous for actually being on the ground "up front" when you least expected it.

As 1972 dawned, the intelligence funding for our agents was being squeezed as US troops accelerated their departure from Vietnam. Now was the first major use of the topical files that were created from scratch months before (and maintained daily) and the first instance of having a key responsibility thrust into my hands. I was informed that we only had so much money to spend, so it was necessary to cut back on the number of agents. I was told that there was no one else who knew what the VC and NVA were doing in I Corps within our unit and even at XXIV Corps/FRAC HQ, so I had to make the call.

Agent handlers were expected to inform the reader as to their credibility as a source and the information they were providing. Time was a key factor, obviously, in determining how reliable the source was while determining how accurate the information they were providing was more problematic. The handler would have to be informed of what was occurring in the area by units, their equipment, intentions, and a host of other potential factors.

Agent Reliability and Credibility Codes (Admiralty Code)

Reliability

An agent is assessed for reliability, using Alpha coding, A–F:
- Reliability of Source
  A—Completely reliable
  B—Usually reliable
  C—Fairly reliable
  D—Not usually reliable
  E—Unreliable
  F—Reliability cannot be judged

Credibility

Information is assessed for credibility, using a numeric code, 1–6.
- Accuracy of Information
  1—Confirmed by other sources
  2—Probably True
  3—Possibly True
  4—Doubtful
  5—Improbable
  6—Truth cannot be judged

Reluctantly, I took at least six months' worth (or more if I needed further information) of individual agent reports (i.e. IIRs), separated them into their nets, and, with maps of their usual operating areas, I compared their individual reporting to my records of enemy units in the area and also compared them to other agents in their net. A typical net had 4–5 agents in different locations. It was interesting to find that some of the reports seemed nearly identical to their previous reports and how many seemed to say almost nothing, especially when there had been some activity almost on top of them. Others were rarely heard from and some indicated things that seemed somewhat impossible, etc. (It appeared to me as I looked at all these nets that it was something that should have been done a long time ago. Proper use of the Admiralty Code would have probably enabled me to complete this task faster than the two weeks it took me to finish.) I then had to state and justify why each individual agent should stay or be dropped. All of this ultimately ended up changing a few of the nets, as some agents were no longer employed. It also probably meant that inquiries would be made to find out who else they might have been talking to.

The new year also brought other changes. All the provisional battalions of the 525th MI Group officially became detachments, henceforth we became the 571st MI Detachment (though "30th CD" remained on our vehicles), 525th MI Group. All our detachments became teams. Changes in command brought Lieutenant Colonel James C. McIver to our unit (officially on April 13, 1972, but he was already in place in March). FRAC was officially established in March 1972 with the assistant corps commander, Major General Frederick J. Kroesen, taking over command from Lieutenant General Welborn G. Dolvin.

The stage was soon to be set for the biggest offensive of the war to date, and one that caught the United States and South Vietnam napping. While the signs of it were present for some time beforehand, it yet again demonstrated failures that often seem to be repeated in warfare: dismissing intelligence that does not buttress the current political and/or military climate; ignoring the capabilities of an enemy; failing to remember that the enemy has constantly lied in what they say and do; and attributing qualities to an enemy that they don't have. These are among the lessons of warfare that the US Army had problems remembering.

PART II

"CRY HAVOC ..."

A note about some of the sources used. When I know about a particular item of information because of past experience, I will comment on it, and generally I will point out disparities between sources and explain why one point of view was probably correct. In most cases, I will select an American source over a Vietnamese one. In the latter case, it is often because Lieutenant General Ngo Quang Truong was the source and he didn't become the I Corps commander until over a month after the offensive began, so he was told or read what had supposedly occurred before his arrival in I Corps. He naturally always attempted to show ARVN in a favorable light. Some American authors, unfortunately, were either unaware of this fact or assume (because he was a general) what he has written to be correct. Again, I will point these examples out and state why I either know better or disagree.

CHAPTER 5

The Laos Prelude

The security of all Southeast Asia will be endangered if Laos loses its neutral independence.

—PRESIDENT JOHN F. KENNEDY, 1961

The seeds of the Easter Offensive of 1972 were largely planted at the end of April 1970, with the highly successful three-month disruption of North Vietnamese activity in Cambodia by US and South Vietnamese forces. Building upon this military success came a plan further to disrupt North Vietnamese operations in early February 1971 by interdicting the flow of supplies along the Ho Chi Minh Trail. This would be accomplished either by capturing or destroying supply caches/depots around the Laotian town of Tchepone (Base Area 604) and possibly the nearby Base Area 611, thereby disrupting or preventing any NVA plans to conduct offensive operations in South Vietnam in 1972. US Studies and Observations Group (SOG), however, repeatedly warned US commanders not to go into Laos because they had been there and understood the depth of NVA strength in the area. Their warnings fell on deaf ears.

It is important to note that there were a number of issues that gave rise to this plan. Vietnamization—with South Vietnam taking over the roles and areas that US and allied forces had commanded—was in full force as the United States was departing. NVA vehicle and human traffic and shipments of ammunition, rice, and other materials were increasing along the Ho Chi Minh Trail, and many feared that these resources would allow the NVA to initiate offensive operations at their convenience, not ours. US forces were rapidly leaving South Vietnam and the ability to assist in ground operations would be even more limited, so an ARVN backstop would soon be absent.

There are many different opinions concerning the origination of the plan for the invasion of Laos, some plausible, some unlikely. Historian Lewis Sorley comments: "On the basis of circumstantial evidence, the small group of young officers working under General Alexander Haig in the White House, part of Kissinger's National Security Council staff, seems the likely source. Perhaps Haig himself was the principal author, a prospect congruent with his later involvement in and reaction to the operation."[1] It seems President Nixon and Kissinger were constantly prodding for some sort of a plan. Max Hastings expands: "Late in 1970, Nixon and Melvin Laird (the Secretary of Defense) faced the prospect of financing the war through the following year with only $11 billion, as compared to $30 billion in 1969. Therefore, it was decided to risk a battlefield plunge: to commit a large South Vietnamese force, supported by American air and firepower, against the NVA in Laos."[2]

The MACV commander, GEN Abrams, thought that Haig was prompting Nixon and Kissinger, as Haig's influence seemed greater than even the senior commanders in the area. Abrams, however, steadfastly refused ever to name the original source of the plan to anyone. Admiral (ADM) John S. McCain, Jr., the Commander in Chief Pacific (CINCPAC), notified Abrams of the President's thinking on Laos on December 6, 1970, with Abrams responding the next day with a general outline of a plan. This corps-level effort into Laos was to become known as *Lam Son 719*. The South Vietnamese Joint General Staff (JGS) also laid claim to concocting the plan. Haig later, after *Lam Son 719*, would state, "President Nixon and *those of us in the White House involved in the planning* were appalled by the Defense Department's handling of the operation."[3] (My italics, giving credence to the probability that Haig was the plan's author.)

Max Hastings has stated that, "The invasion of Laos in early 1971 was a classic military failure: poorly planned, poorly executed, and based on poor intelligence."[4] Captured documents indicated that the NVA knew every detail and change regarding the operation, including all the helicopter landing zones, which goes towards explaining the 60 percent casualty rate amongst the allies.[5] The VC were known to have infiltrated ARVN intelligence and commands for years.

After military operations in Cambodia by allied forces in 1970, US ground troops were prohibited by the Cooper–Church Amendment to participate in cross-border ground operations. *Lam Son 719* was therefore designed to be executed in four phases: the last three were exclusively conducted by ARVN troops and South Vietnamese Marines. The first phase, prior to South Vietnamese units moving across the border into Laos, was conducted solely by US Army ground units in an operation called *Dewey Canyon II*. US units reoccupied Khe Sanh and ended up building a new airfield and clearing areas of approach from which ARVN and VNMC units would cross the line of departure into Laos. US units also assumed responsibility for the tactical areas that ARVN vacated.

USAF, USMC, and US Navy (USN) aircraft struck objectives and NVA concentrations during the operation. US Army helicopters also participated in striking targets, resupplying, and ferrying South Vietnamese units into and out of Laos. These units created and occupied Fire Support Bases (FSBs) inside Laos, primarily to the north and south of Route 9. The Xe Pon River roughly paralleled Route 9 to the south while Route 92 intersected Route 9 almost exactly halfway between

Tchepone and the South Vietnam border, from which a high escarpment ridgeline ran all the way to Tchepone. Extensive vegetation, with little room for even a single helicopter to land, pervaded the area.

In mid-December 1970, there is evidence that the NVA knew that some kind of military operation was being planned, as artillery and antiaircraft artillery (AAA) emplacements were noted in areas where ARVN were to operate. In late January 1971, Abrams (based on MACV intelligence) knew that the NVA recognized some kind of operation was being advanced, as he advised Admiral Thomas Moorer, then the Chairman of the Joint Chiefs of Staff, of this fact. Often the NVA/VC knew about plans or operations in which ARVN were to participate. The planning for *Lam Son 719* attempted to restrict knowledge of its specifics to only a few senior officers before implementing the operation. In fact, many of the commanders who were to put the plan into action were kept from the details until just days before it was conducted.

"However, the troops' movements, logistical preparations and, most of all, the speculations of the American press, had alerted the enemy of the incoming attack," according to ARVN Major General Lam Quang Thi.[6] Despite this, "Enemy units had received orders to counteract a possible ARVN offensive along Route No. 9 five months before it was launched."[7]

Forming a corps organization for the first time, the NVA created the B-70 Corps, which was composed of the 304th, 308th, and 320th Infantry Divisions, which could be reinforced by the 324B and 2nd Infantry Divisions, the 27th and 278th Independent Infantry Regiments, eight artillery regiments, three engineer regiments, three armored battalions, six AA regiments, three sapper battalions, and combat and support elements of Transportation Group 559, the unit responsible for logistics on the trail in this area. It should be mentioned that the 304th, 308th, and 324B NVA Divisions made the initial incursions in I Corps during the forthcoming Easter Offensive of 1972, while the 320th and the 2nd NVA Divisions were two of the three NVA divisions making the opening assaults in II Corps. By January 1971, over 6,000 tons of supplies were to be found in Group 559's *binh trams* (troop stations) in Laos, which would support 50,000–60,000 troops for four to five months. By early February, some 60,000 NVA troops were in the general vicinity of Base Areas 604 and 611. Group 559's communication network had been penetrated by the Americans, beginning with its northernmost outpost on Ho Chi Minh Trail, by at least late 1971. (Later, in early January 1972, four NVA divisions were prepared to move southward from North Vietnam.[8])

The South Vietnamese plan called for a three-pronged attack across the border. The main thrust was led by the 1st Armored Brigade, 1st and 8th Airborne Battalions, 11th and 17th Cavalry Squadrons, and the 101st Combat Engineer Battalion along Route 9. The southern flank was covered by the 1st ARVN Division, while the northern flank was the responsibility of the 1st Ranger Group. The VNMC Brigade acted as the reserve at Khe Sanh. The overall tactical commander of *Lam Son 719* was the South Vietnamese I Corps commander (since 1966) Lieutenant General Hoang Xuan Lam, known to be a "political" general.

On February 8, 1971, the assault began. Striking via QL-9 into Laos was nothing short of an astonishing failure in planning. The invading forces were moving along or through a one-lane dirt road, mountains, double- and triple-canopied jungle, and a lot of bomb craters (some so deep that tanks became stuck in them). Armored vehicles were confined to the single roadway, a situation very reminiscent of World War II's Operation *Market Garden,* where the *Garden* portion of the plan deliberately channelized armor and other vehicles also along a single roadway and easily identifiable bridges, where they virtually became sitting ducks for German guns.

The main objectives of the operation were the Base Areas towards Tchepone, along Route 9. The allied forces were roughly half-way there when ARVN reached the town of A Luoi on February 10. The next day, the tanks halted, and they remained stopped for almost a week afterwards, with no offensive movement. (Later it was discovered that South Vietnamese President Thieu had told his military commanders to halt all attacks when ARVN had taken 3,000 casualties. As is true in many areas of the world, the government kept a "palace guard" to defend against coups. The 1st Armored, the Airborne, and Marine divisions represented the palace guard of President Thieu.) This sudden halt gave the NVA plenty of time to mass against and strike ARVN virtually at will. *Lam Son 719* also enabled the NVA to experiment with operating in a corps-level of command for the first time, something they admit *not* doing in the Easter Offensive.

SOG was first to discover a 6in oil pipeline emanating from North Vietnam into Laos. In fact, on January 9, 1970, an AC-130 Spectre struck two pumping stations west of the DMZ. A F-4 Phantom, carrying 500lb bombs, easily found the large fires and finished the destruction.

ARVN also destroyed several yards of the pipeline during *Lam Son 719.* This pipeline, at that time, was one of two that began in North Vietnam, crossed the "Sky Gate" (the pass through the mountain), went west of the Annamite Mountains, and followed Route 12 to Ka Vat, Nan Xoi and Lang Khang.[9] A SOG team discovered that a shutoff valve was installed roughly every 100 feet, however, so it could be easily repaired. Another USAF source reports that motor oil, diesel fuel, gasoline, and kerosene could flow through each pipe of the 4in pipelines run by the NVA's 592nd Pipelaying Regiment. "The number of pipelines entering Laos increased to six during 1970. By the end of the year, three lines pumped fuel through Mu Gia Pass, serving all truck parks and other installations centered around Ban Phanop. Ban Raving Pass carried a fourth pipeline that paralleled the Banghiang waterway, terminating at a distributing point northeast of Tchepone. From this installation, branches extended beyond the town, apparently leading to a fifth line that linked the Ban Som Peng area of Laos with Lao Bao Pass on the South Vietnamese border.

A sixth pipeline led southwestward from Ban Karai Pass, apparently tying into a branch of the Ban Som Peng-Lao Bao Pass line that approached the A Shau Valley."[10]

As ARVN sat out the week, the NVA began knocking units off their recently created firebases in Laos. President Thieu ordered the taking of Tchepone by the 1st ARVN Division, using 120 US Hueys to transport the ARVN troops the 65km from Khe Sanh to Tchepone. Although some weapons and supply caches were discovered and blown up, the town was virtually deserted, as "the enemy (NVA) had more than thirty-six hours' advance notice of the attack ...."[11] Thieu was able to proclaim a "victory," empty as it was, on March 8, 1971. ARVN troops began to leave the next day. None of the finest divisions—1st ARVN, Vietnamese Marines, and Airborne—fared well against the NVA in Laos, while other units performed much worse (e.g., 1st Armored Brigade).

A major problem remained. In a precursor to the Easter Offensive, ARVN had to conduct retrograde operations under pressure back to South Vietnam, with much disorder. Every time medical evacuation (medevac) helicopters touched down to pick up wounded soldiers, it was observed that able-bodied soldiers pushed aboard in their place, saying much about the conduct of ARVN soldiers.[12]

Lieutenant General James W. (Jock) Sutherland (the XXIV Corps commander in charge of the American effort in *Lam Son 719* and an armor officer who had once served with GEN Abrams, the MACV commander) sent Abrams the following assessment in late March 1971: "Lamson [sic] 719 has been expensive in terms of U.S. support costs, but its achievement so far indicates that in terms of damage inflicted upon the enemy, disruption of his expected offensive operations, evidence of the effectiveness of the Vietnamization program, and benefits which will accrue in the future it has been unquestionably a highly valuable and productive operation."[13] A case for the "disruption" can be made, but the "effectiveness" and "benefits" were a big stretch, as the Easter Offensive was to prove. The NVA also suffered large losses to many of its ground units due to airpower, as yet another presage to the forthcoming offensive the next year.

Perhaps not surprisingly, After Action Reports failed to even mention SOG's warnings and entreaties to not enter Laos. The 571st MI Detachment would experience the same thing the next year.

At the COMUS briefing of March 25, 1971, Sir Robert Thompson (a counter-insurgency authority and consultant to President Nixon on Vietnam, in attendance) stated in response to GEN Abrams' comments, "You were rather cautious in saying that they [the enemy] couldn't mount anything this year. But my impression is that they couldn't mount anything next year either—not that they can sustain. I don't have to be quite so cautious." He went on to say moments later, "What I'm saying is we're going to see the fruits of the Laos operation right through 1972." Abrams was much more circumspect, "And he's [the NVA] been badly hurt. And I think, at the moment—realizing all of the uncertainties of prediction and that sort of thing, which as you know you can get in trouble on that—it is going to have the kind of effect it was supposed to have. The other thing we don't really know is what he [the enemy] had in mind for June and July in MR-1."[14]

There were others who did not agree. James Willbanks wrote, "The operation raised serious questions about the progress of Vietnamization, and Nixon was privately distressed over how poorly the South Vietnamese had performed. As General Phillip B. Davidson, the former MACV J-2 (intelligence) for Westmoreland, later said, 'Lam Son 719 demonstrated that, while Vietnamization had made progress, the South Vietnamese government and its armed forces had deep flaws which made final success of the concept years, probably decades, away. Above all, the operation showed ARVN's complete dependence on the United States forces.'"[15] (GEN Davidson was the MACV J-2 during from 1967 to 1969.) Lam Son 719 was the final straw for ARVN, from which it would only partially recover. In men alone, 7,683 were officially either killed, wounded, or missing. The actual figures are thought to be much higher (closer to 50 percent), despite LTG Truong's contention that it was only "partly due to some tactical blunders on our part."[16] Some? Really?

"In the aftermath of Lam Son 719, General Abrams and his MACV staff accelerated their efforts to increase the combat capability of South Vietnamese armed forces. Unfortunately, they would not have much time—the North Vietnamese were planning a major offensive in South Vietnam for 1972."[17] Lam Son 719 demonstrated a number of problems for Abrams and his staff. Command and control of subordinate forces was a major problem and ARVN was obviously not trained in retrograde operations and its procedures. Many soldiers demonstrated a lack of self-control as they sought individual shelter and safety, forsaking wounded soldiers. This also highlighted an abysmal lack of leadership at many levels.

Note that the NVA did not ignore Laos after Lam Son 719. In mid-December 1971, the 312th and 316th NVA Infantry Divisions (each with three regiments), the 335th and 866th NVA Independent Infantry Regiments, artillery (including a 130mm artillery battalion), the 9th and 18th tank companies (each equipped with T-34 tanks), and AAA, sapper, and Pathet Lao units maneuvered to retake the Plain of Jars in Laos in a campaign designated Campaign Z by the North Vietnamese. The specific objective, in addition to wiping out Lao and Thai forces (under the command of Royal Lao Major General Vang Pao (an ethnic Hmong), who commanded the CIA-backed forces of Hmong, Lao and Thai mercenaries, with General Vitoon "Dhep" Yasawatdi providing support) was also to occupy the Long Tieng Valley.

NVA T-34 tanks, armored personnel carriers (APCs), 130mm artillery guns, and Vietnamese People's Air Force (VPAF) MiG-21 aircraft were used against Laotian royalist regiments, which were backed up by Thai ground units. US B-52s also flew numerous sorties in response, while US F-4 Phantom aircraft fought and sometimes lost to the MiG-21s—three F-4s were shot down on December 17, 1971.[18] An intense fight for Skyline Ridge, which overlooks Long Tieng, was eventually won by non-communist forces in early April 1972 after nine weeks of almost constant combat, despite what the North Vietnamese book *Victory in Vietnam* says—"The Plain of Jars was completely liberated."[19] Not so.

At least one of the NVA units, the 312th Infantry Division, took part in the forthcoming Easter Offensive, but didn't arrive in the I Corps area until four months later, in mid-August 1972, the NVA having been defeated by Lao, Thai, and Hmong irregular forces. The 316th NVA Division remained in Laos during the entire Easter Offensive.

Beyond the communist action in Laos, large offensive operations against South Vietnam in 1972 were anticipated by the VC Provisional Government and the communist government of North Vietnam. Not only hoping to encourage the populace of the South to rise up and assist NVA troops, but to also keep world opinion on their side, the North prompted propaganda aid from their comrades-in-arms on the college campuses, the National Council of Churches, rich foundations, other political associations (including the Vietnam Veterans Against the War), and labor groups in the United States.

News organizations and television media continued their slanted news, but to a lesser degree, as the war was winding down and US forces were leaving country. Still susceptible to manipulation, US television broadcast two supposed documentaries in which manipulated tapes used communist film content and made erroneous "facts" and/or conveniently "forgot" to mention other pertinent facts. Jane Fonda at a NVA AAA site and her 20 broadcasts on Radio Hanoi, John Lennon funding plans to disrupt the Republican National Convention, and a variety of people (such as Tom Hayden, Daniel Berrigan, and Howard Zinn) making their way to Hanoi to show their solidarity with North Vietnam, among others, exemplified the political left's outlook. "Peace" groups, which had sprung-up in attempts to shield their extremism and politics, still attempted to demonstrate their influence.[20]

CHAPTER 6

Foundations of the Easter Offensive of 1972

When you have resolved to fight a battle, collect your whole force. Dispense with nothing. A single battalion sometimes decides the day.

—NAPOLEON BONAPARTE, MAXIM XXIX

The Easter Offensive of 1972 is now the best-known name among many others, such as the 1972 Spring Offensive, 1972 Spring–Summer Offensive (*Chien dich Xuan he*), and the Nguyen Hue Offensive. It was initially called the Eastertide Offensive of 1972 by the United States and the 1972 Summer Offensive by the South Vietnamese.

No sooner had the North Vietnamese pushed the South Vietnamese back across the border between Laos and South Vietnam following *Lam Son 719*, than North Vietnam's Politburo and General of the NVA Vo Nguyen Giap began planning for the next year. In fact, GEN Giap had been working on a new strategy since 1968, a strategy that served as the basis for the Easter Offensive. This third phase of *dau tranh* (armed struggle) incorporated advanced military technology (tanks, long-range artillery, and air defense systems). It would be well-planned and well-calculated in terms of risk.[1] Historian Lien-Hang T. Nguyen notes that "new evidence reveals there was more general consensus regarding the 1972 offensive, and disagreements were only minor ones over tactics .... Once again Giap objected to Le Duan and Le Duc Tho's military plans by urging greater caution, but he failed to alter their strategy."[2] Le Duan and Le Duc Tho, before the 20th Plenum (January 27–February 2, 1972), had changed the leadership of the National Defense Council by appointing them both to the first and second leadership positions, while dropping Giap to the third spot. This allowed planning for the forthcoming offensive to proceed unhindered.[3]

Le Duan had already ascended to the actual leadership of North Vietnam, however, as the First Secretary of the Communist Party. His attitude towards conducting war had also changed because he understood that to take on and defeat the Americans, his country had to have the technology to do so. This meant that North Vietnam had to acquire and become proficient in the use of Soviet and Chinese military equipment and tactics. Furthermore, the NVA had to attack the South before Vietnamization, Pacification, and the transfer of US military arms gained more ground; therefore the offensive should take place before all the Americans left in 1973. This meant that such an attack should take place in 1972, which would also have the benefit of its appearing as if the United States suffered a military defeat, thereby boosting the communist government's image on the world stage.

The success the NVA had in defeating ARVN and VNMC forces in *Lam Son 719* helped to encourage the North Vietnamese populace to fight on against their enemies to the South. Douglas Pike, the well-known Vietnam scholar, counted no less than 15 reasonable, published explanations of the North Vietnamese rationale for conducting an offensive against the South at the time.[4]

There is evidence to suggest that at least some of North Vietnam's initial planning may have already started in Hanoi. Lieutenant General Sutherland, the XXIV Corps commander, sent GEN Abrams a message on March 21, 1971 stating that, "a highly placed VC penetration agent reported on enemy plans to launch an offensive with up to four divisions to take and hold major portions of Quang Tri and Thua Thien Provinces, including Hue and Quang Tri cities."[5] This was undoubtedly the prized "571st agent," who continued to provide key, one-of-a-kind type information through the beginning of the Easter Offensive of 1972. Unfortunately, US commanders did not seem to value this information, which probably cost many lives by their ignorance.

In 1970, allied efforts in Cambodia had great success and severely crippled the North's operations. The VC had been decimated in 1968 and never fully recovered; in fact, the NVA had to fill out most VC units. As General William E. Depuy stated, "Of course, eventually the VC were reduced in strength by the attrition (dirty word) of a decade of combat and were progressively replaced by NVA fillers down to local level. By 1972—the Easter Offensive—the VC and NVA were indistinguishable."[6] Michael Lee Lanning and Dan Cragg also note, "Originally VC, they absorbed so many NVA replacements as to become VC in name only."[7] As Colonel Harry Summers explains, "they did not mass them (the NVA in their VC role) but used them as an economy of force on the tactical defensive."[8] Their center of gravity became the South Vietnamese Armed Forces, though they had underestimated ARVN in its ability to fight and the United States by thinking it would do nothing. "By July 1972, the North Vietnamese had reverted to the tactical defense,"[9] from the tactical offense.

As part of the overall preparations for the coming year, "On July 1, 1971 there was a total change over the entire NVA's communications process. It took us about a month to reconstruct unit communications, but we did it. We could track battalion-sized infantry units coming out of training in the north as they moved south and knew which divisions they connected with in the south."[10]

It would be a mistake to think the NVA Signals Intelligence (SIGINT) was asleep. Their official history would indicate SIGINT units were active during *Lam Son 719* and before the Easter Offensive as well. Consider: "By 1966, US intelligence was well aware that the Viet Cong had an active and effective signals intelligence organization, roughly the equivalent of the US Army Security Agency. The Viet Cong systematically monitored and decoded US, ARVN, and Allied forces radio transmissions on hundreds of frequencies, including those used by aircraft and ground forces. They maintained what we would call a database of call sign and frequencies, from which they had identified the commanders of virtually every Army, Marines, and Air Force unit of battalion size or larger in South Vietnam."[11] The VC were also responsible for luring Major General Keith Ware and his command group to their deaths in 1968 by setting up an ambush using a captured radio.

An example of real-time enemy SIGINT/Communications Intelligence (COMINT) during the Easter Offensive occurred on 9 April. Arriving the day before, the 6th VNMC Battalion command group arrived at FSB Pedro. Instead of occupying the FSB, the commander (Major Do Huu Tung) chose to deploy his three companies to the north and northeast. Intel soon indicated that NVA tanks would arrive along Route 557 for an assault on FSB Pedro. "During the initial phase of that engagement, NVA tanks were flying small red flags on their antennas. A U.S. advisor (Major Easley) talking to a FAC, who could not differentiate between friendly and enemy tanks, was told to 'strike the tanks with red flags.' Shortly thereafter, the NVN (NVA) flags quickly came down."[12] Another example of the NVA's COMINT capability was "NVN's Comint was able to detect changes in the bombline (NGF, SVN artillery, and U.S. TacAir); therefore, (NVA) units tended to hug SVN ground positions to avoid attack by U.S. aircraft."[13] FSB Pedro did not succumb to the enemy until April 27. B-52 Arc Light strikes launched from Guam and Okinawa were picked up by Soviet trawlers, who passed headings and air speeds along to the communist Central Office for South Vietnam (COSVN), who would pass this information along to NVA and VC units along the anticipated objectives.

On the US side, the length of time in which information was intercepted until it reached a unit seems to have varied from never to a "long time." For instance, "… an Air Force EC-47 intercepted a radio message from the B3 Front—PAVN headquarters for the Central Highlands—the commander of the 66th PAVN Regiment. US Army cryptologists at Long Binh decoded it, but it was a long time before I knew anything about it."[14]

Prior to the Easter Offensive, Vietnamization was making headway, while pacification was making great gains in the countryside. In fact, it was briefed in an MACV briefing in February 1972 that the mid-December (1971) COSVN resolution concluded with, "… if hit hard enough, the allies will either collapse or be forced to withdraw, *enabling the revolution to regain access to the population*"[15] (my emphasis). If the VC had to "regain access," then they did not currently have it—quite a statement!

Just a few days before, during the January 29, 1972 WIEU briefing, Mr. George D. Jacobson—MACV Assistant Chief of Staff (ACofS) for Civil Operations and Rural Development Support (CORDS) and the deputy to the Commander, US

Military Assistance Command Vietnam (COMUSMACV) for CORDS—reported on pacification. The Hamlet Evaluation System was developed in 1967 to measure the degree of pacification, measuring six factors (e.g, security, VC activity, etc), in the hamlets, A being the most secure, B being mostly pacified and so forth, with E being the worse. As of 31 December 1971 the percentage in A and B hamlets was 84.3 percent. In A/B/C it was 96.8 percent. The progression for upgrading B hamlets to A: "At the end of 1969 we had 599 hamlets. At the end of 1970 we had 103. At the end of 1971—10."[16]

The older communist cadre longed for a military decision against the Americans, even though there would soon be fewer and fewer Americans left in-country. The younger cadre felt that the wiser course would be to wait a year, when all the Americans would be gone. But the older cadre won out and what the North called the Nguyen Hue Offensive (named for a 12th-century Vietnamese emperor) began to take shape. The decision to make this offensive "traditional" (i.e., armor, artillery, and armor regiments fighting a conventional series of battles) hinged on being able to obtain vast amounts of equipment from China and especially the Soviet Union. Party Resolution #13 of June/July 1971 set the wheels in motion for 1972.[17] Another source,[18] however, states that the Politburo decided in May 1971 to launch a "large offensive campaign," while another source states an overall goal of "20–25 days [which would be from April 18 to 22] to destroy four or five enemy regiments, launch uprisings to liberate Quang Tri Province, and then continue our advance … the Campaign confirmed that the initial mission was to liberate Quang Tri, and only after that was done could we develop a follow-on plan."[19] In June 1971, the Central Military Party Committee approved the plan for three areas—Cochin China, the Central Highlands, and Tri Thien.

What seems to be overlooked sometimes is how the NVA fought in Laos during *Lam Son 719*. The NVA waited for the arrival of South Vietnamese forces with units that were to fight the next year in the Easter Offensive in a conventional manner, even attempting to use the corps concept of command and control for the first time. ARVN commanders seemed so tied to the manner in which they had been fighting (unconventional) that they even constructed firebases along their invasion routes when this operation was meant to emphasize speed and offensive maneuver. After the campaign, NVA units were recalled to North Vietnam, re-equipped, and retrained (this included NVA units operating in southern Laos as well). In December 1971, the 20th Plenum formally approved the invasion of the South and an unnumbered COSVN resolution, of the same month, confirmed that it would use "main force warfare" to accomplish it. This decision was the third and final stage that was also used against the French, the first being defensive (through using terror and guerilla operations to control the populace); the second to form regular military forces to attack remote ARVN and US forces; and third to form larger units to exercise full control over the populace and attack larger formations of US and ARVN units. The people were expected to become part of the general uprising (*khoi nghai*) at this end phase to help in the downfall of the South Vietnamese government.

The Vietnamese New Year (Tet) had become the time of year when the US and South Vietnamese forces normally expected the NVA and VC to conduct some kind of coordinated military and/or terrorist activity. In the northern third of South Vietnam, the northeastern monsoon season runs from November to February. The southwestern monsoon season, generally in the lower two-thirds of South Vietnam, is dry from mid-October until the end of May. The common days of dry weather then are from February 1–May 31.

Perhaps it was fate that Tet of 1972 was the Vietnamese Year of the Rat, with all the descriptions that a rat implies. The Nixon administration had anticipated a need for B-52 and tactical aircraft during Tet (February 15) to return to the theater. Twenty-nine B-52Ds were redeployed to Andersen AFB on Guam. These B-52Ds were the initial group (there would be five more) of Strategic Air Command (SAC) aircraft sent under the codename *Bullet Shot*. Due to generally overcast weather and the fact that most of US aircraft had left South Vietnam, there was a significant reliance on bombing of enemy targets using B-52s stationed on Guam and Thailand. President Nixon, not wanting to redeploy ground forces into Vietnam, sent more B-52s, eventually reaching a total of 169 bombers in May.

The DIA apparently thought that the major commands were still in action in and over Vietnam. "The operational commanders armed with our new intelligence weren't sitting on their hands. They were engaged in an all-out aerial effort to impede, weaken, and if possible, destroy the NVA reinforcements that would be vital to the success or failure of the 1972 attack."[20] Obviously, the Air Force and the Navy didn't get the word from DIA, given all the numbers of USAF aircraft and USN aircraft carriers that had returned to the United States. Units remaining in South Vietnam weren't privy to this information, either.

Approximately 136,000 NVA troops were sent southward along the trail (September 1971–June 1972), with 120,000 destined for South Vietnam and Cambodia, with another 55,000 troops with organic units sent directly across and around the western end of the DMZ. DIA'S COL Armstrong wrote, "South Vietnamese units, while well aware of the impending offensive, were not prepared for the enormity of the Communist's thrust directly through the DMZ."[21] Elsewhere, "The Communists were met by a force that was prepared for them, and the offensive in the three southern corps areas was bloodily repulsed and the NVA forced back to its starting point."[22] In reality, the American advisors and military personnel in all the corps areas had no idea of what lay in store for them. This included Lieutenant Colonel Gerald Turley, USMC, who had had briefings in Saigon before he came north to I Corps to visit Marine advisors attached to the various VNMC brigades, having just become the deputy commander of all Marine Corps advisors in Vietnam.

There was no alert, no rushing of units and equipment to any given area—nothing unusual at all before the offensive began.

The US military and civilian heads responsible for operations in Vietnam didn't seem to be concerned at all as Easter 1972 approached, except for getting a few days of leave. When the offensive began, GEN Abrams was in Thailand with his wife; the head of the USMC advisors in Vietnam, Colonel Josh Dorsey, was with his wife in the Philippines; Ambassador Bunker was also visiting his wife in Nepal (where she was the ambassador); Secretary of Defense Melvin Laird was readying for a golf trip to Puerto Rico; and the MACV US Army Advisory Team 155 (which advised 3rd ARVN) commander, US Army Colonel Donald J. Metcalf, was leaving for the Philippines to visit his wife and children who were living at Clark AFB. So many senior officers and officials were absent or planning to be absent, despite their overall belief that something (supposedly) was going to happen, that it should come as no surprise to find that Major General William E. Potts, the Assistant Chief of Staff, J-2 (the primary intelligence officer in-country), was also on leave in Hawaii.

Just before and for the first couple of weeks during the Easter Offensive of 1972, I was assembling information on who the major NVA units were, where they were, and who commanded most of them. This information was derived from our northernmost agent net's reports. Given this initial information, I was able to deduce what their initial and follow-on objectives were (with the help of our 1:50,000 scale maps). Luckily, most gaps in information were usually filled by the 5×10 topical cards that I had begun to create when I first arrived and by jeep and helicopter observations.

Much of the following NVA Order of Battle (OB) and their movements are based on my memory, which was assisted by contacting various civilian and government authors in the first two decades after the Easter Offensive, and referring back to the articles I wrote, as well. Having reviewed many other authors' OBs for the MR-1/I Corps area at the onset of hostilities, I've found a variety of errors or omissions, both major and minor (one historian failed to mention any B-5 Front units). Most authors, including generals, seem content to use previously published works of civilian and military sources or the interviews of flag officers and repeat these same errors in their books. Using American and South Vietnamese generals' recollections is fraught with risks because there is a tendency among writers automatically to believe their reminiscences, including those who were not present in-country or in the engagement areas. Civilian historians seem even more "starry-eyed" and usually don't seem to understand how the military works.

Before the offensive, the NVA had set almost a tactical pattern, consisting of fighting for a short time, then disengaging. This was not the case on March 30 and the days thereafter, especially relating to their use of artillery. It is also important to understand that the NVA didn't necessarily deploy their units as might be expected in most other countries' armies. The NVA also had several units that bore the same numerical designation. Nowhere was this more prevalent than during the Easter

Offensive of 1972. Though the NVA regional commands had used various units before, since the NVA was conducting conventional, Main Force warfare on a large scale for the first time, some "irregularities" dumbfounded many analysts then and still do today.

The first NVA division to deploy into the South for the Easter Offensive was the 324B Infantry Division—it had deployed west of Hue during the beginning of March 1972 from Laos via Routes 547 and 548. Both roads were used by the NVA in their assault of Hue in 1968. This deployment kept the 1st ARVN Division in Hue, which had suffered much in Lam Son 719, busy and preoccupied. There wasn't any thought of possibly reinforcing 3rd ARVN Division to the north when the Easter Offensive began.

For the most part, NVA divisions consisted of three subordinate regiments. While the 324B NVA Division itself had three regiments, it also linked up with two Military Region Thua-Thien (MRTTH) independent regiments (the 5th and 6th) as it passed through the A Shau Valley. The 5th seemed unknown to FRAC, as it was not reported in the command history (though it is in MACV's command history). As a 571st report stated, MRTTH ordered two of the 324B's regiments (the 29th and 812th) to be detached and act as a reserve while preparing to attack Quang Tri by taking up position south of the city. The units moved northeasterly after they cleared the valley. This also allowed these units to act as a blocking force astride QL-1 in preventing any reinforcement of Quang Tri from the south after the offensive started. The third regiment of the 324B, the 803rd, combined with the attached 5th and 6th Infantry Regiments were to keep 1st ARVN busy in the area west of Hue.

A few relevant technical points of interest are in order at this stage in our analysis. During *Lam Son 719* in Laos, the NVA used a corps formation for the first time. Originally believed to be a newly established Front-level organization, the B-70 Corps consisted of the 304th, 308th, and 320th Divisions (and a few other smaller units). The 304th and 308th led off the offensive in Quang Tri Province during the Easter Offensive, while the 320th arrived in late May. The B-70 Corps was *not* used as a military organization in 1972 (nor were *any* NVA corps formations used anywhere else in-country), as North Vietnam admitted, "… even though we had already organized Corps-Sized Group (Ninh Doan) B70 for the Route 9–Southern Laos Campaign and Group 301 for the Northeastern Cambodia Campaign during the spring and summer of 1971, the fact that we still had not formed regular army corps meant we were slow and that we could not keep up with the requirements of large-scale combat targeted on destroying enemy regiments and battalions."[23] Only one source mentioned a 702nd Command Group HQ accompanying the Tri-Thien Hue Front.[24]

While most intelligence organizations always equated a Front to a corps-level organization, the Easter Offensive of 1972 saw six NVA divisions and the equivalent of two more participate in the northern two provinces. The sheer number of divisions and division equivalents easily equates to an Army or Field Army level. Since this offensive represented the second time the NVA had converted to a conventional way of fighting (*Lam Son 719* being the first), many structures and functions seemed not to have been completely ironed out, let alone implemented.

Most NVA divisions were infantry and, as noted above, each *usually* had three regiments, following the Soviet triangular concept of threes: three companies to a battalion, three battalions to a regiment, etc. There were exceptions in which only two infantry regiments were subordinate to a division, instead of three. Also as noted, the NVA had numerous regiments that had the same numerical designator.

Independent infantry regiments were used extensively by the NVA. Usually this meant that these units were not subordinate to a division, but directly to a Front. For instance, the 270th NVA Independent Infantry Regiment of the B5 Front crossed the DMZ at the onset of hostilities and fought for a while until it pulled off the line and headed west into Laos. It refitted and travelled down the Ho Chi Minh Trail into South Vietnam's Quang Nam Province and became part of the 711th NVA Infantry Division. Another example is the 66th NVA Infantry Regiment, of which there were two: one subordinate to the 304th NVA Infantry Division and the other to the 1st NVA Infantry Division and then, almost seven years later (in September 1972), to the 10th NVA Infantry Division operating in the Central Highlands.

Artillery regiments were subordinate to the Front, which was often compared to a quasi-corps formation specific to a designated area. The Easter Offensive did show that many of the artillery units fought as a corps or Front artillery groups, but were named composite artillery regiments. At least two divisions (the 304th and 308th) both had a composite artillery regiment permanently attached to each (both included 130mm guns). It also appears that tank battalions were at least temporarily attached to some of the infantry divisions throughout South Vietnam.

ARVN divisions were also usually composed of three regiments. There were exceptions, e.g., the 1st ARVN Division had four regiments (1st, 2nd, 3rd, and 54th); its entire 2nd Regiment went to the newly created 3rd ARVN Division on October 1, 1971. This left three regiments until late 1972, when the 51st Independent Regiment was formally brought into the division.

Knowing that there was a US and South Vietnamese preoccupation with the defense of Hue, the NVA found themselves (by design or coincidence) in a win–win situation by keeping the 1st ARVN Division busy: if the 1st ARVN faltered, the safety of Hue was imperiled and ARVN relief forces coming from the south would likely be cut-off at the Hai Van Pass by ground and AAA/SAMs by air—it ensured that that the 1st ARVN couldn't leave the city to assist 3rd ARVN Division to the north. General Frederick C. Weyand (deputy commander of MACV, 1969–72, and later commander of MACV from June 1972) on April 6, stated that, "If we could get that threat to Hue removed, or in hand, god—that would make a difference in this whole situation. But it's that possibility of them getting in there that really gnaws at us." Also, "I really worry more about that than I do the B-3 Front, simply because we don't know enough. We've got the best units in Vietnam opposing the enemy there, but ...."[25] The best units? How little MACV seemed to know about I Corps units (both US and South Vietnamese) and their activities is startling.

The concept of motorized infantry was in its infancy in some NVA divisions. Many different APCs were used during the offensive. As the 304th and 308th NVA Infantry Divisions led the offensive, both also had organic artillery and tank regiments assigned and represent the NVA's first usage of motorized infantry. This was a significant step in converting infantry divisions to a more mobile force. Officially, it appears that the 308th became the first mechanized division in the NVA in 1979.

In mid-March 1972, individual NVA units in each of the three operational areas (I, II, and III Corps) reached their assembly areas.

Tri-Thien:

3 infantry divisions
3 separate infantry regiments
2 composite AAA divisions (367th and 377th)
9 field artillery regiments
2 tank and armored regiments
2 engineer regiments
16 sapper, signal, and transport battalions

Central Highlands:

2 infantry divisions
4 separate infantry regiments
5 artillery, engineer, and sapper regiments
6 AAA battalions
1 armored battalion

Eastern Cochin:

3 infantry divisions
4 separate infantry regiments
2 field artillery regiments
1 armored battalion
2 regiments and 7 separate battalions of specialty branch troops[26]

On January 29th, the 84th Composite Artillery Regiment and the 270th and 31st Independent Regiments conducted operations against ARVN units and installations in the FSB A-4 area. Just before the offensive on March 27, 1972, a friendly VNMC ambush southwest of FB Pedro resulted in obtaining a NVA map showing *all* the trails, streams, firebases, and units in Quang Tri Province. Likewise, a NVA soldier from the 246th Independent NVA Regiment conducting reconnaissance of the area was captured in an engagement near FSB Fuller around this time. He indicated that enemy action below the central DMZ was to begin soon.

Despite a MACV briefer calling the initial NVA attack across the DMZ an "upsurge" in activity on April 2, the Easter Offensive of 1972 was pointedly and significantly much more. Though most of the US combat units had left country, it may surprise some to know that the US Army was very much present at the onset of the Easter Offensive of 1972. In fact, the first two Americans (Bruce Crosby and Gary Westcott) killed during the offensive belonged to an intelligence unit, the 407th Radio Research Detachment. During the early minutes of the conflict a North Vietnamese rocket destroyed their bunker at FSB Sarge (also known as Firebase Dong Toan or Hill 552 by the NVA) where they maintained their post in listening to enemy communications traffic and reporting it up their chain of command.

Major Walt Boomer, USMC, was the senior advisor on Sarge to the 4th Battalion, 147th VNMC Brigade, and checked on the two soldiers after one of the many artillery barrages let up for a while, discovering a blaze in the bunker caused by a direct hit of a probable 122mm rocket. Both men were presumed dead.

Though little has been written about this offensive in the northernmost region of South Vietnam, one can easily get the impression that advisors were the only ones present in South Vietnam, by what little has otherwise been written and repeated, sometimes erroneously. In fact, US Army Intelligence continued to perform, and many performed well during this, the later period of Vietnamization, as US and ground forces were turning over their responsibilities and equipment to the South Vietnamese. Military intelligence continued to operate, while more and more ground units cased their colors and returned home to the United States.

This does not mean that there were not problems, especially not acting on intelligence provided. The year previously GEN Abrams, during a May 22, 1971 briefing, was quite irate when 29 soldiers were killed and 33 were wounded on the previous day at FB C-2. Apparently, the men ran from their mess hall to the closest bunker, where 122mm rockets struck collapsed the roof. He pointed out that common sense dictated that (because they had the intel) they should have been in the various other bunkers on the firebase two to three hours before and (if the time had passed) two to three hours afterwards. He instructed his staff that "I want all this explained to General Sutherland, a message put together on it." He continued by citing another incident on Landing Zone (LZ) English ("or one of those places") where they had the intelligence but failed to take necessary action. "And we had a lot of people killed and a lot of people wounded, and it was a failure—I'm telling you, it's a failure of command!"[27] How prophetic this would continue to be in I Corps.

The Army advisory teams assigned to ARVN divisions and USMC advisors assigned to VNMC units also remained, but were subject to being withdrawn and not replaced. The reduction in advisors was counterintuitive, given the increased need to assist the South Vietnamese as US combat units left country. This decision was made somewhere in the chain of command. As we will see, this is but one of a myriad of decisions and indecisions made or left unreconciled until it was either discovered and/or too late in dealing with because of the political pressure in returning troops to the United States.

The offensive began with an extensive artillery preparation of the battlefield at around dawn (which was at 0544) on what was Holy Thursday, March 30, 1972, striking most of the western-arcing firebases that overlooked Highway 9 in Quang Tri Province. GEN Abrams was briefed on April 3, 1972 (four days later) that the offensive began at "0600 on 31 March 1972"[28] *vice* March 30). The exact time in which the artillery began their destruction of the firebases and other targets, however, depended on who and where you were in the province; various sources state that the artillery preparation of the battlefield began at 0900, 1000, 1100, and even 1200. Some patrolling VNMC units engaged NVA units around 1030; 1100 is the time an NVA source states that the offensive began. 0600 is based on USMC Major Walt Boomer's report that they received heavier than normal in-coming artillery rounds *just after daylight* (my emphasis) on FB Sarge and Nui Ba Ho (where Captain Ray Smith was the assistant advisor to the 4th), located a few thousand yards away.[29]

MAJ Boomer on FSB Sarge indicated that the NVA artillery opened up accurately and with intensity at dawn. As many as seven artillery regiments operated either singly, in temporary pairings (as in Soviet Corps Artillery Groups), or attached to divisions, were prepositioned above Dong Ha in the eastern DMZ, Cam Lo in the central DMZ, and in South Vietnam to the west of QL-9 opposite the western firebases to open hostilities to begin the Easter Offensive. The NVA's 122mm rockets, 152mm field guns, and 130mm artillery pieces ranged the area, paying initial attention to ARVN artillery and allied communications targets. The 130mm artillery (Soviet M46) far outranged (at 27km) every US/ARVN artillery piece, except for the 175mm M107s, which were only located at Camp Carroll.

The Chinese and Soviets supplied the NVA with newer equipment that included artillery guns and howitzers. (Guns shoot at low angles (0–45 degrees), while howitzers fire both low and high (45–90 degrees) angles. Mortars only fire at high angles.) It is believed that the influence of Soviet doctrine also played a part in the NVA approach to utilizing artillery. NVA artillery officers were known to have trained at the Soviet Army Kalinin Artillery Academy of Leningrad. The Easter Offensive is believed to be the first instance where an artillery regiment was assigned to a NVA infantry division. "Two composite artillery regiments were assigned to infantry divisions (the 308th and 304th Divisions)."[30]

The literature on this subject is tenuous, but the 304th NVA Division is believed to have had the 68th Composite Artillery Regiment permanently attached to it, while the 308th NVA Division possibly had the 164th Composite Artillery Regiment permanently assigned to it. Soviet artillery regiments, supporting motorized and tank divisions by the late 1970s, were made-up of two battalions of 152mm howitzers and one battalion of 122mm howitzers, each battalion having 18 guns.

NVA artillery fire missions were obviously well prepared and greatly enhanced by being able to suppress any significant counterfire. NVA artillery primarily concentrated on ARVN artillery and communication locations at first. The Soviets felt that firing first with surprise, accuracy, effectiveness, and mass would allow them to obtain both qualitative and quantitative advantages; "Quantity has a quality all of its own" is a saying attributed to Lenin, Stalin, and a few others. Regardless of its origin, the quote also fits how the Easter Offensive of 1972 began.

"New Soviet equipment became a surprise component in the North Vietnamese offensives in March–May 1972. In addition to Soviet 122-mm rockets, North Vietnamese artillery were able to employ 130-mm field guns and 152-mm howitzers."[31] The 122mm rockets were not new to the offensive—Da Nang was not called "Rocket City" for nothing. In fact, the "flooding" of Soviet equipment into North Vietnam was briefed to GEN Abrams during his January 22, 1972, commanders WIEU.[32] The 575th and 577th NVA Artillery Battalions shelled Da Nang installations and Marble Mountain throughout April.

Using Soviet doctrine as a probable guide, three NVA artillery regiments—supporting the 304th NVA Division's advance through western I Corps—formed a divisional artillery group (DAG), which the NVA called a combined artillery group (CAG), allowing them to coordinate artillery fires. The 241st Antiaircraft Regiment reinforced the 304th NVA Division's efforts.

The North Vietnamese indicate[33] that the offensive began at 1100 their time, on March 30, 1972, leading one to believe that either MAJ Boomer was way off on the time that he and USMC Captain Ray Smith, close by on Nui Ba Ho, both experienced with in-coming artillery. Perhaps artillery prep from Hanoi's viewpoint was not the start because ground troops were not involved? Or that Hanoi might have suffered from the same type of confusion that MACV HQ and Washington, DC all experienced concerning what was happening. Even General Bruce Palmer wrote that the offensive started on "31 March 1972."[34] Others have said March 29, 31 and even April 1.

Even in retrospect, the story is still almost always in error. Kissinger mentions March 30, but didn't quite have the who, what, and where of what was occurring quite right. Correctly, Kissinger wrote, "In Washington, as is usual at the onset of events, it was hard to find out exactly what was taking place. As early as March 31 (Good Friday), Secretary Laird reported that the enemy offensive was a major one. But accounts from the Pentagon were initially soothing. General Abrams, we were told, did not consider that the attack had yet reached a critical stage; South Vietnamese fire-support bases seemed to be holding. There was no need for decisions at the highest level. For two days the attacks were treated as a major enemy probe."[35]

Another Palmer (Dave Richard) had his share of errors, too. Later to be a lieutenant general, he has the Easter Offensive of 1972 starting on March 29, 1972; the 3rd ARVN Division falling back from positions along the DMZ; and "Even more significantly, from the standpoint of surprise, Allied intelligence had also failed to predict either the scale of the offensive or the method of attack ...."[36] Most, perhaps, but not all.

The obvious fact that when enemy artillery deploys forward, offensive action is usually indicated was apparently lost on the generals (or perhaps they were absent from the Basic Course, Command and General Staff, or War Colleges on the days this was discussed?). This "omission" was not limited to the generals in Vietnam. Two weeks before the offensive a Pentagon analyst stated, "The enemy shows no sign of building up for anything big right now." A "Pentagon general with access to intelligence reports from Saigon said, 'There is really only one area where an enemy campaign is expected. That's in the central highlands. In the northern provinces, [there] is a lesser threat.'"[37] FRAC wrote after the offensive, "Preceding the 30 March Easter Offensive by North Vietnamese Army (NVA) forces ... Allied intelligence identified evidence of troop movements and equipment stockpiling, all of which pointed toward an attack, yet the question of when a likely attack would occur remained unanswered."[38]

The North's plan of attack was relatively simple. The NVA's 324B Infantry Division, supplemented by the 5th and 6th Independent Infantry Regiments (all B-4 Front units), would engage the 1st ARVN Division, considered ARVN's best, though it suffered severely during *Lam Son 719*. The 1st ARVN "officers confirmed privately in conversations with their American advisers that they had lost at least 775" soldiers, compared to the official reports of 491.[39] Despite the FRAC official history, the 1st ARVN was not quite battle-ready, though "... ARVN's 1st Infantry Division, an elite Vietnamese unit [was]considered by the U.S. media to be the equal of any American division in Viet Nam."[40]

Operating from its often-used staging area in the A Shau Valley and perhaps other points in the Laotian-South Vietnamese border (see route map in the endpapers), these B-4 Front NVA units would preempt any possibility of relief to the north by applying pressure to the firebases west of Hue and, thereby, to the city of Hue itself. In fact, 1st ARVN had been conducting defensive operations against NVA units since early March, which should have precluded any sort of tactical surprise when the Easter Offensive began, since this was not an unusual occurrence between these two opposing divisions—they had tangled before. It was obvious that the NVA plan was to keep 1st ARVN occupied shortly before the offensive began to prevent any thought of assistance to 3rd ARVN, despite various allied commands stating otherwise by erroneously lumping the 324B NVA Division with those attacking through the DMZ on March 30. The detachment of two regiments to the south of Quang Tri was also enough further to dissuade 1st ARVN from heading north to aid 3rd ARVN, because it would enable 324B to attack Hue openly and allow the independent regiments to possibly assault Hue from the northwest. As it were, the two NVA regiments could continue to apply pressure on Quang Tri from the south and could interdict QL-1 (and threaten FB Nancy). Only the 1st ARVN Division (headquartered in Hue) and the 3rd ARVN Division (headquartered in Ai Tu, just north of Quang Tri), two VNMC brigades (the 147th and 258th), an ARVN tank unit (20th Armored Regiment, similarly equipped as a US armored battalion), and Regional Forces were all that stood in the way of the NVA onslaught in the two northern provinces of Quang Tri and Thua Thien.

CHAPTER 7

Ignoring the Signs—The Buildup and Launch of the Easter Offensive

To direct operations with lines far removed from each other, and without communications, is to commit a fault which always gives birth to a second.

—NAPOLEON BONAPARTE, MAXIM XI

Indications of some sort of moderate offensive were first forecasted to occur during Tet 1972, but when this didn't occur, military intelligence was blamed. A buildup north of the DMZ was only marginally detected at the time, but no serious consideration was given to it. This occurred despite the effects of the American forces pulling out of South Vietnam, which allowed the NVA to virtually roam the DMZ at will.

The South Vietnamese I Corps commander, when presented with the idea of a North Vietnamese attack across the DMZ, bluntly stated, "They cannot."[1] His US counterpart at FRAC agreed, "His appraisal appeared reasonable and well-founded. The NVA had never attacked openly through the DMZ. In the face of friendly air power, armor, and armored cavalry, an attack across the open coastal plain by NVA infantry, even with armor support seemed illogical. Furthermore, the old pattern of movement into western Quang Tri, with unit moves being detected, roads being opened or restored, and a marked increase in anti-aircraft weaponry strengthened the conclusion that the attack would come from the west, possibly as early as May, but more likely in June,"[2] stated MG Kroesen. Regarding ARVN, "It had been our assumption that the enemy attack would be from the west instead of the north, because crossing the DMZ would be a blatant violation of the Geneva Accords."[3] And yet the I Corps commander and his American advisor apparently acknowledge they knew something going on in the DMZ, but neither did anything about it? "There is a tendency for planners and operators to assume that an opponent's past behavior is a good indicator of future behavior. Simple-minded, straight-line projections are always easiest and often the most 'credible.'"[4] This was a prevalent attitude among US and South Vietnamese forces. GEN Palmer, who wasn't present in South Vietnam at the time, wrote that the enemy buildup just north of the DMZ "should have warned the allies of the strong probability of an attack launched directly from the DMZ."[5]

In response to the author's Freedom of Information Act (FOIA) request, a CIA document ("The Communist Winter–Spring Offensive in South Vietnam," dated February 7, 1972) was recently declassified and, while reconfirming that the Central Highlands was to be the main effort of the offensive, correctly identified the presence of the 304th, 308th, and 324B Divisions preparing for action north of the DMZ. This intelligence memorandum has no distribution list attached to indicate which organizations received it; we certainly didn't have it or hear about it.

In a US War College paper, written a few months later, the Team 155 commander, COL Metcalf, wrote, "No official or unofficial forecast, ARVN or American, of enemy dry season activity which was available to me prior to the initiation of the offensive foresaw an attack of this magnitude at this time." Further he stated, "The sources available to me were the G2's of the 1st and 3rd ARVN Divisions, and the American estimates produced by XXIV Corps, and they were in general agreement that the enemy would repeat the dry season activities of previous years ...."[6] Only three sources, and one is part of your own command section? What of the 571's Team A, which was also located on Quang Tri and their IIRs, or when we began producing INTSUMs that even FRAC and MACV had daily?

Vietnamese intel at division and below was usually given to an inexperienced ARVN officer to run and ARVN was generally very unhappy with the intel they were receiving, particularly the absence of US recce information. Compounding the problem even more was the fact that, as FRAC later admitted, I Corps HQ had "never actually functioned as a field headquarters in combat." The situation at FRAC was actually much worse.

FRAC was given 571st intelligence daily and I'm sure they likely received MIBARS readouts and reports, until they closed down. It would also be normal for a major command to receive SIGINT from military units in their area, as well as other in-country assets. It strains credulity that MG Kroesen didn't know what resources were available virtually next door, but perhaps his G-2/G-3 didn't inform him of all the intel assets and completely ignored accurate information on the composition, location, and leadership of the NVA units in the invasion? Or, which is probably much more likely, the general was more like his counterpart in the II Corps/Second Regional Assistance Command (SRAC). "Vann, ever the doubting Thomas, stated on 7 February 1972 that 'Intelligence gathering is the chief problem' and that 'Nearly all reliable intelligence is limited to US S.I. Channels.'"[7] It seems that the LTG Hollingsworth (commander of the Third Regional Assistance Command) also discounted HUMINT, as well.

There were also significant problems with the readiness of ARVN forces. The 3rd ARVN Infantry Division, headquartered north of Quang Tri at Ai Tu, was a recently activated unit created around the 2nd Regiment, taken from the 1st ARVN Division. The 3rd ARVN's other two regiments were well known to be composed of deserters, draftees, and Popular Force elements. Despite this, FRAC's evaluation of

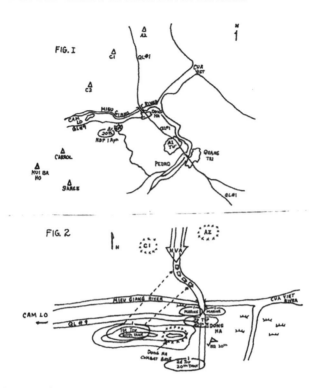

ARVN 20th Armored Regiment's Deployment below Dong Ha. From MAJ Smock's 1974
article in *Armor magazine*.

3rd ARVN combat effectiveness was a rating of "acceptable." This despite Kroesen admitting that the 3rd Division HQ comms and logistical base was not expanded to control Ranger and VNMC elements. Also, "Four battalions, which were to comprise the division's logistic base, had not been activated, and the division artillery was incomplete."[8]

"The 3rd ARVN Division troops on the DMZ were trained and experienced in counterguerrilla warfare"[9] is another statement not based on facts. ARVN's 20th Armored Regiment had just completed its final training only three days before the Easter Offensive started and had only 44 of the 54 M48A3 Patton tanks authorized (the complement of a US tank battalion instead of a US tank regiment) become qualified. The regiment went to Ai Tu for a day before being ordered by 3rd ARVN Division (to whom they were attached) to proceed north to Dong Ha and meet up with the 2nd Battalion/258th Marine Brigade (2/258th). US Army Major James E. Smock was the senior advisor to the 20th Tank and USMC Captain John Ripley was the senior advisor to the 2/258th. Smock later wrote:

> Starting 2 April 1972 the unit fought tank engagements with North Vietnamese tanks. With
> forty-two operational M48A3 tanks it engaged and destroyed at least fifty Russian-made T34/

T54 tanks plus other tracked vehicles and played a significant part in delaying an enemy force estimated at more than two North Vietnamese Army (NVA) armored divisions (regiments) along the Mieu Giang River line for 25 days …. In 30 days (2 April–2 May 1972) it lost all 42 operational tanks: thirty were lost to enemy action and 12 were swamped trying to ford rivers. It was augmented by a 270-man armored rifle unit, but this unit did not function or fight as such, as it was used to provide replacements for the tank crews.[10]

A former ARVN armor officer stated that, "Although only recently established, the 3rd (Division) had bravely accepted its border defense mission and acquitted itself well against NVA units."[11] The problem was that the division had yet to engage the enemy, bravely or not, so it "acquitted itself" well by doing what?

The South Vietnamese command and control problem remained even more fundamental. Inept and indecisive leadership gave way to politics. For instance, the I Corps commander, LTG Hoang Xuan Lam, who commanded Vietnamese forces during *Lam Son 719*, steadfastly refused to have the VNMC regiment under his direct command because this same VNMC officer had refused to take his orders without first obtaining clearance from his VNMC HQ in Saigon. Having suffered no rebuke, remarkably the VNMC officer remained in command of the brigade. This problem resurfaced under the 3rd ARVN Division commander during the Easter Offensive, who was given nominal operational control of the two South Vietnamese Marine brigades operating in his area of operation. Orders of movement to these units were sent by these units to their HQ in Saigon and they didn't comply with any ARVN instructions until they received clearance from their own HQ.

Despite the supposedly known (by some) NVA buildup across the DMZ, and an ARVN report (which now can't be found, but sometimes repeated by ARVN apologists) calling for a countrywide alert for NVA hostilities that were to begin on March 29. If really true, why did the 3rd ARVN commander—Brigadier General Vu Van Giai—decide to swap the positions and areas of responsibility of the 2nd ARVN Regiment at Camp Carroll with the 56th ARVN Regiment at FSB Charlie 2 or C-2 to lessen the effects of something called "firebase syndrome," though they had each only been positioned in these positions for only five months. (One source termed this a *training exercise*.) This was never done before by either ally. Inexplicably, there is no mention of this "swap" in the FRAC command history. This exchange of firebases and areas, which ARVN LTG Lam and US Army MG Kroesen would certainly have been informed about and approved, took place without any detailed planning or experienced leadership in retrograde operations. Coincidently, the 3rd ARVN Division commander and his US advisor, were also incommunicado with these units, as all regimental communications were shut down a half-hour before the NVA shelling began in their area.

There was a report that all NVA units were to be in their staging areas by 1800 on March 29, 1972, in preparation for the commencement of hostilities the next day. It's unclear how this order was disseminated, but it clear that it was a valuable indicator of what would shortly come.

The view from Hanoi: "As for the enemy (US and South Vietnamese forces), even though it had learned of our urgent preparations, it (US and Allied forces) held to the erroneous view that we did not have sufficient forces to mount large-scale attacks on many different fronts. Then, at the time of their greatest optimism, our guns roared out on all fronts."[12] North Vietnam's objectives were potentially many: to prove Vietnamization hadn't worked; influence the forthcoming American elections; reimpose communist control over the South's populace, thereby refreshing the status of the VC (though the NVA had taken over the full manning of many VC units); and initiate conventional battlefield operations for the first time, while securing one or more provinces and/or important cities. The gathering of as much territory as possible was also referred to as the "Third Vietnam," which could be used as a bargaining chip in the Paris Peace Talks.

Completely disregarding the November 1968 Paris agreement, which called for both parties to stop shelling and bombing in and above the DMZ and also to "respect" its neutrality, allowed the North to build massive forces north of the DMZ with virtual impunity. This was permitted because the allied forces were single-minded in thinking the North would abide by the agreement, though their compliance was always dubious. As incredible as it seems, there were physical and sensor indicators of a build-up across the DMZ prior to the offensive that were plainly ignored or not thought of as highly significant. In fact, there were POL Points inside and below the DMZ for tanks and specific routes and corridors for troops and equipment to use.

In late June 1971, Lieutenant General Welborn Dolvin, XXIV Corps commander, reported to Abrams about NVA activity: "He has prudently decided to conduct an intense, though geographically limited, campaign with North Vietnam as his base, the DMZ as his haven and infiltration zone, and roads and trails through the DMZ as direct LOC (lines of communication) to his fighting units."[13] Heavy shelling by NVA units from the DMZ of ARVN firebases had prompted FSB Fuller to be evacuated. Though Abrams requested numerous times for authority to respond to NVA attacks-by-fire, they were ignored or rarely authorized by higher authorities.

Extensive and careful NVA artillery preparations occurred prior to the offensive. The locations of the fire and fire support bases were well known, as US Marine and Army units had constructed and operated from these locations for years. NVA patrols clarified locations and equipment. Artillery observation posts were then pre-positioned, as the NVA maneuvered and secured territory. A full-range of AAA guns (23–100mm) were also positioned along, inside, and below the DMZ. Two North Vietnamese SA-2 Guideline SAM sites and two new airfields were built in the southern panhandle of that country, as were SA-2 sites in northern Quang Tri Province.

Abrams reported that, "Since March 1970, the North Vietnamese have developed roads at the western end of the DMZ and have used them to enable goods to move further south within the sanctuary of North Vietnam before being exposed to allied air interdictions."[14] Further, on the next page of the same briefing, Abrams mentions that, "They're going to try to work that antiaircraft in there, and get it around Carroll and all that, that's become the tactic now." And the NVA did so less than a year later.

The North Vietnamese also established petroleum, oil, lubricant (POL) points along the roads; these would be used heavily by their tanks, which refueled at each location. These were found on:

- Route 6086
- Route 556
- Route 102-Route 556
- QL-9

The roads used for the movement of troops and equipment were as follows:

- Route 608 to QL-9 to Route 556
- Route 102 to Route 556
- QL-1 in Eastern DMZ
- West Quang Tri: QL-9 and the 608-6081/2/3 Network
- Corridor eastbound on Ben Hai River (in DMZ). South along the coast and up the Cua Viet River

Also, supplies were shuttled down the coast of MR-1 (weapons and ammo caches were developed near the coast in Quang Tri and Thua Thien Provinces).

A full moon and overcast skies were present the night before the start of the offensive. Troop movement began with the 308th NVA Infantry Division and the attached 202nd Armored Regiment springing from the central DMZ towards Dong Ha and then continuing towards Quang Tri. Simultaneously, the 27th Independent Infantry Regiments and the 126th Naval Water Sapper Regiment jumped off from the eastern DMZ, attacking southwards between the area east of QL-1 and the South China Sea. This was not the first time that this unit conducted operations in northern I Corps. On January 2, 1971, Quang Tri Popular Forces captured at least 16 126th Water Sappers who were moving a 2,000lb Soviet mine southward from a position north of the DMZ.[15]

Meanwhile, the 304th NVA Infantry Division (which had infiltrated from Laos and the western DMZ, utilizing the road improvements made by the NVA in South Vietnam), with the attached 203rd Armored Regiment, arrived in northwestern South Vietnam and attacked easterly, eventually linking up with the 27th Infantry Regiment on its left flank. This assault from the west allowed the NVA to conduct direct and flanking attacks towards Quang Tri City against ARVN's west-facing firebases and inhibit any support to 3rd ARVN elements. An intelligence report from the 571st MI Detachment indicated that the 324B NVA Infantry Division was ordered to detach two of its three regiments (803rd and 812th, each with four battalions) towards Quang Tri during this period would obviously also serve to hinder any support to the 3rd ARVN from the south, including the interdiction of QL-1. The attached 5th and 6th Regiments remained west of Hue with the 803rd.

With the 304th and 308th NVA Divisions to the west and north, respectively, independent regiments to the east, and the detached 324B NVA regiments to the south, Quang Tri almost became entirely encircled and isolated. While most regions of South Vietnam would encounter NVA ground force activity during the Easter Offensive of 1972, it was the northernmost portion of the country, Quang Tri Province, which would bear the initial and most severe brunt of the NVA's conventional ground campaign.

This was not, of course, a three pronged, six-division, three-division, nor a twelve-division initial assault across the DMZ into I Corps that are found in most histories about the Easter Offensive of 1972. Perhaps it is not surprising, however, when one considers that some historians barely mention that the Easter Offensive was the largest major military action of the entire Vietnam War up to that time; one historian spent less than three pages on the offensive in a decent-sized book, most others barely spend much more.

The allied response was patchy. There was a distinct lack of cohesion in coordinating the efforts between the Vietnamese Army and Marine Corps units in MR-1. (It seemed like last year's Laos example once again.) The 147th VNMC Brigade at Mai Loc (designated Target Z39 by the NVA) and the 258th VNMC Brigade at FB Nancy were technically attached to 3rd ARVN Division. LTG Truong wrote, "The 3rd Division exercised operational control over two marine brigades of the general reserve …."[16] The Vietnamese Marines were considered part of South Vietnam's strategic reserve, a reserve that could ruin a career if it was squandered.

While the long-distances between Quang Tri, FRAC/I Corps HQ in Da Nang, and MACV/the South Vietnamese Joint General Staff (JGS) in Saigon were none too great, "as it turned out, it was up to three days after the enemy attack was launched in MR-1 before it aroused any major concern in Saigon," the Assistant JGS stated years later. The South Vietnamese Security Council met on April 3, 1972. The day before, they worked on a statement concerning MR-1 that three divisions had crossed and violated the DMZ. MACV then corrected this, stating, "It's the equivalent of three divisions, but not three divisions per se. The 304th is the only division thus far."[17] Even MACV wasn't either reading or believing their mail (our INTSUMs). As the USMC history of the period points out, "MACV and the Vietnamese Joint General Staff, lulled into a kind of complacency by reports of the success of the Vietnamization effort and by the intelligence community's forecasts, were very skeptical of these reports, despite evidence that now faced them."[18]

US naval gunfire support was provided by destroyers on the gunline offshore from the DMZ, initially by the USS *Buchanan* (DDG-14)—the destroyers *Waddell* (DDG-24), *Hamner* (DD-718), and *Anderson* (DD-786) didn't return to the area for two more days after the Dong Ha Bridge was dropped. With the *Buchanan*, the Naval Intelligence Liaison Office in Da Nang likely also provided the Commander, Pacific Fleet (CINCPAC) in Hawaii (and the USN SEALS) with our more timely tactical situational reporting than the MACV commander, GEN Abrams, was otherwise receiving from I Corps. The destroyers were not held under operational control (OPCON) to MACV or I Corps and, therefore, reported directly to CINCPAC, ADM McCain, who in turn, relayed information from Hawaii back to MACV in Saigon. "This resulted in Admiral McCain there having more detailed, accurate, and timely information and being better informed on the NVA offensive than General Abrams. Abrams was furious at the inefficient flow of tactical information to his Saigon headquarters from MR-1."[19]

The North Vietnamese were able to maneuver their forces almost at will because the locations of Army and USMC firebases were well-known for many years. Patton's dictum that "fixed fortifications are a monument to the stupidity of man" seems apropos. At the same time, extensive low cloud and rain covered much of the region, thereby keeping most USAF and Republic of Vietnam Air Force (RVAF) ground-attack aircraft from supporting the ground troops. B-52s and US helicopters, with RVAF A-1 Skyraiders, provided the bulk of close air support for the first couple of weeks of the offensive, when the weather allowed. Not everyone agreed about the climatic restrictions. President Nixon was asked about the weather during this time, to which he responded: "It isn't bad. The Air Force isn't worth a ---- I mean, they won't fly."[20]

I remember feeling how the ground shook when the B-52s dropped their load of bombs. The devastation they left in their path is almost impossible to describe. Even those near the target drop would suffer some sort of sudden physical pain. There was never any doubt about what they were, nor the damage they inflicted. Obviously, the B-52 was not normally a tactical weapon platform, but it was fortunate that it was able to operate this way, just as it first had in Vietnam in 1965 over the Ia Drang Valley.

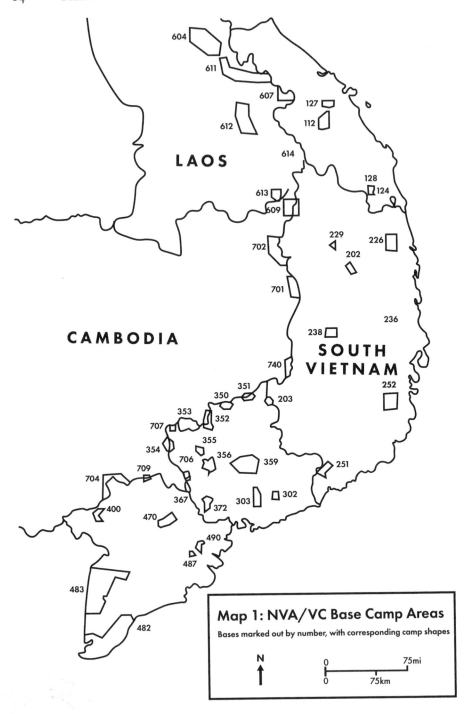

604

611

607

127

112

LAOS

612

614

128
124

613

609

229

226

702

202

701

CAMBODIA

236

238

SOUTH
VIETNAM

740

252

351

350

203

353

352

707

355

251

354

706

356

359

709

704

706

367

372

303   302

400

470

490

487

483

482

Map 1: NVA/VC Base Camp Areas

Bases marked out by number, with corresponding camp shapes

N

0   75mi

0   75km

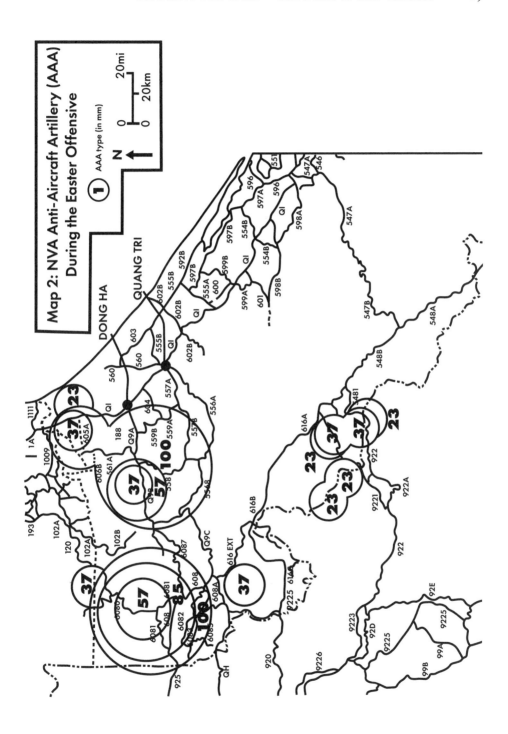

Map 2: NVA Anti-Aircraft Artillery (AAA) During the Easter Offensive

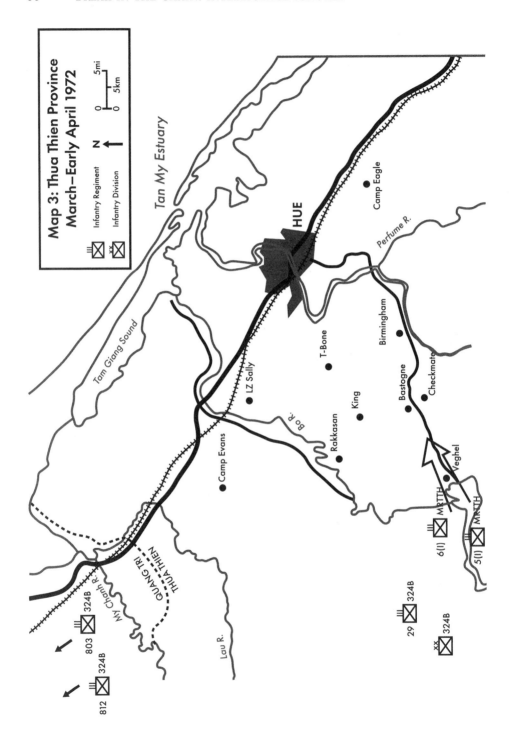

Map 3: Thua Thien Province
March–Early April 1972

Infantry Regiment
Infantry Division

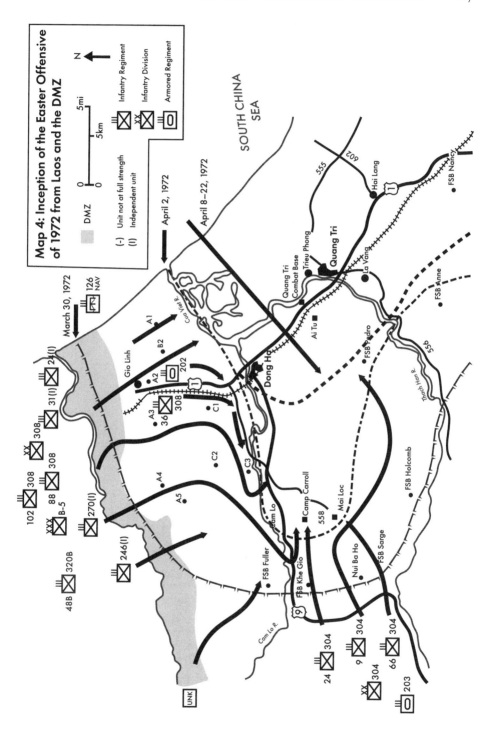

Map 4: Inception of the Easter Offensive of 1972 from Laos and the DMZ

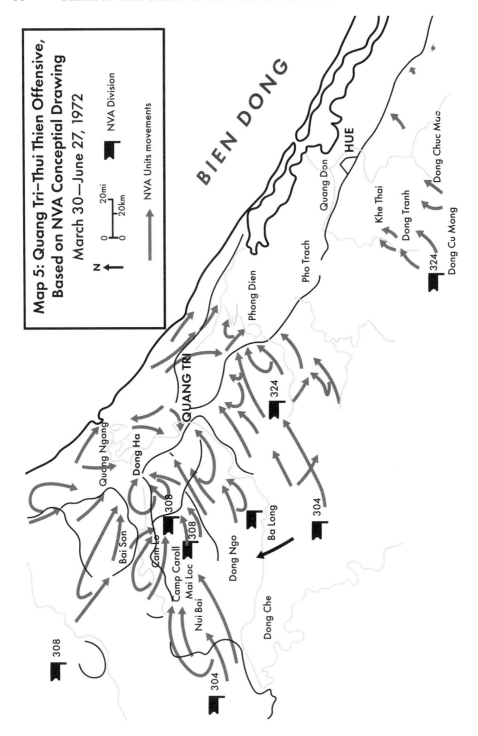

Map 5: Quang Tri–Thui Thien Offensive, Based on NVA Conceptial Drawing March 30–June 27, 1972

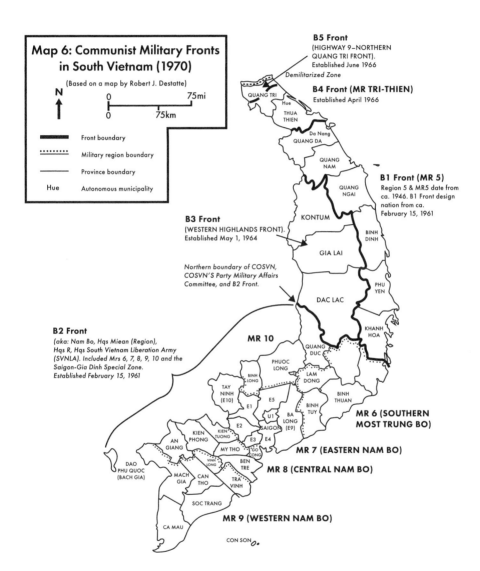

Map 6: Communist Military Fronts in South Vietnam (1970)

(Based on a map by Robert J. Destatte)

N

0   75mi

0   75km

━━━━   Front boundary

··········   Military region boundary

───────   Province boundary

Hue   Autonomous municipality

B5 Front
(HIGHWAY 9–NORTHERN
QUANG TRI FRONT).
Established June 1966

Demilitarized Zone

B4 Front (MR TRI-THIEN)
Established April 1966

QUANG TRI

Hue

THUA
THIEN

Da Nang
QUANG DA

QUANG
NAM

QUANG
NGAI

B1 Front (MR 5)
Region 5 & MR5 date from
ca. 1946. B1 Front design
nation from ca.
February 15, 1961

BINH
DINH

B3 Front
(WESTERN HIGHLANDS FRONT).
Established May 1, 1964

KONTUM

GIA LAI

*Northern boundary of COSVN,
COSVN'S Party Military Affairs
Committee, and B2 Front.*

DAC LAC

PHU
YEN

KHANH
HOA

B2 Front
(aka: Nam Bo, Hqs Miean (Region),
Hqs R, Hqs South Vietnam Liberation Army
(SVNLA). Included Mrs 6, 7, 8, 9, 10 and the
Saigon-Gia Dinh Special Zone.
Established February 15, 1961

MR 10

QUANG
DUC

PHUOC
LONG

LAM
DONG

BINH
LONG

TAY
NINH
(E10)

E5

E1

BINH
TUY

BINH
THUAN

U 1

BA
LONG
(E9)

SAIGON

E2

E3   E4

**MR 6 (SOUTHERN
MOST TRUNG BO)**

AN
GIANG

KIEN
PHONG

KIEN
TUONG

MY THO

GO
CONG

MR 7 (EASTERN NAM BO)

DAO
PHU QUOC
(BACH GIA)

MACH
GIA

CAN
THO

VINH
LONG

BEN
TRE

TRA
VINH

MR 8 (CENTRAL NAM BO)

SOC TRANG

CA MAU

CON SON

MR 9 (WESTERN NAM BO)

CHAPTER 8

Did Intelligence Fail Again?

Historians sometimes cite the failure of intelligence properly to inform and alert the various commanders of enemy intentions as the chief reason for the successful "surprise" achieved by the NVA in the Easter Offensive. Upon closer examination, the true cause lies elsewhere.

The expected Tet Offensive of 1972 in February never materialized. Even so, the Tet Offensive was never expected to be on the scale of the Easter Offensive. "Even during the offensives of 1968, the Communists did not send all of their large units into battle at one time; a substantial portion of them were held in reserve."[1] In March, our agents stated that the postponement was caused by "ARVN's high state of combat readiness."[2]

Though movement activity of the 324B NVA Division was detected in February in their normal Area of Operations (AO) in the A Shau Valley, the only place in which any enemy activity was expected to occur was limited to the area west of Hue. "The enemy's apparent objective is to occupy Hue, the ancient capital, and threaten the harbor and airfield of Da Nang, 60 miles to the south."[3] Hue would surely have to be taken *after* Quang Tri Province fell and the NVA continued southward, but the preoccupation with Hue being the primary enemy objective seemed to transfix both US and ARVN commands to the exclusion of any and all other possibilities. By presenting the obvious, the NVA managed to convince the US and South Vietnamese commands to see what they expected to see. In this case, it was the 324B Division's movement in the A Shau, "… the base from which the NVA always attacked Hue," as the FRAC commander later stated, and the usual enemy movement around Khe Sanh. Many felt that the "disastrous effects" of a military and psychological victory at Hue would have induced an almost catatonic effect, paralyzing the US and South Vietnamese command structure to behave in a predictable way.[4] So deep was the mindset that instantly after the NVA divisions crossed the DMZ, attention to the defense of Hue was almost a rallying cry, as if the assaults across the DMZ were merely feints because Hue had to be the real objective. For weeks afterwards, the press believed that the 1st ARVN had yet to be engaged by the NVA, though they had been for a month west of Hue.

In retrospect, LTG Kroesen wrote, "The NVA has never attacked openly through the DMZ. In the face of friendly air power, armor and armored cavalry, an attack across the open coastal plain by NVA infantry, even with armor support, seemed illogical. Furthermore, the old pattern of movement into western Quang Tri … strengthened the conclusion that the attack would come from the west, possibly as early as May, but more likely in June."[5]

For intelligence analysts, indications of the magnitude of the offensive of the Easter Offensive were obviously present beforehand. All they needed to do was not succumb to the failures that surfaced again in World War II, continued through Vietnam, and continue even today—deferring to a command hierarchy, "stove-piping" intelligence, and relying on one form of intelligence. Telling generals what they want to hear and/or what other, senior organizations say is nothing but irresponsibly neglecting your professional duty. Stove-piping is similar to the practice of deferring to authority, but more implies repeating analysis up through the organizational chain and relying on a particular type of intelligence, running the risk of ignoring, confirming, or negating other forms of intelligence, the latter exemplified through the over-reliance on SIGINT in World War II (at the Battle of the Bulge, for example) to the exclusion of the other forms of intelligence. This example and other parallels were made in my 1997 article for the *American Intelligence Journal* article "Warning Intelligence: The Battle of the Bulge and the NVN Easter Offensive."[6]

Similarly, the same thing happened during the Easter Offensive, which bears repeating and was clearly summarized by John Paul Vann, the SRAC commander, "Nearly all *reliable* [my emphasis] intelligence is limited to US S.I. [i.e., Special Intelligence] Channels."[7] Vann's remark was made almost two months before the offensive began, but serves as a truism of the times in Vietnam, as well. The TRAC commander, LTG Hollingsworth, apparently felt the same way. When he was briefed about the COSVN document of December 1971 indicating a major change in how the North was soon going to conduct military operations, the district senior advisor (DSA) of Ben Cat, along with members of the Ben Cat District Intelligence Operation Coordinating Center (DIOCC), both Vietnamese and American, disagreed with MG Hollingsworth on his intelligence assessment that Tay Ninh was the target of the next offensive. The Ben Cat DIOCC was using HUMINT. Hollingsworth fired the DSA of Ben Cat and, of course, An Loc was the target of the NVA effort in III Corps. Hollingsworth apparently did not entirely take his cue from General Patton who valued, relied, and trusted his G-2, Colonel Oscar W. Koch (who also played an unheralded role during the Battle of the Bulge).

Therefore, all three US commanders of the advisory groups in I Corps, II Corps, and III Corps—which would all feel the brunt of the NVA offensive—didn't think that information from their own attached intelligence people was worthy of consideration because it was HUMINT-derived. The MACV J-2 obviously felt the same. "So I'm supposed to believe that some kind of magic allows a bunch of shaky girbs [acronym for "G.I. rat bastards] distinguished more for their spit and their polish and abetted by a civilian, to use a tangle of antennas and funny talk, to divine the combat plans of the enemy?" So said Major General William Peers (later of Peers Commission fame—the My Lai war crimes investigation) to some National Security Agency (NSA) SIGINT types who were briefing a multi-division attack warning to the 4th Infantry Division commander in 1967, based on the SIGINT information they had gathered. Proving that some generals didn't care for intelligence in general, the general waved their warning away, the NVA struck a few days later.[8]

"General Charlie Corcoran remembered that during his service with Abrams there would be efforts, engineered in Washington, to make the intelligence assessments produced by various agencies agree, thus presenting the President with a single point of view." Corcoran went on to state, for instance, that MACV intelligence estimates should agree with CINCPAC, which would agree with CIA. This was not GEN Abrams' view, as he relied on his J-2 staff.[9] This does not necessarily mean, however, that MACV's J-2 considered intelligence from subordinate organizations of the same value—traditionally HUMINT has never weighed the same as the other types of intelligence. Timothy Lomperis was an intelligence analyst at MACV in the "Tank" (the all-source intelligence center) and wrote to me that, "I will also confirm your point that HUMINT was not highly respected at MACV. There was just this perception that the agents could not be trusted and could only be considered 'actionable' with confirmation from another source, which given the nature of HUMINT, was not often forthcoming, and hence, discarded."[10]

Historically, senior officers and senior NCOs were also once appointed to intelligence positions, instead of being trained in intelligence—the thought apparently being that anyone could fill these positions, maintaining classified documents being their prime function.

Melting multiple sources of intelligence is a necessary learned trait. An NVA soldier was captured in 1970 near Khe Sanh by to a 101st Airborne Division "Pink Team" (a Loach reconnaissance helicopter accompanied by Cobra attack helicopters), who provided unique information on a road being built in the area. "The prisoner explained that his engineer unit was constructing a concealed [camouflaged] road connecting the NW corner of the DMZ and *ban Buc*—a deserted Montagnard village in Laos, NW of Khe Sanh. He explained that the PAVN (NVA) intended to use the road as a western corridor for armor units that would participate in a combined arms assault into Quang Tri Province at some future date."[11] US Photographic Intelligence (PHOTINT) also spotted tank concentrations in the area called Bat Lake, where the Laotian, North, and South Vietnamese borders meet. A 1st MIBARS report on "Road Construction in the DMZ for Route 103 (May–June 1971)" stated that the road was capable of supporting at least medium-tracked and four-wheeled vehicles and "could be used for the introduction of artillery and armored vehicles directly into the northern part of Military Region 1." A later 1st MIBARS report on "Road Construction and Trafficability Analysis for Routes 103 and 120 (Feb–Oct 71)" reiterated the previous report (adding Route 120), but added, "Construction activities and heavy construction equipment have been sighted for the first time as far as far as 6.5 kilometers south of the southern boundary of the DMZ. A strong effort is being made by North Vietnamese construction forces to renovate existing road and trail networks in northern Military Region I and to link them with the DMZ road networks." Lieutenant General Dolvin's warning to GEN Abrams about NVA activity was further substantiated by these observations. Apparently, even the CIA knew about the road network, too. "The 304th NVA Division appears to be almost in place and ready to move against outlying government positions in western Quang Tri Province. It has operated in this area in previous years and can be resupplied by the new road the Communists have constructed into the northwest part of the province."[12]

Sergeant Vern Dreiger was a Vietnamese linguist and Army interrogator in-charge of the XXIV Corps/FRAC POW cage in Da Nang in 1971–72. He related that invariably the most junior-ranking POWs knew next to nothing about their units (except for their immediate platoon or squad leader). "They didn't know shit. This was true of VC and NVA troops alike—it seemed as if it was deliberately done this way." Dreiger also ran into the "not enough rank" and "don't make any work" syndromes that were increasingly beginning to pervade US forces remaining in South Vietnam at the time. No one listened to a mere sergeant. Though he was intelligence trained and wanting to do what he was trained to do, few seemed to care, up and down the ranks, even when he ran across information related to the Easter Offensive.[13] With a few exceptions, I also found that the various intel types were still trying to do their jobs the best way they could. In Dreiger's case, he conducted the interrogations, made his report, and sent it onto Combined Military Interrogation Center (CMIC) in Saigon.

In December 1971, a "usually reliable source" (a *nom de plume* indicating a US-controlled agent, which was the business of the 571st MI Detachment) provided US intelligence a significant unnumbered North Vietnamese Politburo policy document, which stated that the NVA would switch to Main Force (conventional) operations in the following year, as opposed to continued protracted (insurgency) warfare. This document was to change the entire complexion of intelligence in Vietnam completely for the coming year. It caught almost everyone by surprise, but not without some skepticism. However, the recent re-election of Nguyen Van Thieu as President of South Vietnam in early October 1971 and the reintroduction of calling for the mutual withdrawal of all forces to their borders by the US at the Paris Peace Talks may have further caused this reaction by North Vietnam, who probably didn't welcome the thought of returning 100,000 troops that it had sent down the Ho Chi Minh Trail. Obviously, the US position had hardened, though the withdrawal of US forces was continuing apace; perhaps the North decided to strike the South knowing that there would be few US combat troops the following year.

DIA and MACV began to predict a major offensive and chose (primarily based on past history) Tet 1972 as the probable time it would occur. GEN Abrams and

MG Potts, the MACV J-2, are both quoted as fixing the date as February 20, 1972, based on the date mentioned most often.[14] As stated elsewhere, the CIA, though their bags had mostly been packed, agreed with the forecast. Nothing happened. According to General Donn Starry, "*The military objectives were not known*, but intelligence sources reported that its goal would be the destruction of the Army of the Republic of Vietnam. *Not even at the highest levels of government, however, was a major shift in enemy tactics expected.*"[15] The 571st knew better and so should those on its distribution list (e.g., MACV, DIA, PACFLT, etc.).

The press thought that all the warnings given by MACV were "political tricks." GEN Abrams reacted, "I really enjoy it, because it looks like the war is going to finally conclude without them ever deviating from the splendid record of absolute unreliability that they've established."[16]

On March 11, 1972, the Central Military Party Committee accounced "Tri-Thien, which had previously been designated a supporting theater, was now designated as the most important theater of operations."[17] Then, "On March 23, 1972, the Politburo set a resolution and passed a combat plan to launch a strategic offensive across the South Battlefield. The Politburo also decided Tri Thien (i.e., the two northernmost provinces in I Corps) as the main attacking direction while the Southeastern South (i.e., III Corps) and Central Highlands (i.e., II Corps) were the two secondary attacking directions, in an effort to annihilate a major part of the enemy's force, extend the liberated areas, changed the scale of force between our side and the enemy, and turned the power balance in favor of our side."[18] This was a major change of emphasis, not least because the supply lines and ground units would be much closer to the North. The Central Military Party Committee chose Major General Le Trong Tan, Deputy Chief of the General Staff, to be the campaign commander for the Tri Thien Campaign.

"Unfortunately, the lack of a steady flow of information in the fluid situation in northern Quang Tri Province resulted in failure to identify early on the anticipated NVA offensive had been launched. Isolated from the distant battlefield, the MACV staff did not fully appreciate the significance of the sketchy details and generally remained inactive, simply waiting for more details."[19] MACV must not have been reading our INTSUMs, either.

Based on agent reports, the 571st MI Detachment, 525th MI Group, constructed detailed descriptions of the major NVA units and their avenues of approach and accurately forecasted their initial objectives. It was apparent that the NVA's strategic design was to prevent any relief of Quang Tri Province by striking from the north and west, while inserting a blocking force along the Quang Tri–Thua Thien border (to Quang Tri city's south) and near FB Nancy, while maintaining pressure on Hue, thus freezing the 1st ARVN Division. Using the INTSUM for the first time in the history of the 525th MI Group, this predictive analysis was hand-delivered to FRAC/XXIV Corps (who were co-located with ARVN I Corps). Hard copies went to 196th

Light Infantry Brigade (LIB), 1st MIBARS, the CIA, MACV, MACV Studies and Observations Group (MACV-SOG), Naval Intelligence Liaison (NILO), and US Army Special Forces in the Da Nang area. It was sent electronically to HQ, US Army Military Assistance Command Vietnam (USMACV), HQ, United States Army Vietnam (USARV), Seventh Air Force, 7th PSYOPS, the USS *Buchanan*—part of Commander Destroyer Squadron (ComDesRon) 31—and CINCPAC and were sent daily, then twice daily in the weeks ahead.

A South Vietnamese JGS account claimed that there was a countrywide alert for March 29, based on information received in late March by the JGS J-7. "This information was disseminated to all ARVN units as a measure of precaution."[20] If so, it never arrived in MR-1 or MACV, or it was largely ignored by these commands. Otherwise, USAF and RVAF aircraft would have attempted to preempt offensive operations in the days and weeks prior to the offensive, US and South Vietnamese units would have been on alert, with leaves canceled and travel restricted, two regiments of 3rd ARVN wouldn't have been switching firebases and AOs, and generals and other senior members wouldn't be departing or had already have left country.

Though there has been little written on SIGINT reporting, there were indications that something was on-tap, but apparently the information either didn't get routed through the chain of control properly or it, too, wasn't believed. For instance, "the U.S. Army's 8th Radio Research Field Station (8th RRFS) at Phu Bai reported that a NVA artillery headquarters was located only six kilometers southwest of Fire Support Base Sarge [aka, FB Dong Toan]."[21] Given the range of their new 130mm guns, the NVA had all of the western firebases well within range. At the inception of the offensive, the 27km range of the 130mm also allowed it to fire from positions north of the DMZ into South Vietnam, too.

MG Kroesen was only 10 days into commanding FRAC (though he was the deputy commander for some months beforehand) when the offensive started and would remain so for just two months more, until May 30, 1972, when Major General Howard H. Cooksey (another armor officer) took over command. GEN Abrams specifically called Cooksey in the United States to take command of FRAC; Cooksey only had three days in which to take charge from Kroesen. Similarly, the Team 155 commander, COL Metcalf, would only remain until June 3, 1972. GEN Abrams would also be permanently reassigned on June 30, 1972. GEN Abrams had been in-country for years and the others had served the year or so—often in their second tour.

According to one source, "Hanoi, for the third time, decided the circumstances were right to escalate into Phase Three (i.e., a conventional war). On March 30, the NVA launched a coordinated attack of twelve divisions, supported by artillery and tanks, into the northern portion of South Vietnam and the Central Highlands. Once again the Communist attack came as a complete surprise to American and ARVN military intelligence."[22] Not quite 12 divisions and not a complete surprise.

Was it also a mere coincidence that one of the two worst regiments of the 3rd ARVN were swapping positions on the very day and hour of the offensive and that in both regimental communications went down a half-hour before the DMZ portion of the offensive began? Had the commander of the 56th ARVN Regiment planned to surrender during this movement as it moved away from the DMZ, instead of two days later? Was the 2nd ARVN Regiment's movement northward designed for it to be attacked while on the road against the NVA units attacking southward? These are certainly obvious questions that might arise in any serious inquiry, but may never be fully known.

Unfortunately, it took some time for the American command to realize the true intent of the NVA offensive in the north even after inception of hostilities, so intense and overriding was their focus on Hue. It was not until April 27, 1972 (28 days after the offensive started) that the FRAC commander wrote the MACV commander, "Reports are fragmentary at this time but intelligence indicates that the objectives are the capture of Fire Support Base NANCY and to establish a blocking force on the Quang Tri/Thua Thien border. Other NVA forces will then assume offensive operations to capture Quang Tri City." The 571st had first indicated this in an INTSUM during the first week of the offensive, given the actions of the NVA 324B Division and the 5th and 6th NVA Independent Infantry Regiments, which had virtually frozen the 1st ARVN in place, allowing the regiments to strike Quang Tri from the south and interdict QL-1 at FB Nancy.

In summary, the enemy took advantage over the allies by:

- Showing US and ARVN commanders what they expected to see through strategic misdirection
- Using poor weather conditions as cover from aerial attacks (which was virtually socked-in up to 30,000 feet for many days during the first couple of weeks). There were intermittent breaks in the cloud cover, which tactical aircraft would use for reconnaissance and attacks, but there were very few periods when these occurred. There were also few all-weather tactical aircraft in existence. The strategic B-52s were an exception.
- Repairing and extending roads and trails as avenues of approach
- Hitting inexperienced troops and "quiet" areas
- Attacking on extended fronts that were extremely difficult to defend
- Surprising ARVN and US commanders and most intelligence organizations
- Carefully concealing troops and equipment in staging areas.

In World War II, GEN Patton's Assistant G-2 stated this about the Battle of the Bulge: "It was not intelligence (evaluated information of the enemy) that failed. The failure was the commanders and certain G-2s who did not act on the intelligence they had."[23] I would add, "and were given" to the end of the quote for the Easter Offensive of 1972.

HUMINT operations during Vietnam were not usually timely affairs. Most often, information was days or weeks old and, consequently, the tactical value of the material was usually limited. However, there were a few occasions when information was either of such a unique nature or so uncommonly timely that tactical responses could be undertaken.

As the Easter Offensive continued, it was not unusual to see more of a variety of USN aircraft at Da Nang Airbase. The airbase soon, once again, bustled with USAF aircraft as well. Sixty F-4s, five AC-119s and two A-1 aircraft were sent to Da Nang, as were two USMC F-4 squadrons, beginning on April 1, 1972. On April 1, 1972, two squadrons of USMC F-4 aircraft were sent to Da Nang AB. These aircraft redeployed 547km west to Nam Phong Royal Thai Air Force Base (RTAFB) on May 11 because of the manpower ceiling in South Vietnam and all Thai airfields were full.

USAF Air Order of Battle (AOB) In-Area on March 31, 1972

South Vietnam		Guam
Da Nang	Bien Hoa	Anderson AFB
60 F-4	23 A-37	31 B-52
5 AC-119		

Thailand (all RTABs)				
Korat	Udorn	U-Tapao	Ubon	Nakhon Phanom
30 F-4	52 F-4	52 B-52	10 B-57	10 AC-119
16 F-105			70 F-4	15 A-1
			13 AC-130	4 F-4

USAF Air Order of Battle (AOB) In-Area on May 30, 1972

South Vietnam		Guam
Da Nang	Bien Hoa	Anderson AFB
60 F-4	20 A-37	117 B-52
5 AC-119	5 AC 119	
2 A-1	2 A-1	

Thailand (all RTABs)					
Korat	Udorn	U-Tapao	Ubon	Nakhon Phanom	Takhli
34 F-4	86 F-4	54 B-52	92 F-4	4 AC-119	72 F-4
31 F-105			14 AC-130	16 A-1	
				4 F-4	

Source: *Airpower and the 1972 Spring Offensive,* USAF SE Asia Monograph Series, Washington, DC: USGPO, 1976, pp.14 and 30.

The *Coral Sea* (CV-43) and *Hancock* (CVA-19) aircraft carriers were on Yankee Station in the South China Sea with 170 aircraft. Four other USN carriers were also ordered to the area. The *Kitty Hawk* (CVA-63), *Constellation* (CV-64), and *Midway* (CV-41) were in Subic Bay (Philippines) and Japan. The fourth carrier, the *Saratoga* (CV-60), was in the United States preparing to deploy to the Mediterranean. With at least 20 cruisers and destroyers at-sea in the area, it became the largest number of American ships seen since World War II.

Shortly after arriving at my unit, it became clear that it had been content to operate without understanding the tactical and strategic situation in I Corps, relying on XXIV Corps/FRAC for area knowledge. This was easily surpassed as I began by ordering maps and talking with our teams, and keeping accurate files on all enemy (VC and NVA) activities, commanders, operating areas, etc. "The advisory command, recalled Major General Kroesen (the FRAC commander), was 'heavily weighted to provide administrative assistance and logistical advice' *with only a token intelligence and operations section. It was neither manned nor equipped to monitor the combat activity or to provide tactical guidance*" (my emphasis).[24] The general and his staff failed to mention these "little" points to our intelligence unit and I'm not sure this fact was well-known. The rub, though, is that we were the only functioning intelligence unit in all of I Corps and FRAC during the Easter Offensive of 1972 and we didn't know it! I also find it disturbing that Kroesen let this bungling occur, or it was his excuse for being caught flatfooted because he (and others) likely relied almost entirely on "other" (i.e., communications) intelligence, which would be even more problematic (e.g., the classification of SIGINT material) in advising GEN Lam. Shouldn't a commanding major general, with his years of experience, have demanded a fully functioning G-2 organization? Even if XXIV Corps was technically deactivated ten days before (March 19) the Easter Offensive began, and unless it was asleep to begin with, not that much had changed—they were getting our INTSUMs.

To onlookers during the period, it must have seemed as if the FRAC headquarters was in tune with the enemy situation and was trying as best they could to do more.

> Lam's senior advisor, Major General "Fritz" Kroesen, did what he could to keep MACV informed of the situation and to marshal the firepower available from U.S. forces. At frequent intervals he dispatched situation reports back to MACV, describing events and anticipating the next moves by the NVA. By the afternoon of March 31, with the attack a day old, Kroesen was able to send in a more comprehensive survey of the situation. Kroesen identified three axes of attacks: south from the demilitarized zone, southeast from the road network in the western DMZ, and eastward from Laos along Route 9. By this time NVA tanks had appeared in the northwest, and ARVN firebases had begun to fall under the onslaught.[25]

One must wonder how FRAC "suddenly" had such information when Kroesen only had a minimal intelligence section and the only functioning intelligence unit with the information operating and reporting was the 571st MI Detachment?

FSB Holcomb fell first to the NVA on April 1. By the end of the day, the NVA were in control of A-1, A-2, A-4, C-1, C-2, FSB Fuller, Khe Gio, Ba Ho Mountain, and Sarge. It was soon to be Camp Carroll's turn. MG Kroesen saw that "the outpost system had accomplished the classic mission of delaying and forcing the deployment of his forces into battle formation." Withdrawals by ARVN were "carried out in good order .... Only at C1 and C2 were tactical errors made."[26] This doesn't seem to make much sense—forcing the NVA into battle formations is exactly what the NVA wanted to do in the Easter Offensive, letting artillery to keep the ARVN occupied while they headed south.

Others repeated the errors, "… some units conducting orderly withdrawals even under heavy pressure, others fleeing in disorder, still others holding their positions" and the "… South Vietnamese, still using their old propeller-driven A-1 Skyraiders, were able to work in the marginal weather conditions."[27] USAF forward air controllers (FACs) and US helicopters were present whenever the overcast skies allowed and sometimes the A-1s showed up, but not often.

Another major problem was the bombline set up by FRAC. This was a line to help deconflict attacks on the NVA and involved naval gunfire (NGF), USAF, and South Vietnamese aircraft and South Vietnamese artillery. Unfortunately, "the line was set at Danang by FRAC, sometimes without full awareness of the changing battlefield situation."[28]

"On Saturday, April 1, as the NVA pressure grew more intense, Abrams reported back to Washington that 'the situation in Quang Tri is bad and it is going to get worse."[29] The quote continues:

> He could now identify the strength and primary axes of the offensive. The NVA 270th and 31st Regiments were attacking southward from the eastern DMZ. The 308th NVA Division was operating on their west. The 304th NVA Division was attacking eastward from its base area in the northwestern and western sectors of Quang Tri Province. And, southwest of Hue, along the traditional invasion corridor from the A Shau Valley, the 6th Regiment and the 324B Division were beginning to pressure the ARVN defenses. The infantry was supported by elements of two armored regiments, an artillery regiment, and an air defense division.

It was sounding like our initial reports (remember FRAC had nothing and our INTSUM also went to Saigon).

CHAPTER 9

Cut and Run: What ARVN called "Mobility"

When a nation is without establishments and a military system, it is very difficult to organize an army.

—NAPOLEON BONAPARTE, MAXIM LVII

The South Vietnamese Army was often the subject of "unofficial" diatribes on how they fought and conducted themselves. While some units deserved these invectives for specific acts, it is often forgotten that these can almost always be traced to poor performance by unit commanders. The political appointees of generals bred incompetence without correction, leading to eventual unit failure. As ARVN had virtually no military tradition, training of the common soldier was often found wanting, the officers displaying an increasing egocentric self-importance as they advanced in rank, all with a severe lack of continuing military training. As an example John Paul Vann, speaking at the May 29, 1971, at a commanders conference said, "While we have a large number of highly professionally qualified non-coms who are quite capable of advising even battalion commanders, we have almost no Vietnamese officers who are willing to receive one word of advice from an enlisted man of any army. As a result, by and large the enlisted people in the advisory effort represent (only) ration requirements."[1]

William M. Hammond further argued that "U.S. military men used to criticize the South Vietnamese for a tendency to 'cut and run'.... Now, when the South Vietnamese flee, Pentagon spokesmen are inclined to praise their 'mobility.'"[2] Discussing *Lam Son 719*, Hammond adds, "Informed, for example, during a 22 March (1971) meeting that the enemy had released large quantities of rice wine to his troops to whip them into a suicidal frenzy, Henry Kissinger could only remark, alluding to the South Vietnamese army's increasing problem with drug abuse, that '... this ought to be a great battle, one army hopped up on drugs and the other ... on booze.'"[3]

"In 1972, a period that included the NGUYEN HUE Offensive and some of the heaviest casualties of the war, 70 percent of all manpower loses were desertions."[4] As of November 1971, the RVN Armed Forces still couldn't attain a 90 percent manning level.[5] ARVN was 47 percent short of its 66,900-man conscription goal for 1971.

The combat infantry battalions were only at 65 percent strength on November 30, 1971.[6] "The rank and file recognized how senior officials were selected, and their morale and motivation suffered."[7]

In late 1971, Abrams wrote that he considered one ARVN general to be ineffective and one ARVN general to be marginal among all 13 ARVN division commanders.[8] The general, the next May, wrote that "Only ten of them [South Vietnam generals], he [Abrams] said, were truly reliable and earning their pay."[9]

GEN Abrams gave a special background briefing to correspondents on March 21, 1971, where he admitted, "… the enemy had in one case routed a battalion of Airborne troops whose commander had deserted his men …."[10] In the "Ragged Edge of Vietnamization" article by Brigadier General (ret.) John D. Howard, the Airborne Division also had "an unknown number of missing, including a brigade commander."[11]

"General Abrams described the RVNAF's performance in LAM SON 719 and in the early stage of the 1972 spring offensive as creditable. In November 1971 and again late in April 1972, he rated Lieutenant General Lam, who had mishandled the Laotian incursion and soon would be overwhelmed at Quang Tri, as 'outstanding.'"[12] The ARVN Deputy I Corps commander, Major General Nguyen Van Hieu, was installed in April 1971 after almost driving his 5th ARVN Division troops to mutiny in Operation *Snoul 1971*. US Army advisors thought Hieu to be the worst ARVN division commander.

"The primary loyalty of many ARVN soldiers went to their families and villages, not to the government in Saigon or to the Republic of Vietnam."[13] "Villages and hamlets located in northern Quang Tri Province near the ARVN firebases were struck by artillery and rocket fire. ARVN soldiers from the 3d Division and regional forces, seeing their hamlets under siege, left their units to protect their wives and families. Some returned to their units; many did not."[14]

"Some men within both units (3/56 and 1/2) fled the battle (31 Mar 72), in part out of fear for their families caught up in the chaos, while others fought on."[15] Given that there was no possible way to tell who these soldiers were, as most were shedding uniforms, unit patches, and weapons, all within proximity to each other, it became pandemonium. "Specific causes of desertions were numerous, with the most frequent relating to the close family kinship ties existing within the Vietnamese culture." Other factors were intensity of combat operations, poor living conditions, long family separations, low apprehension risk (did not have the mental strength to withstand even a limited degree of combat), limited punishment, and ineffective leadership in combat.[16]

"The ARVN desertion rate during the war was high—averaging from 2 to 4 percent per month … *For one thing, the PLAF desertion rate was about as high as ARVN's* [my emphasis]. For another, few of the ARVN deserters went over to the other side; most returned to their home villages or attempted to lose themselves in the cities."[17]

Only 250 men, "comprising the 57th Regiment," arrived at Dong Ha to supplement the 3rd VNMC Battalion and 20th Armored Regiment. The 57th allowed the NVA to establish a foothold on the southern bank of the Cua Viet.[18]

On April 11, 1972, the Easter Offensive began in II Corps area. In early April in II Corps, the commander of the 40th ARVN Regiment of the 22nd ARVN Division, Colonel Tran Hien Duc, apparently frightened by mortar rounds, rode an M113 APC out the gate of LZ English. Seeing their commander leave, many of the ARVN troops threw down their weapons, stripped off their uniforms, and left the LZ. Others climbed aboard the remaining M113s and escaped southward away from the arriving NVA troops. In the II Corps Tactical Zone at Tan Canh–FB Dak To II, Colonel Le Duc Dat lost the entire 22nd ARVN Division, with the exception of small groups that the Montagnard villagers named "rabbit soldiers" as they ran by them on Route 14.

In part because the SRAC did not believe sighting reports of tanks in the area, the NVA took but 10 hours virtually to eradicate an entire ARVN division. In October 1971, SOG reported tanks in southern Laos, to which John Paul Vann responded, "That's a lot of horseshit!"[19] The following April 23, the crew of a Spectre gunship sighted some 21 tanks. When Vann was told, he responded, "Well, if there are tanks, congratulations, because these are the first positive tanks that anybody has found in MR II."[20]

In II Corps, "part of the 22nd ARVN broke and ran at Tan Canh and Dak To II northwest of Kontum City."[21] "In relating the fall of Tan Canh, north of Kontum, for example, a correspondent for *Time* quoted an American officer who survived the disaster. 'Tan Canh fell,' the adviser said, 'because ARVN never got off its ass and fought.'" And "… a U.S. Army general said of the typical South Vietnamese soldier, 'You can't give a man guts.'"[22]

"MR2 was defended by just two ARVN divisions, the Twenty-second and the Twenty-third, widely considered to be the worst in ARVN. On top of this, the MR commander, General Ngo Dzu, was not up to the job. Even more serious was the fact, unknown at the time, that both the deputy commander of MR2 and the commander of the Twenty-second Division were Communist sympathizers. Seeming, an epic disaster loomed."[23] Later in 1972, General Ngo Dzu, at a US–South Vietnamese officer's conference, was asked how soldier morale could be lifted. His answer was to introduce mobile field brothels, as the French had done. The 22nd ARVN HQ surrendered on April 22, with one of its regiments even defecting to the communist side.[24]

In *The Vietnam War*, Colonel Lung wrote, "On 21 April, based on intelligence reports, the enemy intention to attack the division headquarters became evident. In the light of synthesized data on enemy movements, the division G-2 warned of an imminent tank-supported attack against the division headquarters, probably during the next two or three days. But this enemy capability was rejected by the II Corps commander and his American advisor. On 23 April, enemy PT-76 tanks moved in to attack the 22nd Division headquarters and overran it during the day."[25]

The NVA struck III Corps on April 4. On April 7 in Loc Ninh (III Corps), another ARVN lieutenant colonel attempted to surrender his command, the 9th Infantry Regiment, 5th ARVN Division. Lieutenant Colonel Nguyen Cong Vinh and his bodyguards did manage to run out of their compound's gate and surrender. The commander of the 5th ARVN Division, Brigadier General Le Van Hung, was another of those political generals (of the so-called "Delta Clan") who owed their position to the powers-that-be in Saigon and was well-known for not wanting to make decisions.[26]

Southeast of An Loc (III Corps), two NVA regiments scattered the 1st Airborne Brigade on April 19, 1972. The 6th Airborne Battalion commander, Lieutenant Colonel Dinh, had his men dig foxholes, after which he climbed in one and refused to come out.[27] Also in III Corps, the commander of the 1st Troop/5th Cavalry Squadron (1-5 Cavalry Squadron) "surrendered himself and most of his unit to the North Vietnamese at Firebase Alpha north of Loc Ninh."[28] This unit even drove their tanks and APCs into Cambodia for the NVA. The "commander of the 9th Regiment [Colonel Nguyen Cong Vinh] at Loc Ninh [who] wilted under the NVA assault, and it is likely that he surrendered rather than go down fighting."[29] Consider also the 5th VC Division's successful assault on Loc Ninh, where "the Loc Ninh district chief [Major Thinh] abandoned Captain [George] Wanat as they tried to escape to the south." CAPT Wanat managed to evade capture for 31 days until he was captured and eventually sent to Cambodia as a POW for 285 days.[30]

The reverberations from the surrender of a whole regiment in I Corps were keenly and rapidly felt across the country. American advisors in particular looked askance at the ARVN units they were supporting. "More damaging than the selfishness demonstrated by some of the 5th ARVN soldiers (who looted, fired into houses in An Loc, sold air-dropped food and medical supplies" and "fired on airborne and ranger troops who were attempting to retrieve air-dropped supplies) was the cowardice demonstrated by some officers."

Before anyone thinks that this has been a one-sided summation of the abilities of the South Vietnamese Armed Forces, there were many good units that fought well at various times during the war. The 1st ARVN Division is usually cited as the best division that South Vietnam had. Truth be told, however, the division had suffered badly during *Lam Son 719* and hadn't fully recovered less than a year later when the Easter Offensive started.

What is not usually written by historians and biographers is the fact that when an American "newbie" came to Vietnam, most were told that the life of an enlisted member of any of the US armed services wasn't worth a dime to either the VC or the NVA; they would sooner kill you in a blink of an eye. It was, therefore, obvious that you might as well fight to the death because of the enemy's contempt for the Geneva Convention and their lack of honor in not accepting surrender and automatically killing all those *hors de combat*. There were too many stories of the VC gruesomely torturing to death of prisoners and of the NVA "shooting and machine-gunning our wounded and laughing and giggling."[31]

Americans should have understood from the beginning that the South Vietnamese defended their own families and the area in which they lived, before anything. During the Easter Offensive, the Local Forces/Popular Forces generally fought very well, though their lack of sophisticated weaponry was pronounced and greatly contributed to their combat death totals. To varying degrees, the Vietnamese would lie to your face, as integrity was a Western value they did not seem to fully embrace yet. Their own self-preservation came first, then their nuclear and extended family, followed by their village. Country was a vague notion that few seemed to care about.

The ARVN units were, likewise, very territorial in their own individual makeups. As such, they were, perhaps, more reminiscent of American colonists willing to defend their local and state lands. The 3rd ARVN Division was a newly composed unit, without experience and with commanders who were not up to leading their own individual units, not to mention the sub-par caliber of many of its soldiers, who were not from the local area.

The South Vietnamese Marine Corps tradition of having a general officer whose family came from the North becoming the Commandant of Marines is a bewildering fact, as well. It is worth pointing out, however, that the family of General Giai, the 3rd ARVN Division commander, also came from a village a few kilometers from Hanoi, too.[32] Also unsettling was the favoritism in the political appointments of general officers and their assignments. While senior US officers filed through various units, "command time" was (and remains) essential for advancement, and while there is an amount of political pull within the US military, ARVN had to contend with direct civilian machinations. "The problem with this meteoric promotion (from battalion to corps commander in seven years) was that (LTG) Truong, like many other general officers, didn't have time to attend advanced military training."[33] For that matter, many of the senior military leadership had been at war since their teens, so few had a formal education.

The desertion stampede was to repeat itself in 1975, as Major General Homer Smith stated at the time. He pointed out that:

> The collapse of South Vietnam in 1975 was caused not by cowardice but by the "family syndrome." The fact that the ARVN had their families with them on their battle positions made for great stability on local operations, when the soldiers fought to protect their wives and children, but it was a disaster during the withdrawal from the Central Highlands and the northern provinces in March 1975, when soldiers left their units to take care of their families, causing whole divisions to fall apart. When their families were safe, however, they fought valiantly. During the final NVA blitzkrieg, not one ARVN unit surrendered to the enemy.[34]

There were in fact more South Vietnamese units that fought bravely and well than is commonly thought. "South Vietnamese Combat Performance, A Case Study" by James H. Willbanks provides an example of how well some fought during the

Easter Offensive of 1972 at An Loc. US aircraft support (tactically and in resupply) were essential to ARVN's success as An Loc was, like Quang Tri was in I Corps, surrounded. But as Willbanks points out in his book on An Loc, it wasn't without its share of problematic troops and units, as elsewhere in every corps area.

"When I finally made it out of the camp, the evacuation landing zone was an absolute fiasco. A large number of the South Vietnamese special forces troops—our friendlies—had decided they had priority to get on the helicopters before anyone else, and they were mobbing the helicopters and shooting each other. The NVA was also shooting at us. It was a horrible mess."[35]

"Not all Montagnards were on our side, sometimes the VC and NVA got to some tribes before we did."[36] Sometimes, (Vietnamese) trainees were a little too good, as if they had done things before—"doubtfuls" and probably infiltrators. ("This happened consistently and in large numbers" in all of Medal of Honor recipient BennyAdkins' tours.)[37]

During the evacuation of Camp A Shau, fighting was so intense that half of the helicopters sent to retrieve the defending force were forced to turn back. Those that landed were swarmed by Civilian Irregular Defense Group (CIDG) and Luc Luong Dac Biet (LLDB; South Vietnamese Special Forces) men who rushed for the helicopters. "As they ran, many of the South Vietnamese dropped weapons and also left the wounded behind ... they ... were fighting one another to get on the choppers, and the helicopters became so overloaded they couldn't take off."[38] There were four LLDB soldiers evacuated, only one was actually wounded.[39] The 141st CIDG Company was heavily infiltrated by the NVA; they even fired at a US plane that landed to pick up wounded and resupply aircraft and at the SF troops inside the compound.[40]

"When I was putting Bradford on the plane, the indigenous soldiers were mobbing the helicopter. 'They were hanging all over that son of a gun,' Bradford said. 'The pilot got it up and had to shake the helicopter to get them off. It was a mob scene.' ... In addition to NVA and VC, there were some other force fighting us, too. I can't recall exactly when this happened, but I do know I saw at least one of the enemy wearing a Chinese uniform. He was standing there surveying the situation and I shot at him, but I missed."[41]

Victor Underwood recalled seeing another kind of soldier there, too. "'There was this one big guy I shot.' Underwood said. 'He had round eyes and black hair on his arms, which the Vietnamese did not. He was wearing a silver belt buckle with a red star on it and had a silver thing on his hat with a red star, too. He could have been a Russian or a Frenchman.'"[42]

Americans fought the NVA and VC and sometimes had to physically deal with the South Vietnamese military, as well. Chance encounters with probable North Vietnamese advisors occurred less frequently.

CHAPTER 10

Too Many Tanks

Though various sources, including the CIA in Appendix 9, have indicated five battalions of tanks operated in II and III Corps, and other sources have cited a rough total of 300 NVA tanks operated in I, II, and III Corps during the Easter Offensive of 1972, the most prevalent problem in this regard was an unwillingness on the part of (U.S. and South Vietnamese) commanders to heed warnings of massed armor and heavy artillery.[1]

While the 203rd NVA Tank Regiment was able to cross into South Vietnam to the west in support of the 304th NVA Division making a wide envelopment of ARVN firebases from the west, the destruction of the Dong Ha Bridge derailed, for a time, the plans of the 202nd NVA Tank Regiment's support of the 308th NVA Division's push southward from the DMZ, via QL-1. The 202nd was forced to turn west to make use of the Cam Lo Bridge for crossing the Mieu Giang River. It then apparently regrouped until the morning of 2 April, beginning its approach to Quang Tri, as the 203rd took up positions opposite the western firebases. Blowing the Dong Ha Bridge had ruined the double envelopment of the NVA's original plan, but it did not stop the 304th and 203rd's portion of the envelopment. The 571st theorized as much when the NVA order of battle, which was heavily positioned in the eastern DMZ, was plotted.

Various descriptions of the activity around the bridge include South Vietnamese A-1/Skyraiders flying and knocking out tanks and equipment. No such aircraft were present this day or the *USS Buchanan*'s air search radar would have picked them up.

The use of tanks by the NVA during the Easter Offensive was to be found throughout South Vietnam in I Corps, II Corps, and III Corps. John Paul Vann, the Second Regional Assistance Commander in II Corps, was told about tanks before the offensive but chose to dismiss it. The exact identity of each unit depends on the author of each article, military publication, and book. There have been attempts by many to define the identities of all these units, despite the dearth of Vietnamese information on the subject.

As a former Order of Battle (OB) analyst, I too have spent countless hours wading through the various media for answers about NVA tank units. I quickly found contradictions galore, which caused me to start with the 2002 English version of the *Victory in Vietnam*, which was first written and revised in 1994 by the Military Institute of Vietnam. The Vietnamese *People's Army Newspaper* (online) reinforced what was gleaned from other material. *Victory in Vietnam* served as the baseline for comparing all the US information sources, including some previously classified documents (especially MACV's 1972–1973 *Command History*, Volume 1) and especially in what American advisors who were in Vietnam have written.

In total, everyone erred at some point in their writings. MACV also erred by not listing some units. MACV, CIA, and various authors also got it wrong when it identified the B-70 Corps as having taken the field, as it had during *Lam Son 719*. *Victory in Vietnam* clearly states that, "the fact that we still had not formed regular army corps meant we were slow and that we could not keep up with the requirements of large-scale combat targeted on destroying enemy regiment and battalions."[2]

As pointed out elsewhere in this book, it was not unusual for NVA units to have identical numeric designators. There were many examples of two and even three regiments having the same numeric identifier. This became further complicated when regiments were independent units controlled by a Front, Military Region, or division. Few units would permanently stay in a previous operating area. The 316th NVA Infantry Division, performing its "international duty," remained in Laos during the Easter Offensive and had returned there many times before. As a result of the 1970 Central Military Party Committee plenary session, "the Armor Branch upgraded the combat power of its two reserve regiments, the 203rd Armored Regiment (with T-34 and T-54 tanks) and the 202nd Armored Regiment, and sent two battalions to reinforce the northern and southern fronts in Laos."[3] Notice this was before *Lam Son 719*. The armored battalions may have been the 4th and 195th.

These are my most diligent efforts to identify the main tank units operating in the Easter Offensive of 1972, based on the best available information at this time (and in light of not receiving any reply from the PAVN's Military History Department):

I Corps: At the onset of the Easter Offensive of 1972, two armor regiments struck from behind the DMZ. The 202nd Armored Regiment (the NVA's first armored unit) and the 203rd Armored Regiment both collided with ARVN forces opposite them in the eastern and western portions of the DMZ and Laos, respectively. In the western DMZ, their initiative was made undoubtedly easier by the improved roads that the NVA engineers had built in South Vietnam before the offensive began. The movement of NVA armor through the DMZ and northern South Vietnam was also made easier due to the prepositioning of material and by the oil pipeline that stretched into this same area. The identity of these two regiments has been repeatedly confirmed by multiple sources. The 203rd Armored Regiment was assigned to the

304th Infantry Division and the 202nd Armored Regiment was assigned to the 308th Infantry Division.

II Corps: The NVA sent tanks to the Central Highlands for the Easter Offensive. It is highly possible that the 198th and the 297th Armored Battalions sooner or later became the 273rd Armored Regiment in 1974. Today, there is a 273rd Armored Regiment in their III Corps area in the Central Highlands. Unlike the 202nd and 203rd Armored Regiments, which have become brigades, the 273rd remains a regiment.

III Corps: The 26th Armored Regiment was formed by the COSVN Military Command in eastern Cochin China in early 1972. One of the 26th's subordinates may have been the 171st Armored Battalion, as 97 percent of the unit completed a 1,200km journey down the trail.[4] MACV does not show its presence at any time during the Easter Offensive, however.

It is also known that 12 independent armored companies with light tanks (Soviet PT-76 and the similar Chinese Type 63) were also sent southward to participate in the Easter Offensive. These alone organizationally equate to four armored battalions. In I Corps, a former ARVN armor colonel wrote that a "regiment of amphibious PT-76 tanks" were part of the initial attack[5] based on the former commanding general of 3rd ARVN Division *being shown documents while he was imprisoned* in re-education camps.[6] This assumes that the North Vietnamese knew what they were talking about and the general wasn't being deliberately lied to.

Not surprisingly, CIA documents on this (and other) topics are not only lacking, but outright contradictory. Regarding just armor units, one CIA document does correctly show the 202nd and 203rd Armor Regiments in I Corps/MR-1.[7] The document continues, however, by placing two battalions of the 203rd in II Corps/MR-2 and three 203rd battalions in III Corps/MR-3. That is, then, the 203rd had five *additional* battalions located hundreds of miles away from its parent, surely making command and control somewhat difficult! Part of this confusion can likely be explained by the fact that newly created units often trained alongside the two seasoned units (the 202nd and 203rd Armored Regiments) in North Vietnam. Further, as it is known that individual tank battalions were sent to central and lower Laos at times, it is quite likely that these units kept their old battalion numbers and entered II and III Corps before or during the Easter Offensive. Ironically, the 1972 MACV *Command History*, Volume II, also refers to the 202nd and 203rd Armored Regiments in II and III Corps, as does the CIA.

According to ARVN Colonel Hoang Ngoc Lung, agent sources had reported enemy tanks during the ARVN operation at Krek and Chup in Cambodia in December 1971, revealing a concentration of about 30 tanks around the Chup Plantation, including PT-76s, T-34s, and T-54s, Furthermore, when enemy tanks advanced towards An Loc, COL Lung noted that two new types of armor were identified—Chinese communist (Chicom)-made T-59s and Russian-made BTR-50

APCs."[8] Three regiments of a divisional entity (apparently generated and trained by the 325th NVA Division) were sent to Cambodia and later South Vietnam.[9] Lomperis also places the NVA's 203rd Armored Regiment in II Corps, with the 320th, 2nd, and 3rd NVA Infantry Divisions,[10] but again the MACV *Command History* for 1972 does not show any armored regiments outside of the 202nd and 203rd Armored Regiments in northern I Corps. It was assessed that the 202nd Armored Regiment was composed of the 66th, 198th, 397th, and 244th Armored Battalions. The 66th and 244th Armored Battalions were believed to be equipped with Type 63 tanks. The 203rd Armored Regiment had the 3rd, 4th, and 512th Armored Battalions subordinate to it during the Easter Offensive of 1972. The 4th Armored Battalion may have supported 324B Division operations in April and May with Type 59/T-54 and T-34 tanks. Interestingly, "captured tank crewmen admitted graduating from the Russian Armor School in Odessa in late 1971."[11] In fact, while some 3,000 NVA soldiers were rushed home from the Soviet Union prior to the start of the offensive, many had not completed their tank instruction. It is reasonable to assume that, given the Soviet equipment and training, the NVA likely closely paralleled the Soviet Table of Organization and Equipment (TO&E) of 95 tanks and some 30 APCs per tank regiment.

Part of the unit identification problem with the 203rd rests, again, with LTG Truong, who wasn't in III Corps (and he wasn't in I Corps until May 3). He stated that an NVA tank crewman was taken prisoner in An Loc on April 13 and "declared he belonged to the 1st Battalion, 203rd NVA Armored Regiment. His unit had moved from North Vietnam through lower Laos and then took shelter in Cambodia. Only the day before, his unit was ordered to move into Binh Long Province from the border and participate in the An Loc battle."[12]

A Russian-made T-54 tank was also destroyed on April 13 south of An Loc with its tank records intact. The T-54 was issued to the 5th Company, 5th Battalion, of the 203rd Armored Regiment from the Y1 Rear Service Depot (which received it "before Jan 68"). The tank's records don't show *anything* after December 5, 1971, when the tank practiced turning its 100mm gun—a total of more than four months before it was taken out of action. Additionally, other logbooks were left blank. Great store seems to have been taken in by, "There was no mention in any documents of this tank being handed over to any another [sic] unit. Based on this fact, we can interpret that until the date it was destroyed by RVNAF in An Loc, this tank still belonged to the 5th Co, 5th Bn, 203 Armored Regt, NVA Armor Command." Face value, in light of what has already been discussed and the following paragraph, seems to obviate this conclusion by CDEC.[13] First, the 203rd was still in I Corps during and after this time. Armored regiments, like most Soviet units (who trained the North Vietnamese), had three battalions—not five or more found hundreds of miles away. Third, the 203rd had a storage complex of tanks in North Vietnam. Fourth, a least one PT-76 unit left their tanks in Laos and returned to North Vietnam for a quick training on 203rd tanks in storage. Fifth, the tank in question oddly had no maintenance or other logs. And finally, CDEC joined the choir of Saigon organizations that had no idea of who was fighting in I Corps.

The intelligence gave some other insights. There were reports from at least I and III Corps that NVA tank crewmen were chained to their positions in their tanks. Former South Vietnamese commando Nguyen van Kiet looked into an invading NVA tank and saw a soldier dead and still chained to his tank position in I Corps.[14]

CHAPTER 11

In Retrospect ... A Brief Look Back

Surveying what has been written in the years since the Easter Offensive of 1972, one finds contradictions, equivocations, and blatant lies, as facts seem to erode slowly in favor of popular fiction. With notable exceptions (e.g., *An Loc, Kontum* and *First In, Last Out*), there are few *first-hand* accounts of this, the largest North Vietnamese campaign of the entire war, until South Vietnam was completely taken over by the communist North in 1975. Further, there are far fewer things written about one of the pivotal events that occurred just three days after the offensive began. This is a true chronicle of incompetence, ignorance, betrayal, cowardice, and treason and one that impacted more than just one particular unit or one country.

The firebases in I Corps, the northern portion of South Vietnam, had seen US Marine and US Army combat troops for many years. As Vietnamization of the war proceeded apace and US units left country, South Vietnamese forces became solely responsible for firebases and they occupied many of them in Quang Tri and Thua Thien Provinces by late 1971. (The former province abutted the DMZ, while the latter was the next province south of it, where the city of Hue is located.)

US forces left a significant void in the protection of Quang Tri Province as they vacated these northern firebases. Instead of moving an experienced division up from elsewhere, the South Vietnamese JGS decided to create a new division, the 3rd ARVN Division. The 3rd, with the nickname of the *Ben Hai* Division (named for the river that traversed the DMZ), was under the command of the former XO of the 1st ARVN Division (Forward), Brigadier General Vu Van Giai. The command post of the 3rd ARVN Division was located at Ai Tu Combat Base, just a few kilometers north of Quang Tri.

Why the much-vaunted 1st ARVN Division didn't move north from Hue to defend northern South Vietnam, instead of the JGS creating an entirely new, untried, and untested division is somewhat explainable. Major General Pham Van Phu took over command of 1st ARVN in August 1970 and, in a few months, the division fought in *Lam Son 719*. One of the consequences of the NVA's mauling of so many ARVN units during their incursion into Laos was that 1st ARVN's resulting condition was "so bad that some outside observers believed that the entire 1st ARVN Division was no longer combat ready."[1]

As we have already noted, it was also well known that the city of Hue had a special, historical significance to the Vietnamese and there would be an immediate cry that any military action in the area was really an assault on Hue, as in 1968, one that required the city's immediate defense. This was a common reaction among senior officers in both US and South Vietnamese armed forces and so drove all of their thinking that they were blind to actual events that were not related to attacks on Hue. Stephen B. Young (who served with the CORDS program from 1967 to 1971 as a deputy district advisor in Vinh Long Province and as chief, Village Government Branch), was one among many others who didn't have a clear idea about Hue. "His [Truong's] troops were completely surrounded by the NVA but they held on"[2] in 1968. Returning to Hue in May 1972, he knew the city and the 1st ARVN well, as he commanded the unit in 1968. Hue was not encircled by the NVA when he returned from IV Corps to take over I Corps. Tactical and strategic aircraft were strengthening their returning numbers (USAF and USN/USMC).

US Army Advisory Team 155, the largest advisory team in-country at the time, was assigned to support the 3rd ARVN Division. Lieutenant Colonel William (Bill) Camper and Major Joseph (Joe) Brown were assigned to the 56th Regiment, while Lieutenant Colonel Twichell and Major Figardo were assigned to the 57th ARVN Regiment (commanded by Lieutenant Colonel Do Zeon Gioi). Originally, LTC Camper had been assigned to the 2nd Regiment, but he was subsequently moved to the 56th Regiment because the Team 155 commander, COL Metcalf, felt experienced advisors were needed more in this newly created unit.

The entire 2nd ARVN Regiment was taken from the 1st ARVN Division (a four-regiment division) and served as the backbone of the 3rd ARVN Division, though two of its battalions had suffered greatly during *Lam Son 719*. The 2nd Battalion/2nd ARVN Regiment was hurt so badly that it was tagged as "combat ineffective." The 56th and 57th ARVN Regiments were created almost from scratch. This left 1st ARVN with the 1st, 3rd, and 54th Regiments, until later in 1972 when the 51st Independent Regiment became part of the 1st ARVN's TO&E. The material and personnel impact of *Lam Son 719* on the 1st and 3rd Regiments was such that the 54th Regiment was virtually the only intact 1st ARVN Division fully operational regiment for many months afterwards, conducting operations in the Da Krong and A Shau Valleys.

Truong, transferred out of 1st ARVN in August 1970, was promoted and sent to the Delta where he became the IV Corps commander. He only became the I Corps commander, replacing Lieutenant General Hoang Xuan Lam, on May 3, 1972 (over a month *after* the Easter Offensive began in I Corps). Truong apparently either listened to others or tried to whitewash the real events and activities of the 56th ARVN Regiment because even its own commander tells an entirely different story, and one that others, including myself, had heard at the time. (The turncoat commander of the 56th had also served in Hue in 1968, as did Truong.) In another instance, General Bruce Palmer (who wasn't in Vietnam at the time) proclaimed Truong's leadership in glowing terms, saying that he "supported by stalwart American advisers such as Brigadier General Frederick Kroesen, U.S. Army, organized and fought a successful defense of Hue."[3] Actually, Kroesen was a major general at the time and, by his own admission, his HQ only had a skeletal G-2 and G-3 section and he had tasked his deputy FRAC commander, Brigadier General Thomas Bowen Jr., to handle the advisory affairs.

The 56th ARVN commander was Lieutenant Colonel Phan Van Dinh, of *Hac Bao* fame. The *Hac Bao* (Black Panthers) was considered to be an elite reconnaissance company of the 1st ARVN Division and this unit was the first to raise the Vietnamese flag on the Phu Van Lau Citadel in Hue during the 1968 assault on Hue by communist forces. Dinh became a national hero. As commander of the 56th, Dinh stated that the 3rd Battalions of both his regiment *and* the 57th ARVN were composed of Regional Forces/Popular Forces, People's Self Defense Forces (PSDF) and "hardcore ARVN deserters" (some 700 in number). It was fairly well known that deserters, those who had been absent without leave (AWOL), and prisoners from Saigon (and its vicinity in III Corps) were dumped into the 3rd ARVN. LTC Camper is quoted adding "dissidents" to this pool of "shining" recruits.[4] Even Truong's own assistant I Corps commander, Major General Lam Quang Thi, wrote "The majority of its soldiers were deserters, draft dodgers, and other undesirable elements, who were sent to the northernmost province of South Viet Nam as a punishment."[5] GEN Palmer didn't get it quite right, either. The general wasn't apparently aware that the 3rd ARVN's experienced 2nd Regiment was being redeployed *towards* the DMZ firebases, switching with the 56th Regiment who were going to the positions along the western defense line that the 2nd Regiment was vacating.

The 57th ARVN Regiment's 2nd Battalion was composed of volunteers from the 6th Regiment of the 2nd ARVN Division at Quang Ngai. When not enough soldiers volunteered to go to Quang Tri, the battalion was filled by soldiers who were not necessarily performing well. These soldiers were sent to Dong (probably Dong Da) Training Center for retraining where, ten days later, half of its soldiers had already deserted and returned home.[6]

Supplying, equipping, and training the 3rd ARVN began after it stood-up on October 1, 1971. As the 2nd ARVN Regiment arrived more or less intact, they positioned themselves in the western-facing FSBs, while the 1st Battalions of both the 56th and 57th Regiments manned the northern firebases, while their other battalions continued training in Phu Bai. Early in March, the 56th moved into FSB C-2 from Cam Lo. Training of the battalions did not include conventional Main Force tactics, fighting against tanks, or large (regimental) movements and tactical operations. These training evolutions weren't accomplished because there had never been any foreseen need to do so, though (if nothing else) *Lam Son 719* should have been recognized as what was likely forthcoming. As most operations were anti-infiltration and small-unit insurgency operations, the 56th was pronounced operational only a few days before the Easter Offensive began.

Kroesen, in his "Quang Tri, The Lost Province," wrote that 3rd ARVN "was in good condition; morale was apparently excellent, training had been realistic and effective ...."[7] The official FRAC history for 1972–73 (page 8) states, however, "Replacement and training policies were both inadequate and inconsistent," and a "battalion consisted wholly of Regional Force and Provincial [*sic*—should be "Popular"] Force (RF/PF) personnel—and hundreds of deserters."

With some 550,000 men, South Vietnam's Territorial Forces were composed of Regional and Popular Forces (RF/PF, aka "Ruff Puffs"), the countrywide South Vietnamese National Guard-type units. South Vietnamese RF consisted of 1,679 company-sized units that protected district areas. The PF comprised 8,356 platoon-sized units that guarded their home villages. The RFs and PFs of the Quang Tri Sector during the Easter Offensive were commanded by Colonel Phan Ba Hoa. There were also the 116,000-strong National Police and more than four million people that comprised the PSDF throughout the country.[8]

During the offensive, the RF/PFs quickly turned into an offensive force and were used as such by ARVN units to supplement their operations. It was not unusual, however, for some RF/PFs units to engage NVA forces by themselves. In the first months of the invasion by the North, these units were responsible for over a third of the enemy KIAs, while suffering a similar amount of losses themselves. BG Haig wrote a memo concerning his findings in a three-day trip to Vietnam in mid-April which lauded the RF/PF forces. His discussions with President Thieu also concerned making some of these forces into the much-preferred regular ARVN forces. The head of the U.S. Joint Chiefs did not think the current Easter Offensive was the appropriate time to consider this proposal.[9]

During the Easter Offensive, "unable to defend everything, 1st ARVN (with US Armor officer Colonel Hillman Dickinson as Senior Advisor) constricted its lines and once again ceded control of the western highlands of I Corps to the NVA."[10] This was the situation in the upper two provinces of Quang Tri and Thua Thien in I Corps on March 29, 1972. MG Kroesen is quoted in FRAC's *Command History*, page 12, in his 310415Z March 1972 report to GEN Abrams, "Yesterday's effort also follows closely the recent increase in activity to the southwest of Hue and may have been designed in part to divert ARVN assets from his area to relieve pressure on the 324B Division." Perhaps he wasn't aware of 1st ARVN Division's actions, as he should have been. He certainly did not mention the regiments of the 3rd ARVN Division switching places and being caught in the open. He wrote in this message that the "ground attacks were probably an initial test of 3d Division defenses and reaction capabilities and sizable infantry and artillery forces are now deployed in western

Quang Tri and any ARVN operations to the west will meet heavy resistance," but hours before this message was sent FSB Sarge and Nui Ba Ho had to be abandoned.

Perhaps Kroesen is also responsible for the left hand not knowing what the right was doing. For example, Brigadier General Winant Sidle, who was the head of MACV's Office of Information, contended "that the Third Division was a great success [and] was justified in military eyes because the successful equipping of a large combat force was always a massive undertaking," though "CBS correspondent Phil Jones reported, 'the division's officers were straining to comprehend sophisticated American tactics and equipment and its logistical systems were faltering, and some of its men had not been paid in two months.'"[11]

The very next day, Thursday, March 30, 1972, began with a low ceiling of cloud cover, which added to a day in which coincidences were to exceed all probabilities. COL Metcalf, in his War College essay, did not mention that when the Easter Offensive began the 56th ARVN Regiment was literally on the road, swapping positions with the 2nd ARVN Regiment. Apparently this was a scheduled move between the two regiments (though I could find no such written order) ordered by Brigadier General Vu Van Giai, the 3rd ARVN Division commander, and one that neither of the units or commanders had ever accomplished before. Neither the general nor his American advisor thought it was important enough to be present during the period when both regiments would literally be incommunicado with each other and their division HQ. As noted previously, this swap-over has been attributed to BG Giai's concern to alleviate "firebase syndrome." One would have also thought that *Lam Son 719* would have called attention to the manner and difficulty in which ARVN conducted retrograde (withdraw under pressure, in this case) operations back from Laos into South Vietnam, but it doesn't appear that this "Lesson Learned" was even contemplated. Worse, the FRAC commander stated that the 56th had only spent three weeks deployed along the DMZ, instead of the few months it really had—apparently, he was unsure of what was occurring some 137km away.[12]

The 2nd ARVN Regiment was positioned along the western portion of the ARVN-controlled area, where any perceived NVA attack from Laos would likely come from. The 56th ARVN was garrisoned among the northern DMZ firebases, where not one general officer, intelligence, or major command thought the NVA would attack from the DMZ itself. The least combat-ready and least competent regiment would then assume what was said to be the most dangerous, western-facing responsibilities in I Corps.

The ARVN I Corps commander, LTG Lam, was more a political general than a military commander, and often exhibited inept and indecisive leadership. The Airborne Division commander, Lieutenant General Du Quoc Dong, outranked Lam and publicly pointed out what was wrong with the *Lam Son 719* plan. Dong also never attended any of Lam's briefings or interacted with Lam during the operation.[13] (This was to recur in the Easter Offensive.) "In the midst of *Lam Son 719*, the Airborne

Division senior advisor, Colonel Arthur W. Pence, was relieved. LTG Sutherland, the commanding general of XXIV Corps and the senior American officer in the AO, believed Pence had lost his objectivity and had been thoroughly co-opted by his counterpart."[14] To compound the problem in I Corps, its HQ had "never actually functioned as a field headquarters in combat," as the FRAC commander (Kroesen) later admitted. Nor had it operated as such under Kroesen's command, either. (Kroesen formally relieved Major General James Baldwin, commander of the Americal Division, after GEN Abrams fired Baldwin for the actions of FSB Kate fame (Kate was overrun by the NVA, for which Baldwin and a couple of others were reprimanded for not insuring Kate's defensive security). Kroesen was the last commander of the Americal Division when it was deactivated in December 1971, with two of its brigades withdrawn from Vietnam. He then became the deputy I Corps/FRAC commander.)

Apparently, there were other US generals who were equally or even more confused. GEN Palmer remarkably stated that, "To make matters worse there was no overall South Vietnamese commander of all forces north of Hai Van Pass, which separates the two northernmost provinces of Quang Tri and Thua Thien from the rest of I CTZ."[15] The South Vietnamese I Corps commander was LTG Lam, however, and he commanded *all* of the northern five provinces. A major movement of any comparable size in the US Army would normally take a great deal of preparation; being in close proximity to an enemy demands even greater attention to detail. Troop routes, equipment tear-down, and set-up, military police positioning, and an ability to communicate with all units are essential components of such a move. This was not done as each regiment turned off their communication equipment and moved out separately.

Above all of this was a "supposed" JGS warning of imminent NVA hostilities. "Supposed," since not one I Corps unit mentioned the warning and no US unit that remained in I Corps (MR-1) seemed to be aware of any warning order, either. It is possible that the 571st INTSUM was the basis for this warning, but (not surprisingly) there is no direct linkage revealed or inferred.

The 2nd and 56th Regiments of 3rd ARVN shut down their comms gear at about 0830 that morning. At 0900, the 3rd Battalion, 56th Regiment (3/56th)left FSB C-2 for FB Khe Gio (which they reached); the 1/56th was charged with patrolling Route 9 and then it was to proceed to FSB Fuller (which they did not reach, and the 1/2nd, which was at Fuller, remained); elements of the 2/56th waited at C-2 for the 2nd Regiment to arrive, and the 3/56th tried to make its way to Khe Gio. HQ and HQ company of the 56th (with the regiment commander) and one infantry company arrived at Camp Carroll around 1130. Therefore, the 56th ARVN Regiment left C-2 in battalion order 3–1–2.

It was common VNMC practice to separate a battalion into two command groups, Alpha and Bravo, with the senior advisor with the VNMC battalion commander in

Alpha group and the assistant advisor and VNMC's XO in the Bravo group. Each group had two reinforced rifle companies.

Weather was a constant factor throughout this period and air support was nil. The 9th NVA Regiment of the 304th NVA Division forced Bravo Group and Captain Smith off Nui Ba Ho at 2140 with Captain Smith leading them through the mine field laid beyond the concertina of the FB. Seemingly inexhaustible artillery fires continued the next day, April 1st. Major Walter Boomer, the advisor of the Alpha Group, had withstood near constant enemy artillery and multiple waves of assaults (as had Bravo Group) by the 66th NVA Regiment of the 304th NVA Division on Sarge. When the NVA occupied some of the squad positions in the firebase—it succumbed six hours after Nui Ba Ho at 0330 on 1 Apr. As the Alpha group departed Sarge, everyone scattered eastward. Boomer had no idea what happened to Smith but thought him probably KIA until they stumbled upon each other on their eastward treks. Smith had carried a wounded Marine all the way from Nui Ba Ho, with only one VNMC assisting towards Mai Loc. As they neared the compound around dawn on April 2nd, they stayed outside it until nightfall. At dusk, the 147th HQ and the artillery battalion streamed out headed for Quang Tri with Smith having tied Boomer to him. A Huey was sent to them after contact was later made.[16]

Elements of the 57th ARVN moved from FSB A-2 to FB C-1 at 1400 and then onto the Dong Ha area at 2115, as the NVA attempted to flank this unit. BG Giai ordered both the 2nd and 57th ARVN Regiments to take up positions south of Cam Lo on April 1. Turley wrote that on April 2, "The 57th Regiment, including its commander, had broken under the enemy pressure and, in complete route, had retreated. Its future as a viable fighting force was at best questionable."[17] The 2nd ARVN Regiment withdrew to Cam Lo at 1800 from C-2, minus one infantry battalion unaccounted for. There is no report of the 2nd ARVN until the following Monday, April 3.

Mai Loc was evacuated on April 2 due to dwindling ammunition and supplies. The 147th VNMC Brigade and what was left of the 4th VNMC Battalion moved out with all of their wounded. The recently attached 7th VNMC Battalion (from the VNMC 258th Brigade) was tasked to bring up the rear and had to disengage first from fighting the 66th NVA Regiment (304th NVA Division) as the VNMC and their USMC advisors moved towards Dong Ha or, as darkness fell, towards Ai Tu. The 8th Battalion, 147th VNMC, Marines at Mai Loc were forced out on April 2, primarily by 122mm and 130mm artillery fire.

CHAPTER 12

Prologue to Surrender—Camp Carroll

When you are occupying a position which the enemy threatens to surround, collect all your force immediately, and menace him with an offensive movement.

—NAPOLEON BONAPARTE, MAXIM XXIII

LTC Dinh stated that some 200 artillery rounds had slammed into Camp Carroll (primarily 130mm) during the first hour of the 56th ARVN Regiment's arrival on March 30, 1972. Elements of the 1/56th, 2/56th, and 3/56th (and possibly the 1/2nd) made it to Carroll by March 31. Camp Carroll was subjected to intensive artillery and rocket attacks. Dinh talked with GEN Giai and quickly realized that he had little control over whatever events were to come.

The first human wave assault on Carroll by the 24th NVA Regiment, 304th NVA Division, was preceded by sappers on April 1, 1972, as well. Dinh talked with GEN Lam, who indicated that there would be no reinforcements and that he was to hold his position. The general apparently cut the phone call short as he left for his evening tennis match.[1] That night, Dinh talked on the phone with his wife in Hue, some 65km away. He also contacted his enemy:

> On the night of 2 April [April 2, in this recounting of events, must be April 1st—or March 31st because Camp Carroll fell to the NVA on April 2nd or else the following conversations makes no sense], I was discussing the situation with Deputy Regiment Commander Tran Thong. Thong told me, "This morning an enemy voice repeatedly broke into the radio channel of our forward observation post. The voice kept asking to talk to the senior officer of the Bong Lau Group [which must be the 38th Composite Artillery Regiment]." I told Thong, "I want you to talk to that person. Ask him his name and why he wants to talk to the commander of the Bong Lau Group." Early the next morning, around 0500 hours in the morning, Thong telephoned me. He said, "Son! The guy on the radio says that he is Lt. Col. Pham Van Dinh, the commander of the 56th Regiment at Strong-point 241, which is currently being bombarded by our unit. He asks the Bong Lau Group to cease firing so that he can bring his entire regiment out to join the revolution." I immediately called Hoang Dan, the Commander of the 304th Division, the unit that the Bong Lau Group was supporting in battle. Hoang Dan replied, "You should encourage him to surrender."[2]

At 1400 on April 2, the 24th NVA's second human-wave attack came from the west, near the main gate. A little before 1500, "Dinh received a call from the NVA" about surrendering. This was followed-up a short time later by someone who claimed to be the commander of the communist forces in the area who told him that they would overrun "241" (Camp Carroll) if Dinh did not surrender. (The NVA referred to Camp Carroll as "241," its elevation in meters.) Dinh asked for time to meet with his staff and commanders (1st Battalion commander was Major Ton That Man, the 2nd Battalion commander was LTC Vinh Phong (Dinh's XO), and the 3rd Battalion commander, Major Ha Thuc Mau) to consider surrendering, which the communist commander granted.[3]

This is one of the least-mentioned events that occurred during the Easter Offensive of 1972: the surrender of the 56th Army of the Republic of Vietnam (ARVN) Regiment of the 3rd ARVN Division on Easter Sunday, April 2, 1972. The NVA knew that there were two American advisors assigned to the 56th ARVN Regiment and the enemy knew both were in Camp Carroll. LTC Dinh was instructed by the NVA to ensure they surrendered, as well. Both LTC Camper and MAJ Brown tried to convince Dinh not to surrender, that things were bad, but they could continue to resist for a while longer. Camper and Brown weren't "forced back under enemy fire" as sometimes reported, but left the base by helicopter—a CH-47 (call sign Coachman 005) couldn't land outside the wire, so Camper and Brown headed back to the helipad and were lifted away. Camper and Brown's After-Action Report is located in the Appendix 14.

There is mention of the 308th NVA Division conducting operations in the area[4] (outside their AO), instead of the 24th NVA Regiment of the 304th NVA Division assault on Camp Carroll. There were other units that supported NVA troops across the DMZ and from inside South Vietnam, including the 164th Artillery Regiment, which was believed to have been permanently assigned to the 308th, becoming a composite artillery regiment, and the 365th Air Division (with SA-2s and AAA). Three artillery regiments were formed in January–February 1972 into a composite artillery group, called the Bong Lau Group, likely also the precursor to the divisional artillery as the 304th later became mechanized. The 38th Composite Artillery Regiment (commanded by Lieutenant Colonel Nguyen Cao Son) was equipped with three different field guns, multiple launch rocket systems (MLRSs), and large mortars. This artillery unit supported the 304th NVA Division's (Colonel Hoang Yen commanding) efforts in the Camp Carroll and FSB Sarge areas.

Dinh surrendered Camp Carroll at 1520 on April 2, 1972. Further ramifications of LTC Dinh's surrender have emerged and bear closer scrutiny. The events leading up to this infamous surrender have already been presented. Though the colonels and generals of the US forces and the ARVN barely (if at all) mention the subject, there is at least one supposition that requires further investigation: perhaps the capitulation of the 56th ARVN Regiment was not unplanned, but a portion of a larger conspiracy?

Like *Lam Son 719*, the Easter Offensive was another instance where South Vietnamese security had proven to be a virtual sieve. BG Giai's plan to switch regiments on the exact day and time of the NVA invasion was just too coincidental. There was no real belief that an attack from the DMZ was imminent (or at all) and that the main threat would continue to come from the west/Laos, so why position the most inexperienced regiment (the 56th) in the most dangerous locations while the most experienced regiment (the 2nd) moved to an "easier area?" Why even think that the North would "keep their word?"

If there was an actual alert of some kind, then the MACV, his J-2, the US ambassador to South Vietnam, the Team 155 commander, the 3rd ARVN Division commander, LtCol Turley and other visiting USMC officers, and the Senior Marine Advisor to South Vietnam wouldn't have been out of position instead of somewhere else. The 571st had no knowledge of an alert and we would have been commanded to take special actions from FRAC and/or 525th MI Group HQ if there were. One suspects that this "alert" was an after-the-fact, cover-your-ass exercise for not forecasting the invasion. Kroesen later wrote, "Every estimate relied to some degree on the enemy's past activity patterns to predict his future courses of action." This was true of DIA, MACV, and apparently XXIV Corps/FRAC/I Corps, but it obviously wasn't true of the 571st.

BG Giai believed that an underground communist railroad was in-place in Quang Tri Province which helped the large number of deserters to move southward to their homes near to or in Saigon. "General Giai was particularly upset by the continued endemic desertion, a problem compounded by communist aid extended to the deserters in the form of an underground railroad of safe houses designed to aid fleeing soldiers in their return south."[5] While a Viet Cong Infrastructure (VCI) effort at proselytizing was commonplace in VC-controlled areas, one wonders if Dinh was somehow in contact with them.

Communication equipment of the 2nd and 56th Regiments was shut down at around 0830 on March 30, 1972 and loaded onto trucks. Both units were then incommunicado between each other and 3rd ARVN Division. NVA artillery started shortly afterwards. This gives further support to the belief that the NVA knew about the switching of locations between the 3rd ARVN Division's 2nd and 56th Infantry Regiments. A cursory look at a map at where both units were first positioned and then their *coincidental and simultaneous* movement all but confirms that the start of the offensive awaited their displacement, given the initial objectives of the 304th and 308th NVA Divisions opposite these same two units and the extensive artillery strikes against ARVN troops in the open. The NVA obviously also had artillery spotters south of the DMZ.

The commander of the 56th, LTC Dinh, arrived at Camp Carroll by traveling southwest from C-2. There were limited artillery stocks available on Camp Carroll, according to Dinh. The commander of the 2nd ARVN Regiment, 3rd ARVN

Division, Lieutenant Colonel Huynh Dinh Tung, never made it to FB C-2 (where his Tactical Operations Center/TOC was located). He stayed in the vicinity of Cam Lo, while his soldiers moved forward under artillery fire. The 57th ARVN Regiment was *not* part of the switching of units (though Dale Andrade mentions it in his book), but, by noon on March 30, had retreated in panic with the fleeing civilians southwards to escape NVA ground action. This error was repeated by Wiest in his book, as well.[6]

BG Giai was leaving for a long weekend in Saigon for a "short meeting" with South Vietnam's President Thieu just as the NVA began the offensive. (On the US side, weather may also have been a factor in the senior command element taking time to leave country, much as German Field Marshal Erwin Rommel did when the allies landed in Normandy in World War II.) LTC Camper had related the events of the surrender to Giai and Metcalf at Ai Tu, but Giai refused to believe him, believing the US advisors were cowardly (Metcalf said *nothing* in their defense, though he knew the American advisors did not run away and leave the 56th on their own). Giai did offer an apology to Camper and Brown the next day, as he listened to the Hanoi broadcast. Both advisors were then assigned by Metcalf to the 2nd ARVN Regiment.

Major Ton That Man spoke in a Radio Hanoi broadcast about the meeting Dinh had convened with his officers at Camp Carroll. Dinh "summoned a meeting of particular significance for it decided on the fate of 600 officers and men in this base. Within only five minutes, all agreed to offer no more resistance and decided to go over to the Liberation forces' side."[7] The problem with this account is that the 24th NVA Regiment had Camp Carroll completely surrounded and the 38th Composite Artillery Regiment's observation posts were specifically watching Camp Carroll. Man's ARVN numbers might be erroneously based on Dinh or someone else's wishful estimates. Andrade's deduction of the "rest managed to slip out of the base" seems ludicrous, as does the notion that LTC Dinh was reportedly depressed before his surrender of his regiment. Repeated wishful thinking and excuses for this travesty won't make it so, especially in light of the fact that there is no evidence to the contrary.

Incredibly, there was no sense of urgency about NVA activity (nor of any supposed warning) until Camp Carroll fell, according to BG Bowen (the deputy FRAC commander). LTG Lam, the I Corps commander, kept Saigon from knowing his difficulties. It is reasonable to assume that he knew that two regiments of the 3rd ARVN would be changing areas, as would MG Kroesen, yet both generals must had said nothing at the time to delay, prohibit, or supervise this movement, and LTC Turley, newly arrived in-country, was visiting I Corps USMC advisors in I Corps/ FRAC when the offensive began. He was asked to take over as the chief advisor of the 3rd ARVN Division (Forward) by COL Metcalf on April 2. LTC Turley called FRAC when Camp Carroll surrendered, but wasn't believed, with FRAC asking to speak to Army officers. When GEN Abrams was told that a Marine lieutenant colonel (Turley) was running things in Quang Tri, he demanded explanations. MG Kroesen (who was technically the senior American advisor in the province and should have been the most informed of anyone about the situation) responded that Turley was wrong and had succumbed to panic.

GEN Weyand stated, "The press will be getting to these advisors like Turley and others. I'm sure the security of U.S. personnel is going to be a big story. The advisors are like this, some of them up there. They want out, and they're not going to be let out—in all probability." The briefer said that, "General Kroesen says he has no information that the U.S. advisors are in any trouble there [Quang Tri Combat Base]. He says the combat base is secure now according to his latest information. He recommends no action other than planning. Kroesen says he has talked to the marine lieutenant colonel and the last he told him confirms what Kroesen reported."[8] How different from the "panic" that Kroesen conveyed to Saigon on this date!

The first information that the White House received about the Easter Offensive came from Admiral Thomas Moorer, Chairman of the Joint Chiefs of Staff during *Lam Son 719* and the Easter Offensive, who repeated traffic received from GEN Abrams. In a March 30, 1972 memorandum (Subject: Situation in I Corps Area) from Al Haig to Henry A. Kissinger Haig mentions ARVN FSBs under attack, but Abrams wrote that the situation was "not critical but is developing." Interestingly, Haig wrote, "A further complication is that the North Vietnamese SAM fan [missile coverage area] has been extended well into Northern I Corps ...." Knowledge of this fact was now known to even Washington, but the Seventh Air Force didn't restrict BAT-21 (and others) to fly over and below the DMZ area?

BG Haig's three-day trip to the RVN in April 1972 also mentioned RVN helicopters. "... the Vietnamese Air Force, advised by the USAF, had no knowledge, feel, or first-hand experience with such airmobility concepts."[9] Further, the inadequacies of Vietnamese helicopter assets require ARVN to deploy combat assets to secure the routes of supply to units in combat with the enemy."[10] These inadequacies might be tied to: "A bad, basic mistake had been made years earlier when South Vietnam's troop-lift and gunship helicopters were placed in VNAF with USAF advisers rather than in ARVN with US Army advisers who were experienced in using helicopters to support ground troops."[11]

It must have been much easier for the NVA to begin the Easter Offensive of 1972, when indicators that something major was going to occur in Quang Tri Province were ignored or summarily dismissed, senior commanders rejecting any thought of NVA actions that didn't conform to their preconceptions or the opinions of the commanders above them. Why, too, weren't preemptive actions taken against NVA road construction through the DMZ and well into South Vietnam? The same questions should have been asked concerning NVA air defense positions in South Vietnam.

So, there were two regiments that couldn't talk with anyone, with the most-experienced regiment (2nd ARVN, less its commander) headed directly into the NVA meat grinder, and the least-experienced regiment (the 56th) in movement away from the NVA onslaught (just in time). The soldiers of the last regiment (the 57th) of the division, also replete with deserters, were leaving their posts, stripping off their uniforms, throwing down their weapons, and mixing in with the civilian exodus headed south around noon, all with the division commander (whose idea it was to switch regiments in the first place) coincidently leaving the scene. Most major media outlets took note of this ARVN exodus. No one up or down the chain of command apparently thought anything about the move and it is little discussed today.

Some defenders of BG Giai, who was arrested and sentenced to five years in jail for the fall of Quang Tri, point to the fact that he spent 12 years in re-education camps after the NVA captured Saigon. Though there are many possible explanations, ultimately trusting the communist government to keep their word was always a losing proposition. Giai was not executed by the NVA, nor did he join the many South Vietnamese generals and their families who were assisted in leaving the country by the United States before the NVA arrived in 1975.

Was some sort of faction formed that used communist agents to make a deal for their lives by trading information, such as the date and time of the regiments swapping positions? Are we to believe in so momentous a coincidence? Was this a conspiracy by senior ARVN officers to elude capture or punishment by NVA forces in order to save themselves by sacrificing their men? Were, then, certain ARVN officers told of the forthcoming enemy offensive to enable them to be elsewhere? Did they ask what would happen to their men? (There was a report that many soldiers of the 56th ARVN were executed at or near the former USMC observation post called the Rockpile—see below and Appendix 2).

For his part, MG Kroesen felt Giai did "the best he could with what he had." Forgetting apparently that the Easter Offensive began in the DMZ area with Giai's two-regiment swap that he ordered but didn't stick around for, Kroesen went on to say, "It did very well for a good period of time." What, a couple of days of retreating and surrender? The former senior advisor to the 57th ARVN Regiment, LTC Heath Twitchell, Jr., chimes in with, "I think it is remarkable and a tribute to General Giai's leadership that the 3d Division held together as long as it did under the pressures it faced. I know of no U.S. division that was ever thrown into full scale combat with 6 months of its organization … Under the circumstances, I doubt if *any* general, U.S. or Vietnamese, could have done much better."

Lieutenant General William J. McCaffrey, deputy commander of USARV, told Team 155 that, "I honestly think that the 3d ARVN Division conducted itself creditably during its 28-day battle at Quang Tri and history will eventually record this fact." Continuing, "McCaffrey credited the division with reducing the 304th and 308th NVA Divisions to 'thirty or forty percent strength' and blamed ensuing problems on the higher command levels rather than on the 'poor little bastards fighting on the ground.'"[12] Yet a complete regiment was gone (the 56th, which had surrendered), another had been chopped up badly by the NVA—the 2nd ARVN Regiment, and at least half of another had deserted (57th)—85 percent or so of the entire division was gone.

LTC Dinh has tried to explain his treasonous dealings, blaming ARVN, the US military, the political leadership, and including his depression as part of his rationale. Dinh gathered his 13 officers together on that Sunday and "they" all agreed that surrendering was their best option. A slightly different version is that a "cabal" of officers forced Dinh to surrender. LTC Dinh personally talked with the NVA a couple times on this day, arranging this surrender. The Memorandum for the Record (MFR), dated April 13, 1972, and written by Camper and Brown, clearly points out not only the sequence of events on April 2, but also Dinh's lying and treasonous leadership in surrendering his command. On page 2, Camper and Brown wrote, "He [Dinh] stated that the men had refused to fight anymore and they wanted to surrender." Additionally, Camper personally reported to Kroesen in Da Nang on April 4—surely the 56th ARVN was the main topic of discussion. Interestingly, GEN Starry wrote, "At 0800 on 2 April, after successfully defending the camp against three major enemy assaults, the 56th Regiment inexplicably gave way."[13] Not only is the time wrong and the number of major enemy assaults, but "inexplicably" is completely the wrong word. (It is unclear from where GEN Starry received this erroneous information.)

In the April 7, 1972, COMUS Update, GEN Abrams stated that, "General Kroesen's daily report just breathed impending disaster from the southwest of Quang Tri." Continuing, "What'd they say, five regiments up there?" Followed by Potts affirmation, Abrams asked "… why we're not trying to work the five over."[14] There were actually three times more infantry regiments (three for each division) alone, not including tank and artillery regiments. Kroesen might have meant the 324B and the two independent regiments for a total of five; if so, he apparently didn't mention that they all had been there for almost a month. Some of the 304th regiment had also swung to the southwest of Quang Tri, too. Even months later (March 26, 1973), the FRAC *Command History* incredibly called the capitulation of the 56th and 57th Regiment forces "valiant" and the Camp Carroll fell "after a 2-day pitched battle."[15]

Another Kroesen error also mentions that the 56th lost two of its battalions and three artillery batteries, while "a third battalion refused to surrender and fought its way to Dong Ha."[16] This statement directly contradicts Camper and Brown's MFR (see Appendix 14), as well as any other known document. Further, Dong Ha was the scene of the 308th NVA Division's trek southward; the bridge there was blown up within the same hour of Camp Carroll's surrender and the VNMC made no mention of seeing any 56th ARVN unit soldiers (though there were plenty of ARVN to be seen stripping their uniforms off and tossing away their weapons). MAJ Smock nor CAPT Ripley mentioned seeing this unit at all, as well.

Even more outrageously, MG Kroesen wrote that the surrender of Camp Carroll "had not shaken the morale or confidence of the other defending forces to any noticeable degree."[17] The reverberations of a surrender of a whole regiment were actually keenly felt across the country. American advisors in other areas, in particular, looked askance at the ARVN units they were supporting. In II Corps "part of the 22nd ARVN broke and ran at Tan Canh and Dak To II northwest of Kontum City."[18] There was also, "From the beginning of US involvement in South Vietnam, American participants had speculated about how hard ARVN would fight when the chips were down. Dinh's craven surrender made us wonder about how steadfast our own counterparts would be if they decided the NVA might win a battle we were fighting—or the war."[19]

As previously stated, Willbanks added, "More damaging than the selfishness demonstrated by some of the 5th ARVN soldiers (who looted, fired into houses in An Loc, sold air-dropped food and medical supplies and fired on airborne and ranger troops who were attempting to retrieve air-dropped supplies) was the cowardice demonstrated by some officers. The commander of the 1-5th Cavalry Squadron surrendered himself and most of his unit to the North Vietnamese at Firebase Alpha north of Loc Ninh." This unit even drove their tanks and APCs into Cambodia for the NVA. And the "commander of the 9th Regiment (Colonel Nguyen Cong Vinh) at Loc Ninh (who) wilted under the NVA assault, and it is likely that he surrendered rather than go down fighting."[20]

"Lam confirmed a report officially denied by the Saigon high command that government troops at the infantry regimental base at Camp Carroll Sunday raised the white flag of surrender. It was the only case of cowardice during the pitched battle for the DMZ bases, Lam said. The general told newsmen the regimental commander, a colonel, committed suicide when his troops surrendered."[21] Obviously, Lam had no idea what was going on in the northern part of his command, either.

Another couple of cases include: a Vietnamese soldier/Marine couldn't board a full Huey evacuating US and Vietnamese wounded from A-2. He aimed a thumper (M79 grenade launcher) at the helicopter in an attempt to intimidate and board, and in an evacuation of Ai Tu Combat Base a little later a senior Vietnamese officer pushed his way onto a Huey to board first.

Stars and Stripes, the US military newspaper, had a better grasp on the impact on morale of the ARVN surrender. "The most crushing blow to the South Vietnamese Sunday was the fall of Camp Carroll, which had been pounded with hundreds of artillery, rocket and mortar shells since last Thursday .... Field reports said some government troops may have escaped and those left ran up a white flag of surrender. All American advisors had been evacuated from Carroll by helicopter just before it fell, sources said. It was not immediately known whether the four long-range 175mm artillery guns at Carroll were destroyed or fell into Communist hands."[22] *S&S* actually had better information than Major General Lam Quang Thi, the Deputy I Corps commander, who stated that "ARVN's two 175-mm batteries stationed at Dong Ha and Camp Carroll had been neutralized during the first days of fighting."[23] There was only one battery and it was positioned on Camp Carroll. Unless the general meant that "neutralized" also means given to the enemy, without being spiked, then the surrender of the 56th ARVN allowed the NVA to walk in and take the artillery pieces. One of the tubes that was taken is now located in Hanoi. LTC Dinh states, also, that "the only battery of mighty 175mm guns available along the DMZ" was at Camp Carroll.[24]

"The allies had long detected enemy movements in western Quang Tri Province and patrols west of the Rockpile often heard mechanized activity. Additionally, enemy unit movements were covered by an appreciable buildup of support antiaircraft guns." This information was known prior to February 1972.[25] "By 19 March, the AAA included 23mm and 37mm weapons grouped to comprise at least six high threat AAA areas. In the long run, the appearance of the SA-2 (SAM) missile in MR I was far more critical. In early February, 12 SAM sites were identified in areas near the DMZ, and four approximately 10nm north of the DMZ."[26] In fact, a "USAF gunship … was shot down at 5,000 feet, right over the Khe Sanh air strip, by an SA-2 missile."[27] Where was the Air Force to destroy these sites, better yet, why were they allowed to set themselves up and become operational?

Replying to the PACOM Electronic Intelligence (ELINT) Center personnel studying the SA-2B vs. SA-2F problem (and the lack of any electronic difference between them), GEN Abrams stated, "I'm not so much interested in the Intelligence Community. I'm interested in the fight that's going on and what can be done about it. Well, these people that are studying it—suppose they came down here and flew in the gunships. Wouldn't that motivate them to study it harder?"[28] Obviously, some of Abrams' people didn't either or they didn't like what they were told.

Randolph wrote, "It was clear that the 56th Regiment had surrendered well before the NVA attack had made capitulation necessary … *some members* [my italics] of the regimental leadership had been defeatist at best, communist agents at worst, and they had engineered the camp's surrender."[29]

An ARVN armor officer attempting to restore some of the 56th's grit wrote, "The defenders fought back with ferocity, highlighted by lowering their artillery tubes and firing directly into NVA assault forces."[30] Unfortunately, there is no indication that any of the artillery pieces were fired *at all*, no fire missions requested or responded to, and certainly no fighting back, much less with any "ferocity." Further, the author references another source for this quote and the book does not mention this occurrence at all, though I have read this tale elsewhere.

The surrender of the 56th ARVN Regiment, 3rd ARVN Division, at Camp Carroll on April 2, 1972, will remain one of the unspeakable acts of cowardice to have ever taken place in military history. A "despondent" LTC Dinh surrendered his 1,500–1,800 men and an unknown number of soldiers of the 3/11th Cavalry, and 22 unspiked artillery pieces (including 175mm guns; six 155mm and six 105mm guns were also lost at C-1/A-2.) Interestingly, an ARVN general stated that 1,000 soldiers eventually returned to friendly lines, while another source stated that the men were marched to the Rockpile and executed.[31] This despite Camp Carroll being completely surrounded by the 24th NVA Infantry Regiment, and Dinh talking with his soon-to-be captors on the phone before ordering a white flag be flown at the front gate (and probably prohibiting the spiking of artillery tubes, especially the largest tubes in South Vietnam—a battery of 175mm). It is unlikely the NVA would not know that the guns hadn't been spiked yet, especially since Camp Carroll was under constant surveillance. The next day, Dinh talked with Radio Hanoi, a broadcast heard in the South, asking others to join the North. His radio message was recorded at that time and subsequently translated into English:

> I, Lieutenant Colonel Pham Van Dinh, 56th ARVN Infantry regiment commander have returned to the National Liberation Front forces. My regiment was stationed at Tan Lam (CARROLL) firebase. On 30 March 1972 my unit was receiving a heavy shelling from NLF forces. All of the other friendly forces which were operating around our area or were stationed near our firebase were destroyed one after another. If we continued to fight we would be without all of our logistical and combat support as well as medical evacuation. I was sure that my unit was going to have many casualties. Meanwhile most of the friendly forces and the rest of the 3rd ARVN Division were evacuated to places which were safer. They left us alone under strong pressure of the NLF forces.
>
> Most of the troops of my unit in all ranks refused to fight anymore. I and Lt. Col. Vinh Phoy, who is my executive officer, also decided to refuse to fight anymore. In order to prevent further loss of life of my soldiers, I called for a meeting attended by all my unit commanders. At the meeting we decided to surrender to all of the NLF forces. We communicated this decision to the NLF at 1430 hours 2 April 1972 via PRC-25 radio.
>
> After we left the firebase we were well treated by the NLF forces. The relationship between us and the NLF forces was getting closer and closer.
>
> On this occasion, I advise you ARVN troops that you better return to the NLF, because the NLF fighting spirit is getting higher and higher than ever, and of course, the American-Thieu gang is going to lose the war; the war the Americans called the Vietnamization war. They have been trying to use us against part of our own people's patriots.
>
> The South Vietnam government is also using us to continue the war that they feel can benefit them as individuals.
>
> I think that your continued sacrifice at this time means nothing. Again, I ask you to not let the Thieu-American regime take advantage of your fighting potential. If they send you out to the field you must refuse the combat order. If they force you to go, then you must not fight the NLF. Instead, find out how to get in touch with the NLF forces in order for you to return to the people. Your action will effectively assist in ending the war quickly and also save your life.
>
> My personal feeling is that the NLF forces are going to win the war. The NLF is ready all the time to welcome you back. The NLF is expecting you to return very soon.[32]

Dinh was not the first ARVN officer to broadcast on Radio Hanoi. A year earlier during *Lam Son 719* in Laos, Colonel Nguyen Van Tho, commander of the 3rd Airborne Brigade, became a prisoner and was forced by the communists to make a radio statement denouncing the South Vietnam's incursion, shortly after his capture, and to lay down their arms.[33]

The 147th Marine Brigade "asked" General Giai to leave Mai Loc after Camp Carroll was turned over to the enemy. Receiving authorization, the 147th withdrew to Quang Tri and was ordered to Hue to regroup and refit. The recently arrived (from Saigon) 369th Marine Brigade "replaced" the 147th and took up positions at FB/FSBs Nancy, Barbara, Sally, and Jane—much closer to Hue than Quang Tri.

MG Davidson states that Lam and the JGS assumed "that the major attack in Quang Tri province would come from the west and northwest and not over the DMZ. The brunt then would be borne principally by the marines stationed in western Quang Tri rather than the less competent 3d ARVN Division along the DMZ."[34] Just a cursory look at the disposition before and after the movements of the 56th and 57th ARVN Regiments show that the VNMC soldiers occupied only a couple of firebases that flanked Camp Carroll. The 2nd ARVN Regiment was to take up positions below the DMZ, locations that most of the US and ARVN leadership adamantly decried as having even a remote possibility of receiving NVA ground assault.

GEN Truong wrote:

> Most of the 3rd Division soldiers were natives of the region, familiar with its terrain and hardened to the harsh, cold dampness of its weather. The battalions of the 56th and 57th Regiments, in particular, were *veterans of the DMZ* [my emphasis]. They occupied base camps and strongpoints they had been in for years, and their dependents lived in the nearby hamlets …. The plain fact was that the battalions of the 3rd Division were the most experienced in the DMZ area of any in the ARVN, and they were expected to perform better than any others in that environment …. Two of its three regiments, the 56th and 57th, had been formed and deployed in forward positions along the DMZ barely three weeks before the invasion took place. At that time, the division did not have its own logistic support units and its artillery was still receiving equipment."[35]

In the book *Kontum*, McKenna wrote, "At An Khe, as we talked about the collapse of ARVN units in I Corps and the rout of the 22nd ARVN Division at Tan Canh and Dak To II, we wondered whether our own 44th Infantry Regiment troops would run or stand and fight if they were attacked by tanks. We were not encouraged by descriptions of how the 22nd Division troops threw down their weapons, abandoned their defensive positions, and fled in terror from the attacking Communist tanks."[36] The 3rd NVA Division (and local VC forces) cut QL-1 at the Bong Son Pass and attacked the northern districts, causing the 22nd, 40th and 41st Regiments to abandon LZ English and Bong Son.

"COMUSMACV Personal Appraisal of the Enemy/Friendly Situation" message of March 20, 1972, to the JCS and CINCPAC from GEN Abrams stated that, though activity in the eastern DMZ was moderate, there were no enemy Attacks by Fire (ABFs), though they were anticipated. ABFs were expected to "sustain the threat of an attack through the DMZ in order to preclude ARVN operations against the continuing enemy buildup in the west." The report goes on to mention that the 38th NVA Artillery Regiment was deployed in western Quang Tri Province "possibly to support future major operations. Recent information indicates that all major elements of the 324B NVA Division have deployed or are en route to northern MR1." Still, at that late date, although the 324B had already been operating west and northwest of Hue for well over a week, MACV felt that the activity in the eastern DMZ was to keep ARVN from looking westward, and not NVA operations in or through the DMZ.

In an April 6, 1972, DEPCOMUS update for GEN Weyand, the briefer stated that, "Camp Carroll was overrun."[37] Even though the surrender occurred four days earlier, the truth apparently still hadn't reached all the exalted halls of Saigon.

During the Easter Offensive, "more than 53,000 men volunteered for military service and nearly 18,000 additional were conscripted, while more than 40,000 of those already serving deserted."[38]

There were quite a few factors that might help explain why there were so many acts of cowardice and desertions during the Easter Offensive of 1972. One reason was that actually training a professional military in South Vietnam did not really begin until GEN Abrams became the MACV commander. The changes he ordered were significant and should have been in-place years beforehand. Another reason is that South Vietnamese political appointees were not confined to government offices, but were also found in their military. By Abrams' own account (mentioned earlier), most generals were not very good/incompetent, but remained in place by political connections, though Abrams did inform the South Vietnamese president (who also had his own, individual political favorites). Most South Vietnamese generals also did not have any advanced training, despite their sometimes rapid progress in rank. Self-promotion (self-importance), self-preservation, and corruption (e.g., shadow soldiers, where the officers would receive the pay for soldiers who were not ever there) often prevailed among many—and don't think the average subordinate (of whatever rank) didn't know it. This would also partially explain all their actions on the battlefield.

We did not understand how territorial the average soldier was. Those soldiers from one area of the country could generally care less about another, unless there were relatives in the area. As a consequence, most would fight well against usurpers in their own villages and nearby areas but not necessarily elsewhere. This allowed the communist underground railroads to also exist. At the same time, soldiers generally lacked sufficient pay, housing for their families, and education—one of which is bad enough, but all three do not bode well for a professional military to exist.

Though pacification was working in the South (which worried the North), the concept of being a free (non-communist) country still had not set into the national psyche. People knew and appreciated the reforms that had been made. The VC had already or were becoming less of a problem in most areas, though their military organizations in the South were becoming exclusively filled with soldiers from the North.

CHAPTER 13

The Bridge at Dong Ha

When two armies are in order of battle, and one has to retire over a bridge, while the other has the circumference of the circle open, all the advantages are in favor of the later.

—NAPOLEON BONAPARTE, MAXIM XXV

There was another event that occurred on the Easter Sunday of the Eastern Offensive, at approximately 1630 (4:30 pm). Located to the northeast of Camp Carroll, some 17km away, was the Dong Ha Bridge. The 258th VNMC Brigade's 3rd Battalion, nicknamed the *Soi Bien* (Wolves of the Sea) and commanded by Major Le Ba Binh, was ordered to move to Dong Ha on March 30 to act as 3rd ARVN Division's reserve obviously thinking that the main assault was coming from the west and not from the west *and* the north. CAPT Ripley was assigned to the 3rd VNMC Battalion as its only US Marine Corps advisor.

The NVA had their own plans concerning Dong Ha, however. The 308th Infantry Division's 36th Infantry Regiment had originally planned to lead the way down QL-1 and cross the Mieu Giang/Cua Viet River at Dong Ha and then continue its southward advance toward Ai Tu and Quang Tri. Supporting this effort on April 2 were Russian-built T-54 tanks of the 202nd Armored Regiment, independent companies of amphibious Soviet-built PT-76s and similar, Chinese-built, Type 63 tanks.

LTC Turley asked the 258th VNMC Brigade commander (COL Ngo Van Dinh) to get approval to blow the bridge, but he declined. The 258th was under the operational control of the 3rd ARVN Division, but (as in *Lam Son 719*) Dinh would not act unless he had the okay from Saigon (in this case, from Lieutenant General Le Nguyen Kang, the VNMC commander). Despite Turley pointing out the current situation around Dong Ha and explaining what was likely to happen— "Colonel, we're desperate! You've got to move the 3rd Battalion around to the south side of the bridge. If you don't, we're going to lose the God-damned war!"—Dinh refused to act. Though advisors understood the politics within the South Vietnamese military, Dinh's obstinacy was still unbelievable when the whole course of the war might then be in play—it gave carte blanche to NVA tanks, APCs, and artillery and might have changed the whole course of the war in I Corps, if not throughout the country. As Andrade wrote, "It was this unwieldy command system, with its political overtones, that would ultimately cause the destruction of the South Vietnamese in northern I Corps.[1] Saigon told the 3rd Battalion of the 258th (commanded by Major Le Ba Binh) was move to Dong Ha and to hold it at any cost.

The NVA's targets were two bridges at Dong Ha: an old, partially damaged railroad bridge (which would not support a tank) and the main target, a USMC-built steel, two-lane bridge 300m east of it (the Dong Ha Bridge). There are a few books and articles written about this event, but there are generally three separate stories, *somewhat* consistent with each other, about Dong Ha Bridge's eventual destruction.

#1 ARVN blew the bridge

COL Metcalf, commander of Team 155 advising 3rd ARVN Division, stated, "a great amount of confusion existed about the blowing of the Dong Ha bridges. Eventually credit was given to the 57th ARVN Regiment, 20th Tanks, and the 3d VNMC Battalion."[2] Coincidently, the FRAC *Command History* for the period states the "valiant ARVN 56th and 57th Regiment forces "finally capitulated after intense artillery poundings finally subdued" them.[3] The 57th? Who, among the hundreds of this regiment's soldiers who threw down their weapons, helmets, and web gear, and stripped unit patches from their tunics to blend in with the civilians, do you mean? The men who "looked scared but not terrorized. Unlike the civilians, they knew where they were heading. And they were going to survive no matter what. They'd worry about the rest later, after better men had died to protect them."[4] The 2nd ARVN, seeing the confusion and hysteria, also took part in this flight. The 20th Armored Regiment's commander, Lieutenant Colonel Nguyen Huu Ly, had to be almost constantly prodded to action by MAJ Smock and MAJ Binh.

When Colonel Nguyen Trong Luat, the 1st Armor Brigade commander, arrived he decided to leave the bridge intact for the time being, since the enemy had been stopped and the armor brigade forces were holding. COL Luat was preparing to make a counterattack to the north across the bridge when the bridge charges detonated and dropped the near span, putting an end to any counterattack plans."[5] This included the railroad bridge which some ARVN engineers and Major Smock prepped while Captain Ripley finished the main bridge preparations. Nowhere mentioned is the fact that the 3rd ARVN Division commander had already specifically instructed that the bridge was not to be destroyed because he wanted to use it to counterattack. Two attempts to blow the bridge and there was 400–500lbs of TNT and C-4 explosive awaiting Smock and Ripley when they arrived? COL Luat was going to counterattack, with only the 20th Armored Regiment and his 1st Armored Brigade HQ (with APCs), because there were no other friendly tanks in the vicinity? Further, there was not one other source that mentioned any of this. It is unclear where GEN

Starry received this erroneous information, though it seems likely it came from ARVN sources. This story also differs from the following variant, which states that COL Luat had returned to Camp (FB) Evans 2½ hours earlier.

Another similar version: "When Colonel Luat was present, Lieutenant Colonel Ly personally led him to observe locations of explosives placed on the undercarriage of Dong Ha Bridge. The observation completed; Colonel Luat returned to brigade HQ at Hoa My (Firebase [Camp] Evans) about 1400 in the afternoon." Evans was some 40km away on QL-1. GEN Giai gave the order to drop the bridge, which was done around 1600 on April 2. "Captain Ripley and Major Smock, helped 3rd Division combat engineers place explosives on critical points so the bridge could not be used once the explosives went off."[6] One wonders why CAPT Ripley and MAJ Smock had to set any explosive charges if it had already been done? CAPT Ripley mentions that the NVA arrived at the bridge at 1015, so wouldn't COL Luat have noticed them? One account has five 3rd ARVN Division engineers mentioned, either before or after the bridge is blown, but the 400–500lb of mixed TNT and C-4 must have been deposited next to the bridge by someone. Likewise, the 3rd VNMC had been at Dong Ha for three days already and had been taking fire. MAJ Smock, advisor to ARVN's 20th Armored Regiment is quoted, "Additionally, lack of aggressive leadership and the reluctance of the ARVN tank commander to visit forward positions increased the problems of the tankers' morale and desertion rate."[7] But Ly showed Luat where the explosives were located. In *Trial by Fire*, the 1st Armored Brigade arrived in Dong Ha "sometime around 4:00 in the afternoon."[8]

Smock, in reply to Ripley's question about how LTC Ly acted when they had first met answered, "Bad luck. He acts like we're still in garrison. Treats these tanks like a fleet of Cadillacs, always trying to keep them ready for inspection. Won't take advice and won't take chances. Maybe your major [Binh] can help him strap on a set of balls."[9] Again, LTG Truong (though he had no first-hand knowledge) wrote, "To stall the enemy's armor, the Dong Ha Bridge was destroyed by ARVN engineers at 1630 hours [April 2]."[10]

#2 Combat Skyspot blew the bridge

Combat Skyspot was a bombing system derived from SAC's Radar Bomb Scoring (RBS) system, which used the MSQ-35, a ground-based radar/computer unit that could predict the exact point of impact of a simulated bomb drop. Dale Andrade states that "Most accounts credit Combat Skyspots with destroying the bridge."[11] These accounts include 1st Armored Brigade, MACV, Advisory Team 155, and the coastal zone intelligence officer for Commander, Naval Forces, Vietnam (COMNAVFORV)—none of whom were at the scene when the bridge was blown. "Bippy" was the call sign attached to this mission at 1324, April 2, 1972. Likewise, there is a copy of a request for Combat Skyspot to drop the bridge, though there is no identification of the requestor given.

But what was also seen by FACs flying in the area was the northern part of the main bridge being hit, but still usable for tanks, trucks, etc. "At 1324L, the north end of the vehicular bridge was struck with a Skyspot airstrike and partly destroyed. For the time being, the NVA drive was stopped."[12]

Due to an earlier incident, however, "Combat Sky Spot (CSS) missions would not be requested until a FAC had positively located the friendly elements by overflight."[13] Further, the *USS Buchanan* had maintained a complete radar watch over the area and no FAC aircraft flew over the area due to weather. Also, with the 3rd VNMC and 20th Armored on the southern bank and the NVA tanks and troops on the northern bank, a FAC would certainly have noticed their presence. "The Dong Ha bridge had been prepared for demolition, but the 1st Armor Brigade commander refused to allow its destruction until he obtained a clearer picture of the situation. However, a previously requested Combat Skyspot air strike and sympathetic detonation of the demolitions dropped one span of the bridge."[14]

#3 Ripley and Smock at the bridge

In this version of events, Ripley and Smock blew the bridge. The ARVN general, LTG Ngo Quang Truong, who states that ARVN blew it up, wasn't even the corps commander at that time (he was down in IV Corps, the Delta).[15] Obviously, his information was second-hand and, again, immediately suspect.

Tanks from the 20th Armored Regiment attempted to shoot out the bridge supports and struts with their main guns, but the bridges were too strong. While the ARVN tanks and Vietnamese Marines dueled with their opposites across the river, the advisor to the 3rd Vietnamese Marine Battalion, Ripley and Smock, emplaced additional charges under the south end of both bridges. The detonations dropped the southern spans of both bridges and set them on fire. Both were now impassable. For the time being, the NVA drive was stopped.[16]

There are a few major points that buttress Ripley's version: his photograph, taken by a recce aircraft after the Dong Ha Bridge blew—smoke is emitting from the various segments of the bridge in a uniform, even manner, not like an airstrike at all; looks like smoke is coming from both sides of the structure directly next to each other.[17]

Further confirmation of Ripley's version comes from Lieutenant Commander Gil Hansen, the XO of the USS *Buchanan* (DDG-14) during the Easter Offensive of 1972. The commanding officer at the time was Commander Jim Thearle. Both had served together previously as company officers at the US Naval Academy and had become good friends even before we were both assigned to *Buchanan*. In an earlier tour after the Naval Academy, Jim had been XO of the USS *Waddell* (DDG-24), where Hansen was the engineering officer.

Buchanan's first assignment after arriving off Vietnam on a normal six-month Western Pacific (WESTPAC) deployment was on the gunline at the DMZ, as part of ComDesRon 31 (Commodore T. R. Johnson commanding). There were no other ships present on April 2; apparently the *Buchanan* had been the only USN ship in the area since March 30,[18] although MG Kroesen reported "three destroyers had conducted 37 firing missions, despite North Vietnamese counterfire that had driven the ships 10,000 meters (almost 5.5nm) offshore" on April 2.[19] As Ripley and Smock were setting demolitions under the Dong Ha Bridge, the *Buchanan* was called upon to provide gunfire support to prevent tanks, heavy artillery, and mounted and dismounted troops from crossing the bridge. The *Buchanan* was close enough (within 2nm) to take the NVN forces under fire visually (not needing to use its fire-control radar systems) and engage these targets with both of her 5in/54 automatic guns, each capable of firing 60 rounds per minute.

Gil Hansen remembers:

That day, I personally witnessed us taking out four tanks in about 20 minutes on that bridge—and that stopped them. Meanwhile, we also were firing on the north side of the Cua Viet River with "spotter" fire to keep the NVN from concentrating on Ripley who was then going hand over hand under the bridge laying his explosives. I think he was engaged in that enterprise for about 3–4 hours. And he then blew the bridge.[20]

LCDR Dick Beal, who was our Engineering Officer, volunteered to go ashore and participate in what I think was an undercover "intel" operation on the beach with an "intel" unit. He had been a SEAL and knew that business. What specifically he did, I don't know. I think only the "Skipper", Jim Thearle, and he knew. All I remember is that we launched him in a rubber raft with a couple of our sailors and picked him up a couple of days later. Dick was a bachelor, young, tall, and muscular—he looked like a SEAL. He was a perfect gentleman—quiet-spoken and an unassuming guy. He never talked about that experience and I never asked him.

As far as the three versions of the Dong Ha bridge is concerned, I can confirm it was John Ripley who blew that bridge. There were no aircraft in the area. I was on the bridge of *Buchanan* almost the whole time. We actually took those tanks on the bridge under direct fire. We could see them visually. I remember one of those tanks going forward, then going backward until we nailed him. In the meantime, a spotter was directing our fire while John Ripley was going hand over hand under the bridge dodging sniper fire while laying the explosives under the bridge.

As far as your specific question about intel reports are concerned (as I asked him what information the ship was receiving), I wish I could be more certain. I remember that we had an awful lot of message traffic during that time trying to get a handle on what the North Vietnamese were doing and in what strength they were doing it. We were keeping CINCPACFLT [Commander in Chief, US Pacific Fleet] advised as to what was going on. They, in turn, were letting COMUSMACV in Saigon know that they had a full-scale invasion going on at the DMZ. The South Vietnamese were in charge of communication channels, but I understand, [they] were afraid to tell their headquarters in Saigon what was going on—COMUSMACV was "clueless."

We immediately "radioed" CINCPACFLT as to what was going on—that we were engaged in a full NVN offensive across the DMZ. They, in turn notified COMUSMACV in Saigon, and directed other destroyers to the DMZ. They arrived, as I recall within 24 hours, and joined us in firing against the three NVN Heavy Artillery Divisions preparing to cross the DMZ. We remained at the DMZ as I recall for several days and other destroyers joined us as the days progressed. We were then sent north to engage targets off of North Vietnam as a part of (as I recall) CTU 72.2.1 and CTU 72.2.2.[21]

CAPT Ripley's letter to the USS *Buchanan* can be found in Appendix 6. Seaman Leonard Davis, a member of a damage control team, was killed in action (KIA) by enemy gunfire aboard the *Buchanan* on April 17, 1972. Five others received superficial wounds when a single enemy artillery round exploded below deck as the ship was headed away from the North Vietnamese coast after completing a day-time raid. The *Buchanan* later went North and participated in the mining operation of Haiphong Harbor (known as Operation *Pocket Money*, which began on May 9th). The USS *Buchanan* received the Meritorious Unit Commendation for this period. Ripley was awarded the Navy Cross.

At least three books—*Ride the Thunder* (Botkin), *The Bridge at Dong Ha* (Miller), *An American Knight* (Fulkerson)—and numerous articles have been published describing this action and the events leading up to it stating that USMC CAPT Ripley and USA MAJ Smock actually brought down Dong Ha Bridge. Five ARVN engineers, who probably came from the rear, brought the demolition material (TNT and C4) and then fled the scene. Either way, it is obvious that the evidence seems overwhelmingly in favor of Ripley and Smock's efforts that disrupted the NVA invasion of South Vietnam in 1972.

For some reason, it seems most of the NVA tankers were not inclined to ford the rivers and continue south. Most rivers, while varying in depths, also had swift currents, which could make them perilous for tanks. While the 203rd NVA Armored Regiment was able to cross into South Vietnam to the west in support of the 304th NVA Division making a wide envelopment of ARVN firebases from the west, the destruction of the Dong Ha Bridge derailed, for a time, the plans of the 202nd NVA Armored Regiment's support of the 308th NVA Division's push southward from the DMZ, via QL-1. The 202nd was forced to turn west to make use of the Cam Lo Bridge for crossing the Mieu Giang River. It then apparently regrouped until the morning of April 2, beginning its approach to Quang Tri as the 203rd took up positions opposite the western firebases. Blowing the Dong Ha Bridge had ruined the double envelopment of the NVA's original plan, but it did not stop the 304th and 203rd's portion of the envelopment. The 571st theorized as much when the NVA OB, which was heavily positioned in the eastern DMZ, was plotted.

Soviet Tank Fording Depths

T-32 1.2m/3'11"   **T-55** 1.3m/4'7"   **T-54** 1.5m/4'11"   **PT-76** Amphibious
From ST 7-193 FY82, Ft. Benning, GA

Various descriptions of the activity around the bridge include South Vietnamese A-1 Skyraiders flying and knocking out tanks and equipment. In fact, no such aircraft were present this day or the USS *Buchanan*'s air search radar would have picked them up.

GEN Abrams was briefed during the April 3, 1972, COMUS update. "Re the Dong Ha bridge, 'this was blown by a U.S. advisor, a captain with 400 pounds of

TNT that he personally put under the bridge and wired it up and blew it—uh, while waiting for clearance.' [Laughter] He was being shot at by tanks from the north side of the river at the time."[22] The information on Dong Ha Bridge was obviously passed up to MACV rather quickly with some detail on April 3—the day after it occurred. The necessity to blow up the bridge was obvious, militarily, in light of the number and types of enemy units pouring southward. The humor expressed almost confirms the correctness of the action, as there was no challenging the necessity of the action spoken.

As Dong Ha Bridge was blown, the NVA moved west to Cam Lo to cross and ford. It isn't odd at all to have vehicles crossing by both means when you're trying to rapidly move your forces crossing a natural obstacle, such as a river. Whitcombe claims that "The Thien Xuan bridge was west of Camp Carroll on Route 9 and south of the river."[23] Consulting a UTM 1:50,000 scale, 1971 map, I *only* found a village called Thon Thien Xuan a little over a mile almost due north of Camp Carroll along Route 9, but there was no bridge nearby. I had never flown over that area either.

While there may have been many fording locations west of the bridge, the shear amount of repeated and heavy (e.g., resupply) vehicles supporting two divisions and numerous regiments would swiftly make any location unusable. How many tanks, trucks, APCs, artillery, and troops were able to cross into South Vietnam for the *12 days* it remained standing? How many NVA units then were able to engage ARVN and VNMC units and keep resupplied? Though, undoubtedly, units from Laos came into South Vietnam from the west (as MAJ Boomer saw days earlier), to suggest that, "perhaps the Cam Lo bridge itself was not that important"[24] doesn't make any sense. For instance, the 202nd NVA Armored Regiment attempted to cross the Dong Ha Bridge, and when it was dropped by Ripley and Smock it forced the 202nd and other 308th regiments westward to cross. Obviously, units from the 304th NVA Division were forced to adjust in the traffic jam that surely resulted, as well. Likewise, the attacking independent regiments east of QL-1 were undoubtedly affected by not being able to cross the Dong Ha Bridge, which likely forced a westerly movement, as the Cua Viet's current was swift running. The 48B Infantry Regiment/320B Infantry Division also entered the fight after crossing at Cam Lo, getting beaten up while making its way towards La Vang.

"But Seventh Air Force knew that the offensive was coming."[25] "The Seventh Air Force intelligence system, ponderous at the best of times, failed to get the word out that the situation along the DMZ had fundamentally changed.[26] It also seems that they suffered from a common malady, a tendency to only believe intelligence originating from a single source—SIGINT. The 571st MI Detachment (of the 525th MI Group), had been sending its information out for days. Seventh Air Force, MACV, Special Forces, 196th LIB, CINCPAC, NILO (one conduit which the SEALs also received intelligence) and many other commands and units received this information during this time. "Much of that information came from Washington ..."

is preposterous because Washington didn't want anything to interfere with Vietnamization and troop withdrawals and they had egg on their faces because they had proclaimed Tet as the date any enemy activity would begin. "As late as March 30, an intelligence estimate for Kissinger and the NSC (National Security Council) projected nothing more than intensified terrorism and rocket attacks around Saigon."[27]

Another Kroesen error mentions the 56th losing only two of its battalions and three artillery batteries, while "a third battalion refused to surrender and fought its way to Dong Ha." This statement not only contradicts Camper and Brown's MFR and their discussions with Kroesen shortly after the surrender, but also makes no mention of the soldiers of the 1st Battalion, 2nd Regiment, who were among those who deserted, too.[28]

The FRAC *Command History* for 1972–73 also indicates that on April 4, "… elements of the 308th NVA Division used *sampans* to cross the Cua-Viet River, and approximately *60 tanks* were sighted by US Forward-Air-Controllers (FACs) both south of the river line and north of Dong Ha. *A SAM site was observed five kilometers northwest of that city.* And *by the fifth day of fighting*, the NVA deployed heavy artillery to positions between the DMZ and the Cua Viet. *By this time, enemy intentions were clear*" (my italics).[29] This the only known report of sampans moving NVA troops across the river, the location of a SAM site, and an admission of that it took FRAC an exceedingly long time to divine NVA intentions, though they were provided with this information at the onset. FSB Anne also fell under pressure by the 304th NVA Infantry Division (probably by the 24th NVA Infantry Regiment, which helped to force the surrender of Camp Carroll two days before) on April 4, as well.

Powerful and Brutal Weapons by Stephen P. Randolph, referenced an Arc Light strike that used Combat Skyspot located at Hue on April 10, 1972. The reference used was Charles K. Hopkins in *SAC Bomber Operations in the Southeast Asia War*, vol. III (Offutt AFB: SAC, 1983). The problem is that one of the Skyspot sites was located at Dong Ha until it was overrun on March 31. There was a Skyspot on Monkey Mountain, in Da Nang, however, "which controlled all of the Arc Light and CSS strikes in MR-1 … neither Arc Light nor CSS drops could not be made closer than 1,000 meters of friendly ground forces."[30] Also, it had a range of under 200nm, but if a beacon wasn't abord an aircraft, it could be directed to the vicinity of the target by a skin-paint method, cutting the range by 3/4. The Marines once had a similar system at Phu Bai called a TPQ-10, with a maximum range of 50nm. The USAF Strategic Air Command operated all Skyspot radar sites.

A *Stars and Stripes* article dated April 15, 1972, states that a USN radar site, located 8km west of Hue, took six mortar rounds a day or two before. It may have been an airfield radar for Phu Bai Airfield for returning Marine aircraft or, perhaps more likely, it may have been the Tactical Air Navigation/Distance Measuring Equipment (TACAN/DME). The TACAN DME beacon was used by all aircraft for navigation and could be used for aircraft bombing missions. (There were only two in MR-1/I Corps; the other site was at Ai Tu which was destroyed a few days after the offensive began.) There was an all-weather system that only USAF F-4s and USN/USMC could utilize, if equipped or equipped as the leader of other aircraft (e.g., F-4s) called Loran. Both armed services "flew 291 Loran sorties over northern MR-1 during the first week in April."[31]

"The NVA were very definitely monitoring and jamming our communications." The author cites *The Rescue of Bat-21* as the source.[32]

Meanwhile in the Southern Portion of I Corps

Replacing Major General Nguyen Van Hieu was Major General Lam Quang Thi, who became the deputy I Corps commander to LTG Truong. Truong, in an unusual turn of events, asked Thi to take over operations in the lower three provinces of I Corps—Quang Nam, Quang Tin, and Quang Ngai. This left Truong to concentrate on the major operations occurring in Quang Tri and Thua Thien Provinces.

The 2nd NVA Division moved down towards Kontum (the apparent objective of the offensive in II Corps) with the 1st, 66th, and 141st Infantry Regiments subordinate. The 711th NVA Division was created with the 31st and 38th NVA Regiments. It appears that the 711th waited for another regiment to join and one eventually did—the 270th Independent Infantry Regiment, which was part of the initial assault across the DMZ had operated north of Quang Tri. In an unusual move, the 270th then apparently headed for the Ho Chi Minh Trail, either via Route 9 or by the DMZ and showed up in southern I Corps in June/July 1972. The 711th moved to the Quang Nam–Quang Tin border area and conducted attacks against FBS Ross and LZ Baldy, among others.

Activity in the lower three provinces was generally light, consisting of probing and rocket attacks until April 9, when FSBs West and O'Connor fell to the NVA. On April 14, attacks by fire, interdictions of QL-1, and small-unit actions seemed to indicate that FSBs Baldy and Ross, and the Que Son Valley, might be threatened. Eastern Quang Ngai Province saw 11 villages being entered by enemy forces, causing thousands of people to flee.

CHAPTER 14

BAT-21

The final major event of April 2, 1972, occurred at 1650, some 20 minutes after the Don Ha Bridge dropped. The NVA's 367th and 377th Composite Anti-Air Divisions' AAA and SA-2 Guideline regiments had already moved above, into, and *below* the DMZ. At the same time, a flight of two USAF 42nd Tactical Electronic Warfare Squadron (TEWS) EB-66C aircraft (call signs Bat-21 and Bat-22) from Korat Air Base, Thailand, were escorting three B-52s on a route that took them from Thailand, across Laos, and into South Vietnam. The target objective for the B-52s were to drop their bombs over an area northwest of Camp Carroll. En route to the objective, two F-105Gs (commonly called "Wild Weasels") rendezvoused with the group to provide air-to-air and Suppression of Enemy Air Defense (SEAD) protection.

In Stanley Busboom's case study of the Bat-21 incident, he states that Lieutenant Colonel Iceal E. Hambleton (the navigator on this mission) "had been plotting one site on the DMZ off and on for two months, but the Wing headquarters did not take it as a serious threat because there were no launches."[1] He also notes that "the shadow SAM site was using its acquisition radar (probably the Soviet long-range radar called a "Spoon Rest") but not firing its missiles, and that succeeded over a period of weeks in being ignored as a threat."[2]

As the aircraft neared the DMZ area, missiles were launched and AAA landscaped the sky. The Wild Weasels took on the 100mm AAA radars that were used to direct the fire at the aircraft. As the EB-66C was outbound from Thailand, the normal aircraft procedures, "SAM break procedures of counting off against successful launches and breaking right (south), away from the threat,"[3] would be in order. But this was not to be a normal day.

> The first SAM signals were puzzling to Hambleton. The crew normally got two discreet warnings from the power signals at the site before a launch was confirmed. This day, both preliminary signals were absent and the launch warning (usually the last in the sequence) was the first and only warning the crew got. The timing count was started for a right break but electronic warfare officers shouted, 'negative, negative,' because they saw the SAM was tracking at them from the South, not the North. The pilot dumped the controls away to the left, but they were hit in mid-break.[4]

"… four miles above the DMZ, as the B-52 strike force neared its targets north of Camp Carroll … five batteries of the NVA 365th Air Defense Division loosed a salvo of thirteen missiles at the force, one detonating directly underneath an EB-66 [Bat-21] electronic intelligence aircraft escorting the bombers."[5] No other source identifies the 365th as a Composite Air Defense Division until the later part of 1972, when it also had the 267th and 275th Missile Regiments assigned to it with its five AAA regiments (which it originally had in 1966). The 365th apparently redeployed to protect supply lines along the coast (Thanh Hoa), south of Hanoi. Another problem with this account is that the North Vietnamese sites commonly had six launchers, with single missiles on each.

The SA-2F Guideline missile exploded beneath the EB-66C (Bat-21) aircraft, having been fired optically, with the guidance electronic instructions sent to the missile five seconds after launch from, possibly, the Khe Sanh area of South Vietnam. Only one of the six-man crew successfully made it out of the aircraft, parachuting right into the maneuvering 308th NVA Division's area north of the Mieu Giang (Cam Lo) River, about a mile east of Cam Lo. As Dong Ha Bridge had just been blown, the invading NVA were forced to move west to the Cam Lo Bridge to cross or ford the Mieu Giang River before regrouping eastward, adding to the number of enemy troops in the area invading the South.

An immediate 27km (almost 17-mile) no-fire zone was automatically imposed around the crewman (an Air Force navigator, Lieutenant Colonel Iceal E. Hambleton), who was actually seen floating down above an OV-10 Bronco light attack and observation aircraft. "No one in the rescue center (Joint Search and Rescue Center/JSRC in Saigon) had any idea that there was a major invasion in progress, and it seemed natural to clear out the airspace to protect the downed airman and give rescue forces freedom of action."[6] This occurred on April 2, the 4th day of the offensive, by which time Seventh Air Force, MACV, et al., were all already notified.

Incredibly, in their rush to dismantle American presence in Vietnam, MACV had disbanded the remaining combat recon platoons in Vietnam *six weeks before* the offensive began. "Now there was no means left to react if prisoners were discovered or airmen downed behind enemy lines."[7]

The word that a no-fire zone had been imposed by Seventh Air Force was passed to USAF Major David A. Brookbank, who was running air operations for the 3rd ARVN Division. He immediately went to COL Metcalf, who passed the buck back to FRAC, who, together, played their interpretation of bungling officers who had yet to grasp the situation—so they passed the buck up to Saigon by saying it was out of their hands. We had a variety of Army visitors come to the 571st to look at my maps to get an idea of what was occurring; not one person could understand this lunacy, when so much was at-stake in stopping the NVA as soon as possible.

Lieutenant Colonel D'Wayne Gray, Sub Unit One of the 1st Air and Naval Gunfire Liaison Company (ANGLICO), happened to be in the FRAC command center when the 27km no-fire zone was imposed. Noticing a USAF brigadier general in the room, Gray made the plainly obvious case that Americans and South Vietnamese troops were in danger because of this overly wide restricted area. The general responded, "I would rather lose two ARVN divisions than to lose two US Air Force crewmen."[8] Shortly afterwards, enemy tanks and infantry were sighted, but the no-fire zone enabled them to maneuver at will because cloud cover prevented most Tactical Air (TACAIR) strikes. One of the often-repeated reasons for quickly retrieving LTC Hambleton given was his previous and current access to highly classified material. Hambleton was certainly not the only person to have knowledge that might be valuable to North Vietnam, the Soviet Union, and China—look at the various US intelligence units and agencies that had saturated South Vietnam. South Vietnam's intelligence agencies and commands were pervaded with spies, and they would have certainly known where US intelligence units were, including any CIA personnel. The South Vietnamese military did not understand why this large-area restriction also prevented any artillery missions in/over this area and diverted much-needed tactical strike and observation aircraft to this one area, as well. Undoubtedly, they were probably thinking back a year to the FB 31 incident in Laos during *Lam Son 719*, when a USAF F-4 was shot down in the area. All US aircraft responded to support rescue efforts, which allowed FB 31 to fall to the NVA.

Lieutenant Mark Clark (grandson of the famous World War II commander) and Captain William Henderson were forced to eject from an OV-10 FAC aircraft (Nail-38) that was hit by a SAM, with Henderson soon captured. Clark, who landed in a different area than his pilot, and LTC Hambleton were separately rescued by SOG SEAL Lieutenant Norris. Clark first on April 10 and Hambleton two nights later on the 12th. Norris was an advisor to the South Vietnamese Navy's Sea Commandos and was awarded the Congressional Medal of Honor. Nguyen Van Kiet, one of the Sea Commandos, was awarded the US Navy Cross for this mission, as well. The cost of trying to rescue LTC Hambleton was high, however: 11 were either KIA or missing in action (MIA) and two were made POWs. Two USA helicopters, two OV-10s, and an HH-53 were destroyed.

CHAPTER 15

Independent NVA Regiment Actions in I Corps Area[1]

The 246th and 270th NVA Independent Infantry Regiments initiated offensive operations from the DMZ area with attacks against 3rd ARVN Division bases along the eastern DMZ in support of the 304th Division, while the 27th and 31st Independent Infantry Regiments attacked Gio Linh and Dong Ha in advance of main attack by the 308th Division.

The 5th and 6th Independent Infantry Regiments operated with the 29/324B in Bastogne-Birmingham area along Route 547, releasing the 803rd and 812/324B to keep pressure on FB Nancy and Quang Tri City. (The 324B Regiments that operated west of Hue is different to the unit that appeared in the 571st MI Detachment's INTSUM, which first reported this regiment in early March 1972.) The 803rd and the 29th were often transposed/misidentified probably because only 1st ARVN was dealing with units west of Hue, not the two regiments operating north of the city. In the April 5, 1972, COMUS update, Abrams stated that "They claim that the 6th Regiment, down in that fighting around Veghel, they also broke and ran. They have an intercept message that the regimental commander's been relieved, and the 803rd was brought in to replace them. And the 803rd has issued orders to shoot and kill anybody out of the 6th Regiment that goes to the rear." In response, someone says, "This prisoner also said that the 308th, as we thought for some time, is the strategic reserve division, and that had had to be released by High Command Hanoi to participate in this thing …. And he said that there's also been a new division formed up there to replace the 308th as the strategic reserve. It is called the 315th Division. We have absolutely nothing on it."[2] No 315th Division of any kind could be found then or today. It is, however, one of the very few proofs concerning probable SIGINT activity being used in Vietnam.

The NVA had only moved some 29km into South Vietnam in three weeks. Quang Tri fell on May 1, with FB Nancy on May 3. "The proximate cause of these reverses was withdrawal of the 20th Armored Squadron, ordered by 1st Armored Brigade commander Colonel Nguyen Trong Luat without notifying either higher headquarters or adjacent units. The move spooked other friendly forces into displacing prematurely and opened a convenient hole through which the attacking NVA drove deep into friendly lines."[3]

By April 27, the last NVA reserve infantry division was headed south and stood 2–4 days away—four divisions and independent regiments had already been brought down. There would eventually be (by summer) a total of seven NVA divisions, three independent regiments, and seven artillery regiments (some being combined into artillery groups) that fought in all of the I Corps area—more than III Corps (An Loc) and II Corps (Kontum) combined.

At this juncture, an unexpected laurel came from the April 21, 1972 issue (page 52) in a *LIFE* magazine editorial: "Yet however much everyone longs to be free of the war, it must be noted that the million South Vietnamese troops we trained and equipped, and have called allies, are undergoing a terrible testing (even with American help overhead); are in many places proving their courage and skill, and deserve a cheer. How well they do now, in this test that Hanoi has set for them, will be crucial when peace talks start again."

The entire Easter Offensive of 1972 is usually broken up into segments, usually using these dates:

Stage I from March 30–May 2
Stage II from May 3–June 27
Stage III from June 28–September 16

The exact dates can and do vary depending on the authors. Further, the total amount of time before cessation of hostilities in I Corps far exceeded those in II and III Corps.

PART III

NOT A CRYSTAL BALL

CHAPTER 16

National Intelligence and Surveillance Technologies

Many intelligence reports in war are contradictory; even more are false; and most are uncertain. In short, most intelligence is false.

—CARL VON CLAUSEWITZ

It is interesting to note that some historians have indicated that "the higher levels" of intelligence seemed to have possessed an accurate picture of the forthcoming offensive. Not so, and in reality specific and important intelligence was completely ignored at the national level. In 1971, the "major" national intelligence organizations predicted no more than enemy battalion attacks across most areas of Vietnam for the following year. The DIA, CIA, and State Department followed each other in their evaluations of enemy activity in 1972. "Moderate" was the most commonly used term to describe expected level of NVA/VC activity. "For once there wasn't even any serious differences between the various and very competitive intelligence agencies. Everyone—Central Intelligence Agency, DIA, State, COMUSMACV, National Security Agency, etc.—spoke with one voice. The new year was to be one in which North Vietnam was planning no spectaculars."[1]

Major intelligence organizations could/would not fix another date for the offensive (and then some didn't think it would even occur), nor did most of the generals fully appreciate the enormity of NVA forces that would compose the forthcoming whirlwind. "U.S. Intelligence did not forecast the timing and scope of the NVN offensive. In spite of the many signs of a buildup, there remained a genuine disbelief in the possibility of a conventional type of invasion. This disbelief plagued many U.S. military commanders in Danang and Saigon for several days after the investigation began."[2]

Here we will deal with all the intelligence organizations that had or should have had pertinent information on the Easter Offensive of 1972.

Central Intelligence Agency (CIA)

Some historians have written that all the major intelligence agencies were reluctant to comment if or when the North Vietnamese would conduct major operations. By

1968, some organizations, if not most, had fallen into the yearly trap of thinking that any major hostilities would be tied to the yearly Tet holiday.

For the most part, the CIA had closed shop in Vietnam at the end of 1971. In fact, the CIA's National Intelligence Estimate of April 1971 wasn't followed by another until October 1973. However, in November 1971 CIA issued two draft forecasts of enemy intentions, stating that North Vietnam couldn't launch a big military offensive and there was no indication that they were interested in doing so.[3] However (and probably in an effort not to be left behind the other intelligence organizations), the CIA published an Intelligence Memorandum on February 7, 1972 entitled, "The Communist Winter–Spring Offensive in South Vietnam,"[4] where it forecasted "the Communists hope to stage a major round of attacks sometime around Tet in mid-February and/or during President Nixon's visit to Communist China in late February."[5] This memorandum also postulated that, "The most serious threat, although not the most powerful aggregation of force, exists along the Cambodian border opposite the central highlands."[6] "The buildup in the highlands is all the more serious because the government forces assigned to defend Military Region 2 are among the weakest in South Vietnam, both in numbers and in demonstrated fighting prowess."[7]

The CIA Saigon Station Chief, Thomas Polgar, hadn't been in-country very long during this period, as a March 21, 1972, conversation between GENs Abrams and Potts points out in a briefing Polgar gave that morning. Abrams stated, "Kind of the way he gave it was that this replaces this stuff we've been putting out about [an] impending enemy offensive …. But I'd like to know what he thinks all these regiments and battalions scattered are up to. They're not down here for the Oktoberfest." Potts replied, "He doesn't have a real feel of it yet. He just doesn't know. And so many of his people. I think that's why the ambassador comes to our Saturday morning meetings. He [Polgar] just hasn't been there long enough."[8]

CIA changed their tune when, in addition to "The Communist Winter–Spring Offensive in South Vietnam," they also published "Communist Intentions in The Current Campaign In South Vietnam," dated April 10, 1972, and "NVA Infiltration and Unit Deployments Since September 1971," dated November 1972. All three documents had once contained COMINT information when they were first composed, given the same warnings on each. Since the CIA had only a nominal presence in-country by this time, their documents had the same information as the DIA and NSA's documents would contain.

Defense Intelligence Agency (DIA)

"Each branch of the U.S. military also had its own intelligence service, each mostly concerned with narrow parochial tactical matters. By 1972, the most important of these was army military intelligence, whose analysts serve up facts and figures concerning the location and movement of enemy troops. At the top of the military intelligence heap was the Defense Intelligence Agency (DIA), a confederation of analysts from all services tasked with providing overall assessments of enemy intentions and capabilities."[9] Perhaps it should have been that way, but DIA products were still not known to all, though they received our intelligence.

The DIA, while not mentioning the December 1971 Politburo document, noticed a large increase in men, materiel, and new unit traffic headed south along the Ho Chi Minh Trail at roughly the same time.[10] Sound, heat, urine, and vibration sensors were placed along the Trail to detect movement of troops and trucks. Colonel Peter Armstrong, USMC, wrote, "Our estimate was based on hard intelligence, and as the intelligence business is a very competitive one, I also enjoyed the fact the DIA was first on the street with the new estimate."[11] The 571st, however, never received anything from DIA, nor any reference to their estimate. COL Armstrong also wrote that, "South Vietnamese units, while well aware of the impending offensive, were not prepared for the enormity of the Communist's thrust directly through the DMZ."[12] Well aware? US generals had left country and two ARVN regiments turned off their comms and hit the road to swap positions on the very morning of the offensive, none of which indicates high levels of awareness.

The White House was certainly not aware of it, or so it seemed. They must have been told initially that the NVA were conducting local operations below the DMZ. Surprisingly, the full extent of the invasion only became evident four days later. President Nixon "insisted that it was impossible for the North Vietnamese to have assembled three divisions and support facilities without the Pentagon's knowing about it. Laird, so the President made clear, had deliberately withheld the information." [13] Secretary Laird must not have remembered COL Armstrong's briefing he received in January 1972.

The proverbial cat was let out of the bag when both Americans and allies read the Pacific *Stars and Stripes* ran an Associated Press (AP) article on April 30, 1972, entitled "Nixon Refused to Hit DMZ Buildup." "For weeks before the North Vietnamese launched their invasion, the White House rejected repeated requests from U.S. military leaders for permission to bomb an enemy buildup just above the demilitarized zone … to make sure negotiations still had a chance." Confirming earlier mentioned 1st MIBARS reporting, "When the invasion finally was launched in late March, North Vietnamese tanks and artillery rolled over four such (North Vietnamese-made) roads into South Vietnam."

In fact, the DIA (while making a victory lap years later) had misjudged activity in I Corps and IV Corps, in the former by forecasting minimal activity and in the latter by forecasting way too much. The victory lap included taking credit for actions not taken: "Forewarned, the South Vietnamese broke the NVA's efforts in those areas."[14] There was *no* forewarning in I Corps among American or South Vietnamese forces, at least none that made it down past major HQ in Saigon, and it took many months and lives to recover from some of ARVN's losses.

COL Armstrong also wrote, "Given the poor quality of our intelligence concerning the NVA's activities north of the DMZ, it is unlikely that we could have called their efforts in that area more accurately that we did. However, the egos of intelligence officers are large, and it smarted when the North Vietnamese adopted a course of action in I Corps that was within their capability but not estimated by us."[15] This statement seems audacious, implying that because the big, bad DIA dropped the ball, then no one else could have possibly done any better, despite the fact that the DIA had valuable HUMINT in front of it, which it chose to ignore. "The strongest part of our [collection] system was the technical side. Never had an armed force been better equipped with technology to ferret out the activity of its enemy. However, there were weaknesses, particularly in our human intelligence."[16] A neglect of HUMINT prevails today, but it is ironic that HUMINT "called it" on the Easter Offensive of 1972, despite the various intelligence experts and agencies. Of course, the colonel doesn't mention that DIA would have been receiving the *Vinh Window* information, as well.

Armstrong continues, "What part did human intelligence play in forming our intelligence analysis? I suppose the truthful answer to this question would be 'not as much as we would have liked, but it was not through any lack of effort on our part.'"[17] As the 571st was the only intelligence unit remaining in I Corps, this statement is preposterous. There was never any kind of inquiries or messages from DIA to our unit, though DIA always received our reports.

The Army Assistant Chief of Staff for Intelligence, Major General Phillip Davidson, wrote that, "As 1972 dawned, both the Americans and the South Vietnamese knew a major NVA offensive impended."[18] Though Davidson was the chief of US intelligence in Vietnam from 1967 to 1969, his view that, "ARVN was psychologically ready for the major attack coming at them"[19] is genuinely quizzical. Curious because the 1st ARVN Division had suffered greatly during *Lam Son 719* and the 3rd ARVN division was new, untried, ill led, ill equipped, ill manned, and ill positioned.

National Security Agency (NSA)

NSA is the national agency responsible for Signals Intelligence (SIGINT) and Electronic Intelligence (ELINT). NSA, through its military adjuncts—Army Security Agency, Naval Security Group, United States Air Force Security Service—were present in various locations in Vietnam since the beginning of the conflict, but they were also planning to close their operations by the end of 1972.

"In January 1972, SIGINT began to reflect large-scale movement of equipment and supplies southward into the DMZ, Tri-border, and Panhandle areas, indicating preparations for a major offensive that threatened the phased withdrawal of US forces."[20] "It was the best method of predicting NVA offensives."[21] Not everyone agreed, however. John Prados wrote, "Ultimately Americans could not win the war of the ether—COMINT did not bring victory in Cambodia in 1970, or in Laos in 1971, and it did not predict the massive Easter Offensive launched by the North Vietnamese in 1972. COMINT became one more supposed path to victory in Vietnam that merely terminated in a dead end."[22]

US Air Force Security Service

The US Air Force's 6924th Security Squadron's SIGINT facility was closed out of Da Nang (Monkey Mountain) and the unit was relocated to Thailand in March 1971, as part of the withdrawal of US forces from Vietnam.

Army Security Agency (ASA)

On June 10, 1970, the first Explorer I system was emplaced on Hill 950 (also known as "Hickory Hill") in I Corps (Quang Tri Province). Hill 950 was one of two ends that formed a geographic feature called a saddle. Hill 950 was also used by 1/5 Mechanized to read buried sensors emplaced along the nearby Ho Chi Minh Trail in Laos. The system consisted of four Very High Frequency (VHF) receivers, with a range of around 80km, that acted as a passthrough—automatically encrypting and securely sending voice intercepts 110km southeast to Phu Bai for voice operators to analyze. The SOG/SF and Bru Montagnards also occupied Hill 950.

For almost exactly a year, *Explorer I* remained a valuable asset against tactical units and logistical NVA movements. It faced some technical and logistical challenges. Gas was necessary to operate the equipment, which had to be delivered by helicopter. The equipment was also adversely subject to humidity, dust, and monsoons, and required equipment maintenance. On June 5, 1971, the NVA successfully attacked Hill 950.

The NSA quickly sent new equipment to Vietnam. The first was Explorer II (aka Golf-5 or Leghorn) in Laos. This equipment was also composed of four VHF receivers, which were positioned in Laos, sending its voice intercepts to Pleiku and the 330th Radio Research Company. Explorer III also had four VHF receivers and was emplaced at FB A-4 and FB Sarge in December 1971. Intercepts were then relayed to Phu Bai from each location.

As previously mentioned, the first Americans killed during the Easter Offensive of 1972 were atop FB Sarge; they were running the newly upgraded Explorer III equipment. These men were part of the 407th Radio Research Detachment, 8th Radio Research Field Station (RRFS), Tri Bac Station, Phu Bai. At Phu Bai, there was also an "elephant cage" array for High Frequency/Direction Finding (HF/DF) run by the 8th RRFS. Though the AN/FLR-9 antenna array detected transmissions between 3 and 30 MHz and was considered high-tech at the time, getting a "fix" depended on tipping off other stations using HF Morse to cross DF signal bearings to be able to fix the location of the transmission.

> The NVA had launched their biggest offensive in four years, and in spite of all the indications and warnings from the ASA outposts along the DMZ, the U.S. and ARVN commanders were just as surprised as they had been during Tet in 1968. MACV in Saigon, some 350 miles to the south, refused to believe a major offensive was taking place, even after it had begun. In spite of all ASA's success over the previous ten years, the generals at the top had learned absolutely nothing. Over 30,000 well-armed NVA regular infantry, supported by hundreds of tanks, armored vehicles, missile launchers and long-range artillery had poured across the DMZ into South Vietnam, and the generals and politicians were shocked.
>
> Those in charge had chosen to ignore the intelligence they had been presented and were caught flat-footed again. But, as usual, they were not the ones paying the price for their failures. The outlaying fire support bases, sparsely protected by South Vietnamese troops and Montagnards, and the remote ASA listening posts manned by Viet linguists and Morse intercept ops had become shooting galleries for the invading NVA forces.[23]

In fact, FB A-4 was deserted on March 31, except for the eight ASA soldiers, as the "ARVN infantry company charged with their security had quietly pulled out and left the area during the night."[24]

Airborne SIGINT, Magic, and ground-based sensors

Sensors along the Ho Chi Minh Trail were an integral part of what was known as the *Igloo White* system. Sensor information was relayed to a command center, called Task Force Alpha, in Nakhon Phanom (NKP) AFB, Thailand (equipped with many IBM 360/65 computers and IBM 2260 monitors), via relay aircraft. The attendant data link systems to the recce aircraft (EC-121R and then QU-22s) were the responsibility of Radiation Corporation (now Harris Corporation), while IBM processed the data and compiled the reports for the Air Force. The system enabled the tracking of movement along the trail, and the information gleaned could then be provided to specific attack aircraft, including B-52s. As information was relayed to the command center in NKP, the Seventh/Thirteenth Air Forces created seven *Commando Hunt* campaigns to deal with NVA vehicular and personnel movements along the trail. On March 30, 1972, *Commando Hunt VII/Island Tree* formally ended, the day the Easter Offensive began.

USAF RC-135M Rivet Card aircraft flew flight patterns over the Gulf of Tonkin collecting COMINT activity originating in North Vietnam and Laos. Rivet Card aircraft also had a limited ELINT capability. These six USAF planes flew from Kadena AB in Okinawa and comprised the 82nd Reconnaissance Squadron of the *Combat Apple* program.

A new program called *Island Tree*, was introduced in August 1971. It involved deploying sensors that were directed against the increasing number of troops (instead of vehicles) moving along the Ho Chi Minh Trail, and it proved of great value by year's end. Abrams lauded, "*Island Tree* is producing more than anything. We've really got to stay with it."[25] There was special emphasis given to the 320th NVA Division's movement down the trail, as it was thought to be headed for the B-3 Front (II Corps area).

An RC-135M Rivet Card route over Laos was added due to the increase of trail traffic. These sensors were unusually active with "movers" (wheeled and tracked vehicles) during February and March 1972. In January, there was an average of 25 movers a day which increased to 90 in February. Ironically, another air SIGINT platform also ended its multi-year mission stint on March 30, 1972. The *Crazy Cats* flew Navy P-2E aircraft from Cam Ranh Bay from July 1967 until the end of March 1972. The 12 aircraft were assigned to the 1st Radio Research Company, which was the cover designation for the 1st ASA Company.

From 1968 to November 1972, 1,000 AQM-34 Lightning Bug unmanned pre-programmed reconnaissance drones flew low over North Vietnam, conducting a variety of missions over preplanned routes. They could be rerouted in air, as well. They were the only US aircraft flying over the North from the mid-1960s until the Linebacker II bombing raids began. There was some experimentation with Lightning Bugs becoming electronic listening devices below the 17th Parallel for the *Igloo White* program.[26] Two US Navy Fleet Air Reconnaissance VQ-1 aircraft (EP-3B) flew from Da Nang Air Base, as well. The commander of the Seventh Fleet, Vice Admiral William Mack, rode along on one mission before he rotated back to the United States. The two SIGINT aircraft flew over 1,000 missions in 1972 in support of units of Task Force 77.

After *Commando Hunt VII*, Brigadier General Richard G. Cross, Jr., Seventh Air Force Assistant Deputy Chief of Staff for Operations, said, "This interdiction effort failed to prevent the enemy from positioning sufficient supplies to initiate an all-out offensive against South Vietnam" in March 1972. That was probably the case, although some of the supplies for the Easter Invasion may have been accumulated and stored over a period of years. This failure wouldn't have been due to a lack of trying, however.

Looking back at *Steel Tiger*, *Tiger Hound*, and *Commando Hunt* (different programs concerned with interdicting the Ho Chi Minh Trail), USAF General William W. Momyer (a 7th Air Force commander) said, "The interdiction campaign was able to limit the number of forces the North Vietnamese could support in the South. Not until the interdiction campaign ended with the termination of US involvement could the North Vietnamese logistically support and deploy their full strength of 18 to 20 divisions. Before the 1975 offensive, they never deployed more than 11 or 12 divisions, apparently for fear of the destruction they would suffer by exposure to our airpower."[27] Presumably the dozen of divisions does not include the fact that there were quite a few independent infantry regiments during the Easter Offensive.

In Advisory Team 155's area of Ai Tu combat base existed the only Army ground-surveillance sensor read-out bunker north of Da Nang. A variety of ground sensors were spread in and below the DMZ and along likely avenues of approach by enemy forces coming from the western mountains. Wheeled and tracked vehicle movement in the DMZ and along Route 9 had noticeably increased in early March and was unusually busy during the daylight hours, as well.

The North Vietnamese city of Vinh was a large logistics terminal in the northern part of the Ho Chi Minh Trail. *Vinh Window* was the name given for voice radio interceptions that US SIGINT were able to first decipher in May 1967, based on a HF voice transmission that was associated with the 559th Transportation Group. It wasn't until October 1967 that the breakthrough they were waiting for occurred, when an RC130 Commando Lance aircraft intercepted a Low VHF (LVHF) transmission emanating from lower North Vietnam. A communications liaison system (revealed by a "T" designation), associated with the *binh trams* along the trail to the DMZ, revealed the unit's progress, although the system was not run by the unit itself. In February 1968, the North Vietnamese changed their three-digit location system in the code to a four-digit one. This was of even greater value to us because we could tell where the unit was bound for down the trail (e.g., 20xx meant the unit was bound for COSVN, in the III Corps area, while 90xx meant the DMZ/Tri Thien MR). While *Vinh Window* provided extensive information on unit activity, it also quickly overwhelmed the ability of US forces to translate all of this material.[28]

In the January 15, 1972, WIEU briefing (page 75), the briefer stated that "a major reorganization of the 559th Transportation Group … is underway, involving formation of three new transportation groups: 471, 472, and 473, and several new *binh trams*. Streamlining the system, we feel." In fact, the Front 968 and the 565th Military Advisory Group were combined to make the 559th Transportation Group into a Military Region. The 470, 471, 472, 473, and 571 area HQs (each a division equivalent) were subordinate to the 559th in the 1970–71 timeframe.

It has been estimated that SIGINT information was responsible for some 55 percent of targeting in Vietnam, although combat commanders were generally untrained in this type of intelligence and, as a consequence, ignored or misused the SIGINT they were presented with.

US State Department

Apparently, the British consul in Hanoi, Joe Wright, wrote weekly summaries of North Vietnamese activities, which were also addressed to Saigon, Washington, Paris, Moscow, Bangkok, Vientiane, Phnom Penn, Peking, Ottawa, Canberra, and Wellington. Troops, trucks, and weapons headed south convinced the consul in early 1972 that an offensive of some sort was to be undertaken soon by North Vietnam. Further, Wright reported that Pham Van Dong (the North Vietnamese

Prime Minister), during the second session of the Democratic Republic of Vietnam (DRV) National Assembly in the later part of March 1972, "delivered a violent tirade against the pacification programme," which he described as the "basis of the 'Vietnamisation' of the war." The prime minister claimed that the "new policies of the PRG [i.e. the 'amnesty'] towards the puppet army and administration have helped the political struggle ... in the cities."[29]

Perhaps this last sentence gives even more credence to an underground railroad for deserters in I Corps, discussed earlier. Taking credit for defections (and deserters) of the puppet army (i.e., ARVN) and continuing their efforts to destabilize ARVN and the Saigon government helped in their political struggle.

CHAPTER 17

Theater and Area Commands

The only situation a commander can know fully is his own; his opponent's he can know only from unreliable intelligence.

—CARL VON CLAUSEWITZ

Working down the chain of command from the national level, there were many "fingers in the pie," each with their own intelligence sections and commanders. As you will see, it could sometimes lead to a lot of confusion and withholding of information that was not necessarily pass on to higher, lower, and adjacent commands.

The COMUSMACV sent a message to the CINCPAC and to the JCS detailing the enemy situation above the DMZ. This message was discussed at the March 11, 1972, WIEU briefing.[1] The message described a SAM umbrella that stretched as far as 30km below the DMZ and well into the Laotian panhandle. The MiG and SAM coordinated network prevented our gunships from operating in the pass areas of the north (where NVA equipment and troops entered the Ho Chi Minh Trail), and greatly increased the risk to our fighter aircraft operating in the area. In addition, the B-52s were generally stopped from entering these areas, though CINCSAC said they would fly if and when the target justified the risk. The message continued by stating that long-range artillery, tanks, and infantry units were positioned in the area just above the DMZ. In what turned out to be a most prophetic conclusion, the author of the message stated, "If he initiates his offensive at the outset of a protracted period of bad weather, we risk serious losses in northern Military Region 1." The rules of engagement (ROEs) at this time were that aircraft could return fire, but not initiate it, despite the known fact that the SAMs and MiGs were controlled by integrated control systems that stretched across southern North Vietnam.

Intelligence had continued to see a buildup and prepositioning of men and material, which prompted GEN Abrams to decide on February 5 that the expected offensive was in the immediate offing. A 48-hour maximum air effort against the MR-2 (Central Highlands, where the main effort was expected to come from) and then in I Corps (MR-1) began. The Pentagon suspended further action on February 16, 1972.

In fact, General John D. Lavelle (Seventh Air Force commander and the commander of air operations for MACV) wrote in "The SAM Threat" that in the first three weeks of February, almost a dozen SAMs were in or near South Vietnamese territory. Lavelle's interpretation of North Vietnam's ground-controlled intercept (GCI) radars, the emissions of which alerted USAF aircraft to watch for planes and SAMs, was therefore, within the ROEs. This was because the GCI radars were netted between each other and were used to guide North Vietnamese planes and/or SA-2 SAM systems to intercept USAF aircraft. BAT-21 was downed by an SA-2 missile which was manually tracked, and the SA-2 system's GCI radar may have also provided initial guidance to it. Lavelle knew then that USAF aircraft flying over North Vietnam were tracked and might expect air or SA-2 reaction, or both—this was not necessarily known to others, especially to some US politicians playing military expert.

During the April 8, 1972, COMUS update, GEN Abrams asked about B-52 strikes in MR-1 and was answered, "Sir, every strike up in MR-1 is targeted against a target that is recommended by the FRAC commander ...."[2] The day before, in relation to these strikes, Abrams posed the question, "What'd they say, five regiments up there?" To which his J-2 (LTG Potts) responded affirmatively.[3] There were *over* three times as many infantry regiments (the two NVA divisions attacking through the DMZ alone had three infantry regiments apiece), two tank regiments, and multiple composite and regular artillery regiments operating north of the Hai Van Pass (northern I Corps) by this time. Saigon was getting our INTSUMs because when the 525th MI Group staff duty officer would log them in when the evening ones arrived and taken over to MACV. Didn't Kroesen pass this information onto MACV? Was no one reading the 571st's INTSUMs, including BG Thomas Bowen, FRAC's deputy commander? They probably were, because there were a few items that Kroesen included in a few of his daily reports to Abrams) but they probably didn't want to believe our HUMINT information, but had egg on their faces when they found out we had accurately forecasted the NVA approaches and initial intentions.

Military Assistance Command Vietnam (MACV)

Even after the offensive had begun in I Corps, "intelligence sources" in Saigon (and perhaps elsewhere) on Monday (April 3) still had no idea of the extent of the offensive. The Pacific *Stars and Stripes* cited "intelligence sources" theorizing that the NVA might "be staging a dress rehearsal for a future general offensive."[4] This theory was supported by the meticulous communist planning that went into the 1968 Tet offensive. The lack of activity elsewhere in country supposedly backed this theory.

Other theories quoted by the newspaper included: using the two northernmost provinces "as a bargaining lever to end the war;" influencing the forthcoming elections in the United States against President Nixon; proving that Vietnamization wasn't working; influencing public opinion to stop aid to South Vietnam; and returning the Vietnam War to the front page everywhere. Ending with, "the motivation behind the Quang Tri attacks of 1972 may have to be discovered by historians," it seems obvious that the "intelligence sources" (whoever they might be, if not invented) must not have seen the DIA and CIA pony show reports and the ARVN countrywide alerts, nor have been aware of MACV and FRAC's lack of complete analysis and lack of confidence in their very own subordinate intelligence organizations. Looking at what the NVA and VC had done prior to Tet 1968 condemned the logical analysis of current events to a historical perspective, once again. Tet 1968 stood as the guidepost of American involvement in Vietnam, it still remains so today.

According to the MACV J-2, "Military intelligence was highly effective in predicting enemy actions prior to the Easter Offensive," during his tenure as chief. According to Potts, the only weakness in intelligence estimates was the selection of the tri-border region in the west and not the Demilitarized Zone as the initial point of enemy attack."[5] Apparently, the "effective" predictions didn't also include both where and when, however. Given the massive numbers of troops and equipment that the NVA initially and subsequently employed, pre-emptive actions were obviously wanting, as well.

Likewise, USMC Captain O'Toole, "as the senior Marine intelligence officer in Vietnam, had access to upper level intelligence briefs. Nevertheless, he related to [US Army Captain John M.] Oseth (Team 155's intelligence advisor to the 3rd ARVN Division) upon his arrival in Quang Tri on March 31, 1972, that nowhere along the line had he heard any word of an impending enemy drive in Military Region 1."[6] Oseth continued, "Similarly the suggestion that the invasion was anything less than a total surprise is false. After the fact writings have alleged that this or that level of command or person knew something large was going to happen sometime somewhere. My answer to that has always been what O'Tool [sic] told me when the magnitude of the offensive was starting to become clear. He said he sat in on all the MACV situation briefings every day, and nothing, nothing ever indicated a full-scale invasion was in the works. Similar observations are made on interview tapes at [the Military History Institute at] Carlisle [Barracks] by Colonel Raymond Battreall, an armor officer who participated in the Saigon deliberations that put a new division along the DMZ, and LTC Heath Twichell, one of the 3d Division's field advisors who also knew the Saigon Perspective."[7]

Despite the January 10, 1972, Secretary of the Army Briefing[8] where GEN Abrams remarked that "We've got to continue the intelligence activity, and we've got to have communications," troops began to leave country. Unfortunately, none of this seemed to apply to lower echelons of intelligence. It was a fact that *none* of this information and "analysis" ever filtered down to our unit (for I would have seen it) and presumably the other non-Saigon-based 525th MI Group detachments—instead we got plenty of nothing. In the end it was probably lucky that none of this contradictory information was disseminated because it might have weighed on the validity of the intelligence being produced by the 571st MI Detachment's reports that were being sent daily, especially during the Easter Offensive. According to some USARV intelligence personnel, MACV "froze" them out too.

All of this does, however, point out that lessons learned, at least as far back as World War II, continued to be forgotten or ignored. The intelligence fallacy that, "The combat 2 (as in S-2, G-2, and J-2) is not, as is sometimes propounded and widely believed, working entirely for his immediate commander. This 2 business is *all-for-one-and-one-for-all* … It's not a cloak-and-dagger business society but it is, or should be, a tightly knit club, a fraternity of hard-working people who are all working for themselves and for all their brothers as well."[9]

Reading how Lomperis states MACV operated in an "unspoken, military etiquette of hierarchy whereby analysts and desk officers could comment on facts, but only field grade officers were supposed to offer analysis and interpretation"[10] in briefings only makes one think of the military adage, *it's not what you know but what your rank is.*

Many MI soldiers of the 525th MI Group served at its HQ in Saigon, as well as various MACV assignments in the area. One such place was called The Tank, which was where a variety of different types of classified material was used for assessments to inform the generals and MACV staffs. At least at the time of the Easter Offensive of 1972, an officer assigned to The Tank explained the priority of the various kinds of intelligence they used in assessing enemy intentions, capabilities, etc. From highest-to-lowest, the most reliable were: open source (media and library), imagery, SIGINT, HUMINT, troops in contact (TIC), and POW reports.[11] MACV's Tank had spaces for the four MRs, headed by a colonel with a major in charge of each region's desk. MACV's reports consisted of a Daily Intelligence Summary (DISUM), Weekly Intelligence Estimate Update (WIEU), and Monthly Intelligence Estimate Update (MIEU). This is where the generals and admirals were briefed with "massaged" intelligence, so as not to offend. "… CYA Intelligence reporting was ritual." Supposedly, "the central concern of each desk was to keep track of its Order-of-Battle."[12] (In retrospect, I would be greatly surprised if their maps and files had as much information as the maps and 8/5 cards I maintained.)

While the intelligence personnel were usually intelligence trained, the operations (J-3 at MACV) personnel were from the combat arms fields (armor, infantry, and artillery). The field and overall commanders, in this case GEN Abrams of World War II tank fame, were and always are from one of these branches. (A common-enough joke made light of the fact that an "intelligent officer" would never be allowed to command, or become the J-3 of any large formations of troops.) The operations head at the various Army levels always outranked all others in the same organization, and the MACV J-3 was no exception. The J-2 at this time, GEN Potts, was a commissioned armor officer before the Army assigned him to various intelligence organizations, which was a common occurrence. "… Whatever the demands of J-3 for the 'best intel,' intelligence was never going to be perfect, and J-2 wanted to be sure that some huge operational disaster could not be blamed on faulty intelligence. The J-2 reports on enemy intentions came down to a continuum of four predictors: unlikely, possible, probable, and likely. All of these terms came with appropriate caveats. The difference between probable and likely lay in the density of these caveats, but they were never absent, even for likely. There were no 'slam dunks' coming out of intelligence in Vietnam."[13]

"On the allied side MACV intelligence officers nailed every significant enemy offensive on their watch ... from the mini-Tet in May 1968 ... to the Easter Offensive of 1972" and, "Clearly Potts was justified in his conviction that Vietnam was 'an intelligence war.'"[14] There are many examples which can be used to refute this assertion. Why were Abrams and Potts visiting their families out of country at the time of the invasion? Why didn't the J-2 take note of the 571st MID's reports, etc. Perhaps, it was simply general officers knowing better?

The differences between the higher HQ and a little intelligence unit almost 644km away could not have been more pronounced, though Team 155's CPT Oseth wrote that "the suggestion that the invasion was anything less than a total surprise is false"[15] though our Detachment A was virtually co-located at Quang Tri and our INTSUMs were sent countrywide. GEN Abrams knew what was forthcoming when he stated the evidence so far (which included 130s in the DMZ and western Quang Tri), leading to the conclusion that "Hanoi is making an all-out military effort in 1972. That's what the story is. That's what the facts are."[16] The question remained when?

ARVN, VNMC

For the most part, ARVN depended almost exclusively on intelligence given to them by US intelligence. South Vietnamese units that knew their AOs might know a lot about the NVA, VC, and the villages, but this information was probably not normally available to US forces.

FACs

Several FACs had noticed NVA activity in the DMZ area in the weeks preceding the Easter Offensive, calling-in strikes and dutifully reported what they had seen, though other FACs did not. South Vietnamese FACs were known to orbit away from enemy activity and, hence, could not call in accurate strikes.

1st MIBARS/PHOTINT

US PHOTINT missions detected a large concentration of tanks near what was called Bat Lake, where North and South Vietnam borders met with Laos. The 1st Military

Intelligence Battalion Aerial Reconnaissance Squadron (MIBARS), which was active country-wide until early-1972, found that roads in the western DMZ during the spring and fall of 1971 had been widened and improved so it could sustain tracked vehicles (discussed elsewhere in this book).

SOG

The Studies and Observations Group (SOG) began to shrink organizationally on March 31, 1972, becoming an advisory team attached to the South Vietnamese Strategic Technical Directorate. For those that remained in-country, they probably did take on some missions that are not generally known.

SEALs

The Naval Intelligence Liaison Officer (NILO) regularly received all the 571st intelligence reports and INTSUMs. This office was also a direct conduit by which US Navy Sea-Air-Land (SEAL) teams received this information, as well. In Da Nang, the SEALs were located at Camp Fay with the cover designation of Naval Advisory Detachment, Da Nang, while actually they were the Maritime Studies Group (SOG) 37.

A confidential SEAL Intelligence Support, dated July 20, 1971, delineated the "19 months of experience to direct-action U.S. SEAL platoons operating in the Republic of Vietnam. Certain intelligence support functions described in the enclosures have been assumed by Naval Intelligence Liaison Officers (NILO) in Vietnam …." The document also specifically calls upon the SEALs to establish liaison with the "local 525 M.I."[17]

Though there was no personal contact with the SEALs, all our reports and INTSUMs went to FRAC every day, where other organizations, including the SEALs, also received them or special items, too.

CHAPTER 18

Diversions and Deceptions at the Onset

Often considered backward in technology, the NVA often proved they were not. Though not often discussed, the NVA became well versed in misdirection activities and in not calling attention to themselves.

In 1969, a dozen members of the NVA's Technical Reconnaissance Unit A-3 were captured on the Michelin rubber plantation northeast of Saigon. Voice and manual Morse intercept operators were among those captured. US AN/PRC-25 and AN/PRC-77 radios ("bought from our South Vietnamese allies or third parties") and several Chinese R-139 HF receivers, and other commercial equipment were obtained. Unit A-3's records disclosed detailed American protocols and procedures, and verbatim transcripts of radio transmissions over a period of four years were also part of this intelligence bonanza.[1]

FRAC/I Corps

The 324B NVA Division entered the South from Laos in early March 1972 and proceeded towards its usual AO in the area west of Hue against a usual opponent, the 1st ARVN Division. On March 5, 1st ARVN began an operation called *Lam Son 45-72* to destroy an NVA logistical base near Cu Mong (southeast of FSB Veghel).[2] Soon afterwards, "unable to defend everything, 1st ARVN constricted its lines and once again ceded control of the western highlands of I Corps to the NVA."[3] Coincidence, just a short while before the Easter Offensive was to begin? This was the situation in the Thua Thien Province, in I Corps, on March 29, 1972.

This initially caused no real alarm because it was the "usual" movement of the 324B. Two independent infantry regiments (the 5th and the 6th) and the 29th Regiment of the 324B, however, kept the 1st ARVN engaged west of Hue, as the other two regiments of the 324B (803rd and 812th) moved northward to establish a blocking force south of Quang Tri, to prevent assistance from coming northward along QL-1, and to keep pressure on Quang Tri City from the south. Even the CIA (who were receiving our reports and INTSUMs) recognized this earlier than FRAC when it stated in a April 10, 1972, Memorandum, "… it seems more likely that for the time being it will basically continue to put on enough pressure to make the threat credible, tying down the 1st ARVN Division while the action proceeds to the north around Quang Tri," as we stated two weeks before.

SRAC/II Corps

Before the offensive began in II Corps, the VC conducted diversionary attacks, beginning on April 5 in Binh Dinh Province. Keeping local ARVN forces busy along the coast was an attempt to assist NVA forces beginning operations in the western part of the province. Before the offensive began, II Corps was cast by Hanoi as the primary area in with the NVA would strike. The NVA knew well that their radio traffic was being monitored, so as part of their own deception schemes, the 304th NVA Division moved into a forest in North Vietnam, before the Easter Offensive, under radio silence. An element of the division (perhaps a couple of platoons or a company) moved down the Ho Chi Minh Trail, making phony radio reports four times a day, as if the division was en route to the Central Highlands.[4] This continued until they reached *binh tram* 40.

TRAC/III Corps

Just as the 324B NVA Division kept US and South Vietnamese eyes on Hue, so did the NVA create a diversion in III Corps. "Prior to the launch of the main attack into Loc Ninh, two independent NVA regiments attacked outposts in Tay Ninh Province, to the south of Binh Long. This was the *traditional* Communist attack route toward Saigon. These attacks were meant to focus the allies' attention in that direction while the North Vietnamese launched their main attack against Binh Long Province."[5]

Photographs could sometimes "lie," too. Lomperis wrote about a "set of photographs coming to the MR-3 desk of a concentration of T-54 tanks just across the border from Tay Ninh in Cambodia. It turned out these tanks were literally made of cardboard and were designed to deceive us into thinking that the major line of communist attack would be directed at Tay Ninh, rather than Loc Ninh."[6]

CHAPTER 19

571st Military Intelligence Detachment

The whirlwind and its vortex may have confused others, but not one intel unit—the 571st MI Detachment, 525th MI Group. It was considered a "minor" unit, though the "major" organizations certainly embraced its information as their own and, just as quickly, ignored its information when it didn't suit their "analysis." The 571st also benefitted from having numerous Vietnamese-speaking linguists and even one who spoke Mandarin, unlike the author of *Capabilities and Intentions* who bemoaned his intel assignment to Vietnam where his unit had no Vietnamese speakers. Our Mandarin-speaking linguist was a pipe-smoking major who was naturally assigned to Hue. "Naturally," because Hue had a Chinese-speaking community and the knowledge and importance of any Chinese advisors for the North was well-known, probably since the *New York Times* article of November 17, 1965, where NVA POWs were quoted as saying a Chinese communist officer was assigned to every NVA regiment. General William Westmoreland, then the MACV commander, made it known shortly afterwards that any mention of Chinese advisors was a forbidden subject.

The Easter Offensive of 1972 is usually just a footnote in the Vietnam War. Even today, a 2012 DIA report entitled, "The Vietnam Cauldron: Defense Intelligence in the War for Southeast Asia" only cites the Easter Offensive once in the entire document. Though the information of a forthcoming changeover to a conventional war by the NVA first came from a 571st "usually reliable source" in December 1971, DIA coincidently noticed a large increase in traffic along the Ho Chi Minh Trail at roughly the same time.[1] We thought it only made sense, after all, why would the NVA give up what they learned in Laos using tanks and 130mm artillery, etc.? Other "major" intelligence and command organizations likewise began to slowly change their minds, as well.

"As the crucial year of 1972 approached, MACV and the Vietnamese Joint General Staff worked overtime to get the nation's defenses in a better state of readiness to meet the next NVA invasion. It was expected to come in January or February 1972 and to hit hardest in the northern provinces of South Vietnam."[2] On December

31, 1971, General Cao Van Vien, Chief of the JGS, attended the WIEU with GEN Abrams. Discussing the current situation, Abrams stated, "If he moves the 304th, the 308th, and the 324 Bravo into Quang Tri and Thua Thien, that ain't protracted war. That's main force. That's a big battle."[3] Two months later, however, Abrams and Sir Robert Thompson heard this—"Briefer: It is believed that a countrywide return to main force warfare is unlikely at this time. Some main force warfare may possibly be employed in the Tay Ninh area. Most likely: B-3 Front, and to a lesser extent northern MR-1."[4]

These projections and their new attitudes were generally unknown at the detachment-level (in part because there was always a tendency to over-classify and closely hold information emanating from outside Vietnam and at MACV), and little information (but for historical) was received from the group HQ. Since the 571st was the source for this and similar reports to come, it was probably best that their intelligence was not received, because it did not hold any sway in the interpretation of the information from the detachment's sources. For the 571st, our reports would become the lynchpin of future efforts for 1972 and the gathering of as much information as possible and ensuring that this information was widely disseminated, despite US withdrawals.

One 571st report, dated February 28, 1972, stated that the "general offensive plan of the National Liberation Front of South Vietnam" would go into effect on March 10, 1972 and consist of "four main fronts." Military Region Tri-Thien-Hue (MRTTH) "would commit three NVA divisions against ARVN bases, Dong Ha City and RF/PF bases along QL-1 in Quang Tri and Thua Thien." This report went on to discuss the Plateau, Wam-Ngai, and Plain Fronts.[5]

"Some officials thought that Hanoi had abandoned its plans for a major offensive altogether. Even during the last days of March when gradually increasing levels of enemy artillery barrages were noted in addition to continued infiltration and supply movement, and in spite of at least *four separate human resources* (571st MI Detachment agents) *who claimed that there would be a "great offensive" in the near future*, American military personnel for the most part were dubious about any impending large-scale attack."[6] The delay seems to have been, "In northern Military Region 1, two agents indicated that the cause was ARVN's high state of combat readiness."[7] Notice that MACV took heed of agent reports and this was from a briefing on March 11, the day *after* the hostilities were to begin. (The actual report would have taken a couple of days to be typed and sent over the wires, processed by the 571st, sent to our group HQ, and into MACV—this would likely have been a report I may have called down to Saigon about over the secure phone.)

As new information was received, our detachment's UTM maps started to become more populated with the standard military symbols of FM 21-30. Historical information was sought from XXIV Corps, with little reciprocity, and even less was ever received from anywhere else outside of the 525th MI Group. CIA had essentially closed shop by 1972 (and never shared their information anyway) and none of the MACV J-2, DIA, or CINCPAC reports trickled down to the 571st. Our enemy unit, personnel, and equipment index cards that were created months before became invaluable and remained so as more of our agent data was collected. These reports were enough to alert FRAC and the group HQ in Saigon when they were initially received, but were obviously ignored.

The following are from the 525th MI Group Operational Report Lessons Learned (ORLL):[8]

> (18) A March report revealed the Hqs, Military Region Tri-Thien-Hue (MRTTH) recently issued a directive to all military and political cadres on MRTTH's policy for the recently launched Spring Campaign. The Spring '72 Campaign "was to have been initiated" at the end of March 1972 and was to continue to the end of April 1972. The campaign was to be called XUAN LY SON (translated as: Spring Mountain). The objectives as reported were:
>
> Military: NVA military units will move toward increased operations against ARVN base camps and outposts. NVA Artillery units will move guns into the DMZ to provide maximum firepower to units operating in the area. Local armed guerrilla units will try to maintain their presence and increase their effectiveness by attacking and harassing RF and PF outposts in the rural areas.
>
> Political: Parallel with military activities, proselyting units will make an all-out effort to support the peace plan proposed at the Paris Talks. (Perhaps, the Camp Carroll surrender and the underground railroad are indicative of these instructions?)
>
> (22) On 1 Apr 72, a VC officer in Thua Thien Province reported that "the objective of the attacks initiated in Quang Tri (P) was to draw ARVN units into the northern province, weakening the position in Thua Thien (P) for operations to cut off Thua Thien (P) at the Hai Van Pass. The 29th NVA Regt was reported to have been given instructions to secure bases in the A Shau Valley from which attacks using tanks would be introduced into Thua Thien (P).
>
> (19) The "812th and 29th Regts of the 324th Division were ordered by MRTTH to prepare for an attack on Quang Tri City" in another report. Each regiment had four battalions of about 1600 men and were given specific avenues of approach. The C-14 Sapper Company was also ordered to attack the ammo dump on Ai Tu Combat Base. Another report confirmed this same information.
>
> (23) One of our agent reports stated that detailed planning and coordination was necessary for NVA/VC offensive operations. As such, there was a VC cadre meeting of the Quang Da Special Zone (QDSZ) on April 9, 1972 which called for increasing political and military proselyting activity in anticipation of offensive operations against South Vietnamese activity in Quang Nam Province and Da Nang city and Airbase. "Civilians were mobilized into labor groups and transportation units to assist labor and transportation units to assist local and main force units from the projected offensive.

Virtually all detailed collateral information leading up to (and for the next couple of weeks afterwards) the Easter Offensive of 1972 in I Corps came from the 571st MI Detachment's agent reports (the "usually reliable sources") and our analysis contained in these INTSUMS. Despite being snubbed by these major HQs, the INTSUM was a quick way to distribute intelligence information rapidly and as needed (usually at least daily) when the offensive began. There were no specific requirements on what had to be contained in an INTSUM. This means of conveying intelligence had never been done by the 525th MI Group in Vietnam. The intelligence we were receiving and analyzing was highly important, time sensitive, and tactical in nature. FM 30-5 was consulted, and it stated that there is "no prescribed format except that the word 'INTSUM' will be the first item of the report." Capabilities, vulnerabilities, conclusions, and showing a Date–Time–Group were also mentioned as well as, "The INTSUM reflects the ... interpretation and conclusions as to enemy capabilities and probable courses of action." It also stated that non-essential detail should *not* be added, which made it perfect to use in getting the intelligence out quickly and securely.

Many SOG reports were first dealt with in the same manner as the 571st ones were, "In Saigon there was a hesitance to accept SOG's warnings by minimizing and nitpicking intelligence reports, which came to a head during a briefing for General Abrams." After "a MACV staff officer began demanding arcane details before the intelligence could be accepted," Abrams erupted and verbally ensured there would be no further challenges to SOG recon team reports.[9]

MACV wasn't the only command to screw-up. XXIV Corps had somewhat of a history of screw-ups too. Take January 1972 (while Kroesen was the deputy I Corps commander) when SOG had pictures of NVA soldiers cultivating a field outside Da Nang. A plane flew low over this activity and ended up photographing an American looking up at the plane. GEN Abrams looked at the photos and messaged I Corps to mount a battalion-size rescue mission. Nothing happened. Another message was sent offering JPRC assistance—no reply. Finally, a third message was replied to stating that "they assigned a battalion to that matter and the battalion they assigned was a Marine battalion which was on ships off Danang, headed home." Too late then for any rescue attempt.[10]

At least at that time, US Army agents were extremely proficient in using manual typewriters (in the age before electric typewriters and computers). Not only were INTSUMs quickly turned out and released, but our method also allowed for on-the-spot corrections and clarifications. What occurred was an Army major (my boss) typed what an acting-jack sergeant (me) was writing or dictating. The major acted as a sounding board—if things weren't clear to him, then the confusing part was rewritten. The maps covering the walls also brought greater understanding to what was being conveyed by text, as well as UTM coordinates used to pinpoint enemy locations, routes of advance, objectives, etc. Perhaps sounding somewhat arcane and probably not heard much today, the "Mission" came first (and this remained true in my other [joint] intelligence assignments afterwards). We also all knew that lives were always potentially at stake, which gave greater importance to our best efforts. Our twice-a-day INTSUMs later became standard practice for all the 525th detachments after about a week.

Today, this "officer-enlisted" familiarity linkage is often looked at askance, but it was an example of the bond of mutual respect that existed at the time and most of my time in Army intelligence. While some military and civilian people can't fathom this kind of professional relationship having existed, it's important to point out that it was also a prevalent idea among most in the MI field. The same obviously didn't apply to the South Vietnamese, as Vann stated, "Enlisted men, no matter how well qualified they are to advise, we do not have any Vietnamese officers qualified to receive advice from enlisted men."[11]

In the years that followed, similar professional and familiar relationships between other Army, Navy, and Air Force intelligence officers existed. I was not the only example, to be sure. Perhaps it was the fact that any educational differences between us were slight, intelligence training was rigorous at the time, selection for the intelligence field once had to be investigated (security and character) and demonstrated by past actions. The realization of the high value of the information we reported and that people's lives might depend on the intelligence we developed quickly became an internalized norm and responsibility. "Intelligence errors in combat, if serious, were measured in terms of lives lost. If they led to wrong tactical decisions, an intelligence officer was readily available for reassignment."[12]

By contrast, before the offensive began in II Corps, the senior advisor for Kontum Province, Colonel Stephen W. Bachinski, plainly ignored a six-and-a-half-year MACV SOG veteran, MSG Lowell Stevens, who had seen the North Vietnamese building roads through the jungle. After riding along in an OV-10 for a couple of months, Stevens reported his sightings to the US Army colonel, who scoffed at the report and did not inform MACV HQ.[13] Just as in I Corps, even 100-percent accurate information was ignored. One wonders if it had been an officer who had reported the information instead whether it would have changed the colonel's mind.

From the staff duty officer (SDO) logs (which were a means to track events occurring on evenings and weekends) of the 525th MI Group located at Building 616, Tan Son Nhut AFB, there are six times in the March–April period in which the 571st was in direct secure telephonic or RTT contact with the group concerning the tactical situation occurring in I Corps. The first *recorded* contact was at 1800 on March 31, when Quang Tri Combat Base (3rd ARVN Division and Advisory Team 155 HQ) information was discussed over a secure telephone. Two hours later, at 2000, the SDO duly recorded my name and the current intelligence information that I personally conveyed to him, and that an Ops Immediate (OO in message parlance) INTSUM message was waiting for the 504th Signal Battalion to "come up" (receive). In an ironic and "interesting" twist, the 525th MI Group's SDO log for March 30, 1972, couldn't be found by archivists in the national military commands and civilian agencies and is presumably lost or stolen.

Not coincidently, MG Kroesen sent a message (FRAC 311215Z Mar 72, "Quang Tri Situation,") to GEN Abrams. Given the +8-hour difference between Zulu (Z) time and all of South Vietnam, it was surely our message, which Randolph describes:

> By the afternoon of March 31, with the attack a day old, Kroesen was able to send in a more comprehensive survey of the situation. It had become clear that this was a major effort by the NVA—not harassment and not a diversion, as previously suspected, but the opening of the long-awaited major offensive. Kroesen identified three axes of attack: south from the DMZ, southeast from the road network in the western DMZ, and eastward from Laos along Route 9. By this time NVA tanks had appeared in the northwest, and ARVN firebases had begun to fall under the onslaught.[14]

Further, Abrams is quoted stating, "General Kroesen's daily report just breathed impending disaster from the southwest of Quang Tri ... What'd they say, five regiments up there? I mean, I'm not trying to become a targeteer, but I was just listening to what the staff is presenting here, and what the reports say, and [laughing] I don't know why we're not trying to work the five over."[15] This must have been at least partially from our INTSUMs because *Kroesen had nothing* (by his own words)—no intelligence section, the weather kept planes from flying, etc. What other information he could have received would have come from 1st and 3rd ARVN Divisions and the I Corps commander, but they were in a fight. The only other American unit who might have provided information would have been the 8th RRFS at Phu Bai, though classifications of their information would have caused difficulties. Many references indicate that the major HQs had few answers for days after the offensive started.

As for MG Kroesen, he recalled that "The advisory command was heavily weighted to provide administrative assistance and logistical advice with only a token intelligence and operations section. It was neither manned nor equipped to monitor the combat activity or to provide tactical guidance."[16] I also find it disturbing that Kroesen let this vitally important situation occur, and/or it was his excuse for being caught flatfooted because he relied on "other" intelligence. The rub, though, is that we were the only reporting collateral intelligence reporting unit in all of I Corps/FRAC during the Easter Offensive of 1972 and we didn't even know it, though we suspected it.

The FRAC *Command History* for 1972–73 is dated March 28, 1973—the day after the command ceased to exist—and makes only two references to MG Kroesen and nothing about COL Paris (the FRAC G-2) or the 571st MI Detachment. The document is only 111 pages long (including maps and references) and has only 24 different endnotes! How the Easter Offensive began and major actions that occurred, for the most part, are missing. It also has numerous mistakes in the text and maps and the reader will be left wondering why, when so many NVA divisions and regiments invaded this area of northern South Vietnam and it lasted far longer than any other corps area, there is so little written and why it has so few references?

"One example of the close-mindedness of some senior military commanders was the total disregard Kroesen and Westmoreland among others showed toward intelligence predictions of an enemy frontal assault along the Demilitarized Zone. The enemy had never done it the past, and so they were never going to do it in the future? This position persisted even when reports came in almost daily of sightings of tank tracks or 130-mm field guns positioned along the Demilitarized Zone."[17] Senior leadership, both American and South Vietnamese, also seemed to think that the NVA would not use tanks and 130mm guns that they used effectively during *Lam Son 719*.

Our messages that were sent daily (and later, twice daily), received by the 525 MI Group during weekdays, were not recorded, as the SDO log was only used for evenings and weekends. An April 3 SDO log entry at 2140 shows that the command element of the group was notified of the tactical situation in MR-1, with an Army major leaving two minutes later with our 0700 INTSUM, presumably en route to the MACV Tank. The next recorded entry wasn't until April 8, which shows an INTSUM, Part II, being taken to the Tank at 1958. The last April SDO entries occurred on the same date, April 17 at 0400 and 0620, note the separate arrivals of our INTSUMs, which were delivered by 504th Signal Battalion couriers (the last instance also having six additional messages). Two copies of each were then taken to The Tank. As with FRAC, MACV intelligence makes no mention of our efforts in using an INTSUM to spread the word, though the SDO logs clearly show that they did receive our intelligence.

Just as in the Battle of the Bulge, "The fact remains, however, that all the intelligence information on which the Third Army G-2 Section based its predictions was available to other commands. Our intelligence reports were widely distributed to higher, lower, and lateral echelons of command (… a full week before the German offensive began.)"[18]

The need for rapid tactical communications was also a topic of the 525 MI Group's Lessons Learned for April 30, 1972. The senior US advisor to the 1st ARVN Division, Colonel Hillman Dickinson, stated that this division, operating in the A Shau Valley, had, "found much evidence that … the main attack would come from Laos. (Note: This is undoubtedly the 324B NVA Division which traversed the A Shau.) Dickinson also said that not until after the offensive had begun did he learn of intelligence that indicated the enemy plan to come through the DMZ."[19]

COL Dickinson has been the only person to claim that he learned, from an MACV intelligence report, that the NVA invasion of the South was to occur on April 1. This is but one of two references to a specific invasion date, though no such report has ever been found or referenced. It is doubtful that so many senior American officers would have left the country deliberately if an offensive was in the offing and that 1st ARVN had just ceded control of the western highlands of I Corps to the NVA, again.

The South Vietnamese JGS supposedly issued a warning. "Late in March 1972, information was obtained by the J-7 (Plans and Development office) of the JGS that 29 March was to be the D-day of the general offensive. This information was disseminated to all ARVN units as a measure of precaution." "As it turned out, up to three days after it was launched, the enemy general offensive in MR-1 still failed to arouse any major concern in Saigon."[20] This could have been the 571st MI Detachment's first warning to everyone, as it was widely disseminated across Vietnam and would certainly have been shared with the senior ARVN leadership.

"General [Cao Van] Vien, Chief of the Joint General Staff, later acknowledged an important debt to Abrams at that juncture. 'It was he again who, in the confusion of the first few hours after the NVA crossed the DMZ in early April 1972,' said Vien, "personally informed me of the critical situation and the debacle of the 3rd ARVN Infantry Division. Had it not been for his insight and solicitude, the JGS would have found itself in an embarrassing position after I Corps had apparently lost effective control.'"[21] The DMZ was crossed, and the Easter Offensive began on *March 30*—the "first few hours" had long since passed.

As part of Operation *Countdown*, all intelligence operations ceased on January 28, 1973; all 525th MI Group's IIRs were destroyed by February 10, 1973. Since all the IIR copies were destroyed, hard copies may still exist in the individual commands or agencies that were operating at the time, including PACFLT and its subordinates. All documents of this era have since been retired. Some organizations will only respond to FOIA requests on reports that they issued, not any information that they possess received from any other organization. The CIA is one such organization and is also one that still redacts entire pages, though almost half a century has passed—they were very cooperative with the author, however.[22]

CHAPTER 20

Observations, Reflections, and Conclusions

The hordes of analysts at the PACFLT, DIA, CIA, and MACV's J-2 certainly gave the "bum's rush" to the 571st MI Detachment—they did so by disregarding the reports made before and throughout the Easter Offensive. One has to wonder what the real consequences were of their inaction? How many people became casualties because of their failure to act?

There is an inbuilt "bias" that, though less so in the intelligence field, still predominates in how information is formed into intelligence (usually sources) and how it may then be reported (classifications). Each service is different (and a couple are extreme), but each tends to have certain characteristics in common, especially in the real or imagined reputations of the organization and the seniority of the personnel making the judgments. This also occurs in the non-military departments/agencies, though experience and rank may matter less than where a person went to school or their rank when they left the military service or civilian agency, if appropriate.

Almost all the 571st MI Detachment's reported information was "only" classified at the "Secret" or "Confidential" level. In the intelligence world (then, as it is today) how the material was classified is often thought to equate to its value, especially by those who are not in the intelligence field. As the SRAG commander John Paul Vann bluntly stated on February 7, 1972, "Nearly all reliable intelligence is limited to US S.I. Channels" (S.I. stands for Special Intelligence—SIGINT.)[1] This viewpoint was true as far back as World War II and it remains so today.[2] "Generally, the higher the command echelon, the greater the dominance of SIGINT in the intelligence picture."[3] GEN Abrams was quoted the year before stating (about MR-1), "What this needs now is really getting the headquarters going up here and getting the all-source intelligence and really getting to work on targeting. You've got a lot of power, but it isn't any good unless you have intelligence."[4] Contrasting Vann's outlook on intelligence, but supporting GEN Abrams' statement is an exchange in summer 1973 between General Bruce Palmer, Jr. and Lieutenant

General Phillip B. Davidson. The following is from a letter from Davidson to Palmer, dated July 18, 1973:

> ... Why—how come? One answer seems to me that we were too reliant on signal intelligence. I recall some figure like 80–90% of our intelligence came from this source. But this kind of intelligence, of course, can be tricky and misleading unless confirmed by some other source. Moreover, it is more strategic in nature and not suited to lower unit tactical operations (Division—Brigade—Battalion). In any event, despite all our air superiority and aviation, surveillance technology, etc., we could not reliably find our enemy.

Palmer responded, dated August 24, 1973:

> ... MACV J-2 was particularly well organized. My only reservation here is that again, because of the role played by SIGINT, certainly in part, the tendency seemed towards over-centralization at that level and insufficient attention at lower levels, especially Field Force/Corps and Division. There was a tendency for COMUSMACV to tell his subordinate commanders what the enemy was up to (largely based on SIGINT) rather than vice versa.[5]

Why didn't MACV J-2 also listen to Abrams? Ironically, the Son Tay Raid (Operation *Ivory Coast*) failed, at least in part, because of this same "compartmentalization" of intelligence in November 1970.

Lam Son 719 was a precursor to the Easter Offensive, in more ways than one. The after-action summation, mentioned earlier, of the I Corps commander at the time, LTG Sutherland, could have been transplanted into an Easter Offensive report. Without massive US air support, it is highly doubtful that ARVN would have been able to withstand the NVA assaults throughout the country in both operations. A year later, the NVA withstood more US air bombardment in South Vietnam and was still able to bring down their reserves and engage South Vietnamese troops. Undoubtedly, the new equipment the NVA received from Russia and China greatly helped, but the political and military leadership of South Vietnam only saw what they expected to see or dismissed what they didn't want to hear, as did the American generals and admirals and their respective HQs. As GEN Palmer wrote, "Many Americans who served in Vietnam were aware of the shortcomings of the South Vietnamese ... and many of us had serious doubts as to whether we would or could be successful in the conduct of the war."[6]

Vietnamization (which as GEN Abrams noted as far back as 1967, was necessary for US troops to be able to leave the country) did not include fighting a maneuver-style of warfare. Since the US built the FBs and FSBs and the South Vietnamese then occupied them, fixed fortifications became the norm. Obviously, US and ARVN forces would conduct sweeps, involving multiple units and types of equipment, but they would all return to the base camps after the operations were over. Partly due to a lack of a "frontline," the Patton axiom remains that fixed fortifications are a monument to the stupidity of man.

NVA units that had fought in *Lam Son 719* returned to their often-used AOs to fight a year later. Obviously, their recovery of men and materiel received a top priority and was probably, at least in part, provided by Base Areas 604 and 611 that ARVN/VNMC failed to destroy.

During *Lam Son 719*, command and control orders by the VNMC commander were ignored by his divisional commanders on more than one occasion, sometimes due to conflicting instructions and sometimes by insubordination. For instance, the corps commander ordered the 1st Armored Brigade to withdraw and ordered two US Air Cavalry troops to support their movement. The airborne division preempted this, having used the helicopters to support their battalion operations. The armor brigade had to make two unnecessary river crossings as it returned toward South Vietnam; unnecessary because the route had been cleared but they were not told. In ARVN's haste, some ARVN tanks were also simply abandoned.

Operational Plans (OpPlans) often went awry. For example, the 1st Armored stopped at A Luoi and it took days to restart the offensive, but by then, the initiative had switched to the NVA. "The most important problem to be solved was insubordination on the part of general reserve unit commanders who like many other generals considered themselves to be pillars of the regime. The unsubmissive attitude of the Marine and Airborne division commanders was actually inexcusable in that they placed themselves above the national interest and let their personal pride interfere with the task of defeating the enemy. At least, the I Corps commander should have been given the authority to require that his orders be strictly carried out."[7]

It was well known that US Army officers needed to have "command time" in Vietnam. Half a year in a staff job and half a year commanding a company, for example, was normal. It is also obvious in looking at how long the general officers commanded a corps (or military region) that a few months sufficed, unlike GEN Abrams who commanded MACV for four years. For the XXIV Corps commander, MG Kroesen, two months seemed to have been enough (in fairness, he spent four months as deputy commander of the corps under LTG Dolvin, who spent nine months as XXIV Corps commander). Kroesen initially took over as the commanding general of the 23rd American Division in July 1971, replacing MG Baldwin, who was relieved for the FSB Mary Ann incident of March 28, 1971. GEN Palmer, Jr., in a book review wrote, "The short command tour policy in Vietnam, ironically a decision taken to maintain morale and not … to provide command jobs for 'ticket punchers,' compounded the problem … of our continuity of effort, because unit leaders were too briefly on the job to gain a thorough knowledge of either the enemy or our South Vietnamese allies. Under such a policy, it became too easy and tempting to pass on responsibility for an unfinished job to one's successor."[8]

Commanding a corps that never took the field and a command structure that couldn't care less for intelligence that ran counter to the "prevailing wind" seemed to be the case in I Corps/FRAC. In peacetime, these officers rise up the ranks by the politics they play. In wartime, many seem to do the same, but quicker. The very senior military are not always trained in what the other services do and how they do it. For instance, ADM Moorer signed off on the *Lam Son 719* plan, though GEN Westmoreland maintained that he was never personally consulted as a member of the JCS staff.

There seems far less written about the Easter Offensive than other actions during the Vietnam War, though it was the biggest battle of the entire conflict. Distorted views of what occurred during the Easter Offensive among former ARVN/VNMC personnel are contained in some histories and analyses of the period written by South Vietnamese officers, and these views have been repeated by US generals and historians.

"A reduction in U.S. Combat forces and military support created tensions between South Vietnamese units and American advisers—co-vans in Vietnamese."[9] There were other reasons, as well. "Unlike many of the higher-ranking ARVN officers, (few) had a reputation for being honest rather than corrupt."[10] "But then a rigid adherence to truth has never been a Vietnamese characteristic, either North or South."[11] The reasons are many, but the passage of time has not shed light on many of the things that occurred, nor refuted erroneous accounts, now regarded as fact, written by some who never served in Vietnam and, consequently, take what is told to them as truth.

A. GEN Lam had command and control problems with the VNMC commander during *Lam Son 719*, who suffered no ill effects for his insubordination. Lam refused to have the VNMC and the redeployed Ranger Command under his I Corps control during the Easter Offensive.

B. The 258th VNMC Brigade needed Saigon to approve the move to Dong Ha (though it was OPCON to 3rd ARVN) and was already present in the I Corps area. All VNMC brigades (including their subordinate battalions) apparently operated this way in I Corps because they didn't take orders from ARVN commanders. This time, however, obedience to a lawful order wasn't with a corps commander (as it was during *Lam Son 719*), but with an ARVN division commander. One might reasonably assume that USMC advisors and advisory command would likely have known about this obvious breakdown in command and control. CPT (writing as LTC) Oseth wrote that "USMC advisors, to the extent they did not work to break that tendency down [the VNMC "stovepipe" in command and control issues between VNMC units and the 3rd ARVN commander], were themselves implicated in the 'coordination difficulties' that helped to account for the collapse, and ultimately for BG Giai's disgrace."[12] That said, the 3rd ARVN commander was not GEN Lam and their previous position as the strategic reserve undoubtedly was probably almost a reflex action. It would appear then that the VNMC commandant should have stepped in to stop or, at least, modify this practice.

"There was an unwritten rule, however, that the commandant of the Marine division was traditionally an officer from the North, possibly because the majority of the soldiers in the division were from North Viet Nam." I wonder how many soldiers and marines came from the North and how many are responsible for passing along where and what the ARVN/VNMC were up to?[13]

Perceptions of American military in Vietnam were also present in retrospect and during the war. Historian Dale Andrade wrote, referring to USMC CAPT Ripley, "The credo of elite units demanded courage above and beyond the standard for ordinary soldiers ...."[14] I don't have any dispute with him concerning Ripley's courage, but Andrade seems to say that only US Marines, Navy SEALs, Special Forces, etc., have more courage than "ordinary" soldiers. I'd bet that those common soldiers and US Army Medal of Honor selectees in Vietnam wouldn't appreciate this slap to their honor by a civilian military historian, nor would their units.

An unexpected incident occurred during the end of April, where "a large number of US Army NCOs who were the remnants of logistical units with no further mission in Kontum." Though they wanted to stay and fight, all they had was logistical "rather than combat arms experience. To *retrain and organize* them would take too long ...."[15] There were apparently many *senior* officers who must not have thought a lot of Army basic training (though they never went through it themselves during the Vietnam period), or who thought that engaging the enemy never occurred except to infantry types. Perhaps their limited exposure to non-infantry soldiers had something to do with it. Either way, there were many who were called upon to defend themselves and others who didn't qualify for a Combat Infantry Badge or whatever because they didn't have an infantry Military Occupational Specialty (MOS). Not wanting American soldiers to fight, considering the countrywide problems ARVN was having with desertions, is amazingly narrow-minded and personally insulting to those who were prepared to stand and fight.

"One thing I learned about the South Vietnamese was that they always left their enemy an opportunity to escape. When Americans get into an action, you aim to kill 'em all. But the idea of a battle of annihilation was not part of their culture and I had to accommodate my plans to take this into account," according to Lieutenant General Bernard Trainor, USMC (ret.).[16] This might have been true of the South Vietnamese, but it certainly was not true of their brothers in the North.

Seventy percent of all RVN military manpower loses were due to desertion (which averaged 130,000 each year); during the Easter Offensive the desertion rate was 43 percent higher. The many observations and news pictures of ARVNs taken during the offensive (and *Lam Son 719*), pulling their rank and unit insignia off their uniforms, tossing their weapons away, attempting to grab the skids of helicopters or blending in with the civilian populace fleeing the area are easy confirmations. Cowardly behavior "infected the common soldiers as well. This was seen, for example, when the 'olympic wounded' abandoned their wounded compatriots in order to clamber aboard medevac helicopters in the panic to get out of the city."[17]

"At the top of the military intelligence heap was the Defense Intelligence Agency (DIA) ...."[18] The question mark over DIA's competency can be epitomized by Secretary of Defense Melvin Laird's refusal to believe a January 1972 DIA briefing on North Vietnamese activity in what was to become the Easter Offensive. (The DIA cannot seem to find this briefing after two years of FOIA requests and a phone call. I was told they don't have any Easter Offensive information—none! They also could not explain the DIA Report "The Vietnam Caldron" that I held in my hands during the phone call.) It is fascinating that Laird told Congress in February 1972 that, "the NVA lacked both personnel and logistic support ... they cannot conduct a large-scale military operation for a substantial period of time." Moreover, "Admiral Thomas Moorer told the same hearing that the NVA had the capability, if they chose to accept the casualties, to generate a 'high point' type guerrilla offensive during Tet, or at the time of President Nixon's projected visit to the People's Republic of China."[19]

"Had there been any reports of major reinforcements in that area [I Corps]? The answer was, yes, there had been reports of that nature. However, these were discounted by the fact that the reports had been given a low level of credence (F-6 category)."[20] As noted previously, "F-6" was a means, using the "Admiralty Code," by which a source was judged (A-F) and how credible the information was (1-6). It seems DIA didn't bother to look up what "F-6" meant: "Reliability and Credibility cannot be judged," not "a low level of credence" at all! DIA, the citadel of military intelligence, evidently suffered the common intelligence malady of belittling HUMINT, a problem that most intelligence agencies suffer from, even today.

As a matter of fact, when I first encountered the term "Admiralty Code" it wasn't identified as such in FM 30-5 *Combat Intelligence*. I asked why all our reports indicated F-6 ratings? It appears it would have required our agent handlers to look at each agent's past, which I had at least partially been asked to do when we had to pare down the number of agents we had. As previously mentioned, I had to compare the information our agents were providing in each report with known or suspected intelligence information—at least partially by all our OB maps and our intel files. This would have provided for the "credence" of the information in the IIR, but it would have proven to be a difficult matter to accomplish given the distance between all of their locations throughout I Corps and ours. On those occasions when the agent handlers were in town, their agents and the value of their information, as well as the current NVA and VC activity in their area, was always discussed.

US Advisory Team 155's COL Metcalf's (the senior advisor to the 3rd ARVN Division) wrote a War College document later in 1972 and it is another interesting bit of equivocation. The first few pages have to do with why he didn't know the offensive was coming and the role of intelligence. "Past activity patterns," he wrote "can cloud the observer's vision [and] may have led informed persons in the intelligence community to give less credence than was warranted to (other) indications ...."[21]

This seems to be a not so nice way of blaming intelligence for the mistakes of a professional combat commander. Continuing, he wrote:

> First, a summary of the pertinent intelligence available prior to the initiation of the offensive and it will include a discussion of the deficiencies in the overall intelligence effort which appear in retrospect. It is not my contention that insufficient intelligence was available prior to the offensive, but I do hold that examination of all the available information would not necessarily have led an analyst to the conclusion that an offensive of this nature and extent was imminent. I contend that among all the items of intelligence produced prior to the attack, a small fraction indicated that such an offensive might occur, but other equally sizable and equally believable fractions indicated that something less might occur.
>
> No official or unofficial forecast, ARVN or American, of enemy dry season activity which was available to me prior to the initiation of the offensive foresaw an attack of this magnitude at this time … every intelligence estimate I saw, or hear, settled upon as most likely a course of action involving more limited attacks at a later date. The sources available to me were the G2's of the 1st and 3rd ARVN Divisions, and the American estimates produced by XXIV Corps, and they were in general agreement that the enemy would repeat the dry season activities of previous years ….
>
> It was not anticipated, however, by any source available to me prior to March 30, that the enemy general offensive would occur so early and would take the form, in Quang Tri, of a multi-division invasion across the DMZ and from western areas of the Province. Again, I am speaking of estimates as to most likely courses of action, not the broad spectrum of enemy capabilities. Assessments of enemy capabilities were accurate; estimates of most likely courses of action were not. The difficulty at the time, however, was that in all categories of information there was no preponderance of believable and persuasive items supporting the invasion alternative, or any other alternative, and an objective evaluation of the available information did not inexorably lead to one conclusion in lieu of all the others. The "maximum effort/effort" items amounted to a comparatively small fraction of the available information. Every estimate relied to some degree on the enemy's past activity patterns to predict his future courses of action. It is true, however, as I noted above, that even an "enlightened" appraisal of the available information might have rejected the "maximum effort/invasion" fraction. It was a question upon which reasonable men might reach different conclusions.

Undoubtedly, there are and were a lot of retrospective and selective memories by individuals and organizations regarding their actions or inactions during the Easter Offensive of 1972. Why? Because, if their hindsight is or was in fact true, then they neglected to ensure that adequate reconnaissance and military forces would remain in South Vietnam until the danger of the Easter Offensive had passed, and they are responsible for the deaths of many American and South Vietnamese troops and civilians. Is this too harsh a judgment? By ignoring the evidence of PHOTINT, SIGINT, and HUMINT collections, the major field and national commands displayed either complete ignorance, incompetence, or deliberate malfeasance towards what was about to take place on the battlefields. In their desire to appease their political masters, the flag officers running the major commands (and their staffs) were responsible for providing the best intelligence in order to make the best decisions, while *also* warning of any consequences resulting from these actions. The fact that not one officer lost his job or resigned his commission lends credence to the assumption that the United States was too much in a hurry to leave South Vietnam and that shifting responsibility was the order of the day. The generals won their promotions and their medals and did indeed sleep while the Easter Offensive of 1972 passed them by. General Douglas McArthur's dictum that we "never fight a land war in Asia" remains only partially true, especially when governmental and military politics stand in the way.

One rumor was verified as true by Team 155's S-1, then Major, Robert Wells, who recounted the facts to me. "Sometime in early 1972, Metcalf had a two-bedroom brand new, furnished mobile home air-lifted by chopper to the compound for his housing. A month later, his wife showed up and spent about a month. That tells you a lot about our commander."

MG Kroesen (who, by the way, was COL Metcalf's boss) states that the intelligence community, the government of South Vietnam, and the military commanders (US and ARVN) "predicted confidently that 1972 was to be a year of showdown, a test of Vietnamization, and a major Communist effort to establish control in the South." Then, later in the same paragraph (because the communists didn't strike during Tet) "it was believed that enemy activity would be limited to an increase in terrorism, rocket and mortar attacks, and guerrilla efforts to destroy bridges, and lines of communication." So, it appears that the NVA were expected to mount a major effort at Tet, and when they didn't it was left to the VC (which was hardly a major threat at the time, due to the success of pacification) to take the lead in 1972? Continuing in the same paragraph, Kroesen states that, "Only a superficial study of the map, the foot mobility of the enemy, and the history of prior years was needed to conclude that these preparations would require two to three months."[22]

"Foot mobility"? There was a huge increase in trucks, tanks, and troops passing through the trail. There were many reports of Ho Chi Minh Trail activity and NVA activity above the DMZ, but let's not forget the 1st MIBARS reports that stated the NVA were expanding and improving roads *below* the DMZ, too. I believe that most analysts would have assumed that all 1st MIBARS reports which provided specific target information in South Vietnam—such as NVA construction activity below the DMZ—would have been passed to air or ground units as targets to destroy. Given the many different pre-offensive failures, however, this might not have been the case.

On December 28, 1971, at the COMUS and commanders update in Saigon, MG Kroesen (at the time, the Deputy MR-1 Commander) responded to GEN Abrams' question of how he saw things in MR-1. "Well, sir, in MR-1 I think there's a general agreement between General Lam and General Dolvin [then the MR-1 commander] that we are facing a main enemy force threat at Quang Tri that's been pointed out, and we think that this new division in Que Son [Quan Tien?] Mountains may be exercised against one of the outlying districts, Hiep Duc or Duc Duc. But we are concerned with the main force units in only those two locations. Our biggest concern in MR-1 is the increase in terrorism, increase in sabotage, the harassing attacks on

QL-1, the loss of additional bridges. General Lam thinks the Territorial Forces are perfectly capable of coping with this, except they're in for a greater fight than they've had in quite some time." In speaking about MR-3, GEN Abrams added that "The situation is somewhat different in MR-1. Most everybody up there'll fight."[23]

> There was no plan and there were no positions built for defense against an invasion by a conventional attack. This is difficult to justify in hindsight, but the explanation is quite simple: the defensive outposts and firebases had served the US Army and US Marines well for more than five years; who in the ARVN or among the US advisors is to be held responsible for not revising a proven concept of operations? The answer, again in hindsight, must assign the responsibility to the command chain, i.e., the 3d Division and I Corps commanders principally, and to their advisors who accepted, perhaps too readily, the logic of the popular assessment. But this assignment must be tempered with an understanding of the intelligence evaluations presented to them and the history of the war in the area.[24]

Kroesen, in addition to stating that there was a lack of conventional defensive positions in I Corps, appears to be, at partially, blaming the US Army and Marine advisors assigned to Vietnamese units, forgetting he was the senior advisor in the I Corps and he was responsible for the intelligence he and they received. Using the old canard "It's always been this way" regarding the history of the area (e.g., North Vietnam promised not to violate the DMZ) is an incredible statement!

Colonel Harry Summers once wrote, "Contrary to the accepted wisdom, we did not create South Vietnamese regular units in our own image. With the exception of their marine and airborne units, the South Vietnamese Army was much like the American militia at the beginning of the Republic. Stationed in their home areas, with their families with them on their battle positions, they had great stability for counter-guerrilla operations (as our early militia did in protecting settlers from the Indians)."[25] This was certainly not true of the 3rd ARVN Division.

Kroesen's War College paper gives some other items not mentioned elsewhere, such as: "Four battalions, which were to comprise the division's logistic base, had not been activated, and the division artillery was incomplete."[26] The 3rd Division HQ, comms, and logistical base was not expanded to control Ranger and VNMC elements. "The contemplation of a counteroffensive erased from the minds of the Corps commander and staff any thoughts or problems connected with assuring the defense of Quang Tri and the even more important questions involving the defense of Hue."[27] ARVN did not patrol at night. The 3rd ARVN and I Corps commanders "erosion of mutual confidence" developed around the end of April.[28]

Based on the above, it seems obvious that 3rd ARVN was ill-prepared to fight for any duration as a unit, let alone have the ability to support other units. The corps commander had an unrealistic preoccupation with counterattacking the NVA, the defense of Hue was obviously all-important, not patrolling at night would obviously become very apparent to the NVA (allowing them to reequip and resupply during the evening without fear), and the loss of trust and support between the corps and division commanders began much earlier than Kroesen seemed to think.

Lewis Sorley wrote, "Although there was general agreement in the intelligence community—Vietnamese as well as American—that an offensive in early 1972 was highly probable, some observers of the Vietnam scene, perhaps those *not as well informed as those of us privy to the most reliable estimates* [my emphasis], were influenced more by what seemed to them to be the illogic of a major North Vietnamese attack at this time."[29]

"Although the three areas of the enemy's major concentrations—northern MR-1, Kontum, and north of Saigon—were clear indicators that the heaviest attacks would occur in these regions, it was impossible, on the basis of available intelligence, to determine the priority the enemy assigned to the three objective areas. Neither could we tell which attack would be launched first, or if they would occur simultaneously."[30] (In other documents, the NVA attacking through II Corps from the Trail and Cambodia was the "likely" scenario. This supposition was apparently shared with the press, as well.) Mistakenly, GEN Thi stated that the offensive in Quang Tri, Kontum, and An Loc all started at the same time on March 30.[31] In fact, the offensive in III Corps began on April 4 and in II Corps on April 23. IV Corps in the Delta, despite the DIA claiming that the NVA were "planning a major effort" there, saw little enemy activity.[32]

The 324B NVA Division moved into the A Shau Valley in early March, heading for its *usual* AO to the west of Hue to keep the 1st ARVN Division occupied. The 324B was a Military Region Tri-Thien-Hue (MRTTH) subordinate unit. As it moved through the A Shau, it linked up with the 5th and 6th Independent Infantry Regiments, also of the MRTTH. As time progressed, it was obvious that at least two regiments were moving in a northeasterly direction and could act as a blocking force along QL-1 (the main north–south highway in the country), while the three regiments confined 1st ARVN to FBs Bastogne and Birmingham. There wasn't much left to defend Hue as the 324B clashed with ARVN, but the NVA knew that 1st ARVN would never leave Hue and assist 3rd ARVN as long as they maintained pressure on the city. FSB Bastogne fell on April 29.

During the COMUS update briefing on April 5, GEN Abrams is quoted as stating, "They claim that the 6th Regiment, down in that fighting around Veghel, they also broke and ran. They have an intercept message that the regimental commander's been relieved, and the 803rd was brought in to replace them."[33] This is the only instance of such a report and it contradicts MACV's history for 1972 and 1973 on page A-9, which shows the 29B Regiment of the 324B operating with the 5th and 6th Independent Regiments, while the 803rd and 812th Regiments of the 324B were positioned south of Quang Tri.

In the days before the offensive began, MAJ Boomer noticed and reported wooden crates being stacked in the distance from FB Sarge along the sides of Route 9, indicating the resupplying of NVA forces. These would quickly be gone by morning. GEN Giai was informed and responded 3rd ARVN didn't have the strength of numbers to aggressively check it out.[34] This valuable Indications and Warning (I&W) indicator was apparently ignored.

CHAPTER 21

Lessons Disregarded

"On the major front south of the Demilitarized Zone, other North Vietnamese battled to cut off the provincial capital of Quang Tri from the south while advancing from the north and west on the city base 19 miles south of the DMZ" (Pacific *Stars and Stripes*, April 7, 1972). This was already in a 571st INTSUM before this date and well before Kroesen's message to Abrams of April 27, 1972.

In the end, the Nixon administration's implicit tolerance for corruption served, as with other elements of its policy toward Vietnam, to maintain a short-term stability in the government at the expense of its long-term prospects. The fall of South Vietnam stemmed from a range of causes. But, among those closest to the events, corruption was considered the most damaging, "largely responsible for the ultimate collapse of South Vietnam."[1]

In the August 2016 issue of *Vietnam* magazine, Colin Powell was asked if South Vietnam would "have prevailed against the North's invasion if the United States had continued to fund them?" Powell replied that this was the view of "a lot of Vietnam veterans—that it was the Congress who lost this war. I can't buy into that. By that point, it didn't make any difference whether we could have [won] because the American people had made a decision. We are a people's army."[2] Powell goes on to state the American people had lost their will to fight, there were racial problems, Watergate, a recession, and a counterculture that forced us out of the war.

As an Army intelligence analyst during the Easter Offensive of 1972, I usually look for books and histories that include this event. I normally expect only a few pages by an author who writes about the Vietnam War, though it is the biggest and longest battle of the entire war. Karnow's *Vietnam: A History* is the most prone to error and misunderstanding.[3] Its errors include:

The Mekong Delta "was to suffer most severely from its consequence." It was virtually untouched during the Easter Offensive and it was not further explained.

"Despite the advance intelligence they [American and South Vietnamese] had received …." Not so, despite what some of the generals say in their memoirs. Some have indicated they knew, but nothing happened (especially at Tet) or there was an alert that no one knew about.

"... a three-pronged pincer (in the northern provinces)—eastward from Laos, up from Cambodia through the Ashau valley and directly down from North Vietnam across the demilitarized zone." There were no NVA units that came up from Cambodia; the 324B NVA Division operated in its usual area of the A Shau and then held the 1st ARVN Division static in Hue. The 304th NVA Division came in from Laos and the western DMZ, the 308th NVA Division and many regiments of the B-5 Front came through the eastern and central DMZ.

LTG "Truong, who didn't take over I Corps until May 1972, could not rally one of his two divisions, a raw unit that panicked in the face of the onslaught." The 3rd ARVN had its 56th Regiment surrender at Camp Carroll, the 57th broke and ran as it streamed through Dong Ha (with only 250 soldiers that could be used in a defense), and the 2nd Regiment is rarely mentioned in any reporting. "Rally" is certainly an odd word to use for a division that had at least half of its soldiers KIA, WIA, captured, or who deserted—who was left to rally?

The first two Americans who died during the Easter Offensive of 1972 were on FSB Sarge and they were also in Army intelligence. There were others killed throughout the offensive and they all deserve better treatment in this book.

US and South Vietnamese aircraft did not strike the people evacuating from Quang Tri along the Horror Highway (QL-1). While there was one South Vietnamese aircraft that accidently drop ordnance on the highway, it was again, an accident. As Karnow mentions, North Vietnamese artillery killed many people trying to escape, NVA infantry units were ordered to fire on everyone along the route.

And another author wrote, "... thousands of Vietcong guerrillas ..." though the VC were very few in number and the VC units, after 1968, were primarily filled by NVA soldiers. "More than 130,000 troops, the elite of PAVN's combat forces, were thrown into battle, their numbers swelled by thousands of guerrillas."[4] Actually, there were very few VC units, let alone "elite" units. The hopeful rising of the populace in support of the North never transpired during the Easter Offensive.

"Although the Easter offensive was not an unexpected, sudden turn of events as alleged by some war correspondents, the direction of the attack in the north, straight through the DMZ, did come as a major surprise because the invasion was expected to only come from the direction of Laos. Apparently, the consensus of allied commanders and intelligence officers was that the enemy would not even consider violating the DMZ for fear of giving the United States a good reason for resuming the sustained bombing of North Vietnam."[5] Some others understood how the enemy operated in that the NVA had no hesitation in violating any rules, "The PAVN respected no rules of engagement" such as firing across political boundaries, etc.[6] The list could easily go on.

MG Davidson states that Lam and the JGS assumed "that the major attack in Quang Tri province would come from the west and northwest and not over the DMZ. The brunt then would be borne principally by the marines stationed in western Quang Tri rather than the less competent 3d ARVN Division along the DMZ."[7] Just a cursory look at the disposition before and after the movements of the 56th and 57th ARVN Regiments show that the VNMC occupied only a couple of firebases that flanked Camp Carroll. The 3rd ARVN was to face north, west, and northwest, all of which were the directions in which the NVA would come.

"The DMZ area, moreover, was tied into the North Vietnamese POL pipeline system and could therefore provide the large quantities of fuel required by modern conventional forces."[8] Little discussion is ever made concerning the POL pipelines that NVA tanks and other vehicles used as they poured through the DMZ. Taking three years to complete, this pipeline, like the one discussed in *Lam Son 719* (above), eventually crossed the Gianh River, followed Routes 10 and 18, crossed the Se Banh Hieung River to an area north of Route 9 in South Vietnam.[9] Apparently, NVA forces were able to build this pipeline unmolested, just as they were able to improve and create roads into the South. "Sustained operations with tank units larger than a company were considered impossible without establishment of large fuel and supply caches in the border areas. The activity required to establish these stockpiles would reveal enemy intentions and subject the forces and supplies to devastating air attacks."[10] This and other engineering efforts were improved and extended for the next three years when *all* of South Vietnam eventually fell.

The NVA had an "initial advantage of a large cache of prepositioned supplies." Between October 1971 and March 1972, they moved 4,200–4,700 tons of ammunition and equipment into Quang Tri and Thua Thien Provinces giving them about two months' worth of continued fighting.[11] The use of the Soviet M46 130mm field gun seemed to surprise some, but it shouldn't have. These field pieces (with tanks) were used in December 1971/January of 1972 by the NVA attempting to take possession of the Skyline Ridge in Laos.

"Interviewing GIs is the worst way to find out what's going on …. The People in the middle of … [a battle] have the least idea of what is happening," said Henry Kissinger.[12] And politicians have no idea at all.

"Meanwhile, the South Vietnamese commanders of the incursion continued to fight among themselves, prompting General Sutherland to tell Abrams, 'We can take [the South Vietnamese] … only so far; beyond that point they must go on their own …. Today I am not sure of how much further we can take them.'"[13] Though said of *Lam Son 719*, it remained so later.

It seems apparent that the press wasn't entirely informed on what was going on in I Corps, either. Hammond states that a major attack to the west of Hue occurred when 1st ARVN had been engaged by the 324B NVA Division since early in the previous month. Further, it mentions ARVN "troops on the move" below the DMZ, but it does not say where or why.[14]

The press was known to promote problems in the past, so when they did so during the Easter Offensive it wasn't too surprising when "officers from the Second

Battalion, First Infantry, 196th Infantry Brigade (Light), alleged in signed affidavits that newsmen had caused a near mutiny. In mid-April, learning that a planned airlift had been canceled and that troops would be moving overland by truck, correspondents at the scene had supposedly passed along rumors to the men that the road they would be traveling was mined or booby-trapped … whether any had promoted a combat refusal was difficult to say."[15] There was a definite air, however, of not doing anything that could be seen as stupid or wild because of the withdrawal of Americans. For instance, in II Corps, Brigadier General George E. Wear (Vann's second in command) told an Air Cavalry captain in April, "Your mission is to not get another American killed."[16]

Quang Trung 729

On April 11, 1972, GEN Abrams visited MG Kroesen in Da Nang. We weren't invited, perhaps because we had "the goods" on what the NVA was going to do before they did it and the generals in both Da Nang and Saigon would be reminded of that fact if we were invited. Can you imagine something like, "As we reported every day since 30 March …" what might have happened? Abrams was treated to GEN Lam's plan to kick the NVA out of Quang Tri, however. Obviously, this plan would have been disastrous and luckily Lam was dissuaded from pursuing it further. Instead he was guided to look westward.

Quang Trung 729 was born using the 147th VNMC Brigade, three ranger groups, two armored cavalry regiments (ACRs), and two of the original three regiments of the 3rd ARVN Division, with the object being to take back the high ground to the west (i.e., Carroll, Mai Loc, and Holcomb). Kroesen rather dubiously believed, somehow, that the "3d Div, 2d and 57th Regts have recovered fairly well …." Each regiment supposedly had 1,700 troops, a figure that no one really believed, especially in the 57th. With the action originally scheduled to jump off at 1300 on April 14, GEN Lam upped the time to 0100 on account of his horoscope. The next day, Kroesen reported that, "Excellent results were reported by the TACAIR Forward Air Controllers yesterday and the appearance of US air provided a significant lift for 1st and 3d ARVN Division forces."[17] There was little territorial gain anywhere along the Forward Line of Troops (FLOT) for a week and a half. Extensive US and South Vietnamese airpower at least helped prevent the NVA from decimating South Vietnamese troops, despite their supposed westward movement, which could be counted in yards and feet, not miles.

"Interviewed about the battles of April 1972, Colonel Luat (commander of ARVN's 1st Armor Brigade) had this to say: 'During the period when the situation temporarily subsided Lieutenant General Hoang Xuan Lam, commander of I Corps, and Major General Nguyen Van Toan, chief of the armor branch up from Saigon, called me back to 3rd Division headquarters to discuss the option of attacking straight across the Ben Hai River because the northern communists had violated the Geneva Agreements, but American advisers did not agree. Worried that I Corps would press forward, the advisers blocked it by … issuing the 1st Armored Brigade only twenty gallons of gas each day for each vehicle, limiting artillery rounds … to five rounds per day for each gun and stopping supply of combat rations to the group.'"[18]

ARVN must not have grasped the fact that attacking northward into the DMZ exposed their flanks and might have allowed the NVA to encircle and cut off these ARVN and VNMC forces. The rationing of petroleum, shells, and combat rations has *only* been mentioned by this one South Vietnamese source. Likewise, only one American source mentions a 201st NVA Armored Regiment on April 18, "stationed just inside North Vietnam … on its way south to reinforce the front." Unfortunately, there was no 201st Armored Regiment, though there was a 203rd NVA Armored Regiment assigned to the 304th NVA Infantry Division and the 202nd NVA Armored Regiment assigned to the 308th NVA Infantry Division—nor was there a 204th Armored Regiment "committed" at the time (or ever).[19] Thus, *Quang Trung 729* was initiated 12 hours earlier than it was originally scheduled due to Lam's horoscope![20]

Apparently, the FRAC, MG Kroesen, and many others knew of LTG Lam's belief in horoscopes when he reported to MACV that Lam continued to plan for a counteroffensive because his "horoscope was favorable for such a move."[21] This belief was also known to GEN Abrams. For instance, it seems Abrams had a discussion with Major General Ellis Williamson, the commander of the US 25th Infantry Division, in January 1969 concerning a joint operation with the 5th ARVN Division. Apparently, Williamson was aloft in his command helicopter and noticed the ARVN soldiers were not to be seen. Contacting the US division advisor to the 5th Division, he was told that "the 5th division is asleep. The division commander consulted with his astrologer, who told him this was not the right day to go on an operation." Williamson was contacted later by Abrams who asked if he had called General Lee a son of a bitch? To which he replied, "Well, certainly not to his face, because I have not seen him for several days."[22]

The belief in astrology was not restricted to Lam. When GEN Truong came up from IV Corps to take I Corps, he gave command of the southern three provinces of I Corps to Lieutenant General Lam Quang Thi. "The day after General Truong took over I Corps, he asked me [GEN Thi] to assume the command of Southern MR1 Theater which covered Quang Nam, Quang Tin, and Quang Ngai Provinces. At that time, beside the 3rd Division (which was regrouping and refitting in Da Nang), I had the 2nd Infantry Division with two regiments (the 4th Regiment had been sent to Hue to reinforce the Northern Theater), and one Ranger Group."[23] The HQ of the 2nd ARVN had recently moved to the former US Americal Division HQ at Chu Lai against two (and later, three) regiments of the new 711th NVA Division. FSBs West and O'Connor were lost on April 10, though attempts were made to recapture West for the rest of the month.

Thi's appointment isn't mentioned very much at all, as all the attention was directed towards GEN Truong. Thi had his family join him in Da Nang during the summer of 1972, but there was a problem. The official residence of the deputy commander was the site of bad luck, according to Chinese geomancy experts. The port director of Da Nang, also a believer in geomancy, insisted that Thi and his family stay in his villa. Colonel Duong Thai Dong, "who represented the artillery command at I Corps Forward CP, came to see me [General Thi] in my office. Dong was known in the Army as one of the best *tu vi* (astrology) experts. He disclosed that he had been requested the night before by Saigon to look into my *tu vi* to see if I could defeat the current NVA offensive and that he had filed a favorable report for me."[24]

I wonder how extensive chiromancy and Chinese geomancy were among the South Vietnamese military and navy (President Thieu and Prime Minister Khiem were into chiromancy, too)? How much of an impact might this belief have had on military operations?

Quang Trung 729 stepped-off on April 14, 1972, and continued for 10 days, ending on April 24. The operation's frontlines moved no more the 500 meters in any direction.[25] This was hardly what the FRAC *Command History* called moving, "westward slowly and methodically, searching and clearing enemy from their paths."[26]

CHAPTER 22

Early Lessons, Still Disregarded

While it can't be called an intelligence organization, per se, there was a small *sub rosa* organization that William Stearman, a career Foreign Service member who went over to the National Security Council (NSC), put together before the Easter Offensive. This group was composed of NSA, CIA, and DIA members, as well as Dr. Steve Hosmer of RAND and Dr. Stearman. Using Open Source Intelligence (OSINT)—the Hanoi newspapers—they had they first inkling of the Easter Offensive in the fall of 1971.

Men who were previously exempted (both skilled and physically unfit, Chinese, and Montagnards who didn't speak Vietnamese) were all being conscripted in North Vietnam. "This meant only one thing to us: the enemy was scraping the bottom of the personnel barrel to mount a major offensive. We checked the seasonal weather patterns and concluded that it could come off in the spring of 1972."[1] The NSA member of the group, analyzing "communications shifts," arrived at the date of the invasion 10 days before it occurred on March 30, 1972. This analysis was passed to Henry Kissinger's deputy, General Alexander Haig. "I wrongly passed this on to Al Haig who seems to have ignored it, since our generals were caught by surprise. I should have given it to Henry and to John Negroponte," wrote Mr. Spearman.[2]

The White House sent a "U.S. Message to North Vietnamese" on April 1, 1972 (delivered on April 2) calling out the North Vietnamese for launching an offensive across the DMZ and calling for a plenary session of the Paris conference for April 13.

The Easter Offensive, often relegated to a "by-the-way" treatment by historians, continued to see American soldiers being killed. One 525th SDO entry stated that on April 8, seven WIA, one MIA, and two KIAs (an officer and an enlisted soldier) were found shot with the hands tied behind their backs in Nui Ba Din (III Corps), yet another example of how the NVA and VC often treated our soldiers.

The Easter Offensive was won by South Vietnam with American airpower combined with some determined and courageous ARVN and VNMC. Douglas Pike cites the "terrible punishment … visited on PAVN [NVA] troops and on the PAVN transportation and communication matrix. PAVN force could not mass sufficiently in front of Hue because of devastating air strikes. PAVN's line from

Kontum to the sea, which cut the country in half, could not be held. And, most important, ARVN troops and even local forces stood and fought as never before. An Loc—probably the single most important battle in the war—held, and with its holding went General Giap's hope for a knock-out blow."[3] Le Duan held the reigns of the military and ARVN/VNMC held in the north to prohibit the NVA from not only Hue but the port of Da Nang.

Each area of South Vietnam was important, though the fall of each would accomplish different things. An Loc was closest to Saigon and US and South Vietnamese HQs. Its fall would have an immediate effect countrywide. Dividing the country in half in II Corps would have allowed other NVA to enter from outside the country and isolate those ARVN units remaining in I Corps. The fall of Hue, which would vindicate the NVA and VC's failure in 1968, would have allowed NVA resupply and reinforcement efforts a straight shot southward from North Vietnam. Temporarily halting at the Hai Van Pass, if necessary, NVA forces would then be able to capture Da Nang and its port and air facilities before continuing southward to join up with NVA units in southern I Corps and II Corps.

In a strikingly similar manner, the Battle of the Bulge had many of the same features as the Easter Offensive of 1972. "Ultra uncovered some of the deception measures, but not the true reason for them. Signals intelligence such as Ultra had its limits …. The abundance of Ultra encouraged complacency. It created a belief, after Mortain, the Hitler couldn't pull off a really big surprise if he tried. That belief prevailed at SHAEF, at Bradley's headquarters and at Montgomery's … Ike's intelligence chief, as well as Bradley's and Monty's had handfuls of dust that they threw in each other's eyes,"[4] remarkably like MACV, FRAC, and ARVN did 28 years later.

"On Saturday, April 1, as the NVA pressure grew more intense, Abrams reported back to Washington that 'the situation in Quang Tri is bad and it is going to get worse.' (COMUSMACV 011400ZApr 72, 'COMUSMACV Personal Appraisal of the Enemy and Friendly Situation.') He could now identify the strength and primary axes of the offensive. The NVA 270th and 31st Regiments were attacking southward from the eastern DMZ. The 308th NVA Division was operating on their west. The 304th NVA Division was attacking eastward from its base area in the northwestern and western sectors of Quang tri Province. And, southwest of Hue, along the traditional invasion corridor from the A Shau Valley, the 6th Regiment and the 324B Division were beginning to pressure the ARVN defenses. The infantry was supported by elements of two armored regiments, an artillery regiment, and an air defense division." The 5th Independent Regiment, which the 571st MID had identified, is missing from this report, as are all the artillery and air defense units. Eight hours earlier, Kroesen's Commander Daily Evaluation, 010544ZApr 72, mentions nothing about the NVA divisions and regiments in Quang Tri Province, except for the 5th and 6th Independent NVA Regiments in Thua Thien Province, which we had identified three weeks earlier.

ARVN's LTG Truong, who did not participate in *Lam Son 719*, wasn't commanding I Corps when the 3rd ARVN Division was created, hence calling its soldiers the "Veterans of the DMZ," though few of its soldiers had actually lived there before, is curious. Likewise, LTC Turley also mistakenly wrote that, "Most of the troops were native to the region."[5] General Bruce Palmer, Jr., echoed this with "the bulk of its personnel, recruited from the northern provinces, were green and had received only minimal basic training."[6]

It also, however, naturally questions Truong's second-hand observations of I Corps in April 1972, including who controlled the RF/PF forces, especially since he had yet to take over command of the region. "Under the supervision of the 3rd Division, but not directly controlled by it, were the Regional Force (RF) elements which manned a line of outposts facing the DMZ from QL-1 to the coastline ...."[7] The 57th ARVN Regiment manned outposts in this area, too. MG Kroesen apparently disagreed when he wrote, "The 3d ARVN Division Commander was an interested monitor of their [RF] actions and dispositions, but he had no direct responsibility for either."[8] It's interesting that both high-ranking generals had distinctly different command and control perceptions, but neither had a complete understanding of the function or capabilities of the 3rd ARVN Division and control of the RF.

LTG Kroesen, in his "Quang Tri, The Lost Province" wrote that 3rd ARVN "was in good condition; morale was apparently excellent, training had been realistic and effective ...."[9]

Perhaps Kroesen is responsible for "[Brigadier General Winant Sidle, who was the head of MACV's Office of Information] Sidle's contention, for example, that the Third Division was a great success was justified in military eyes because the successful equipping of a large combat force was always a massive undertaking." Though "CBS correspondent Phil Jones reported, the division's officers were straining to comprehend sophisticated American tactics and equipment and its logistical systems were faltering, and some of its men had not been paid in two months."[10]

Why were two regiments that had only been positioned in their assigned firebases for only five months (where the 56th was rarely at full-strength) were ordered to trade places with each other has been attributed to BG Giai's concern to alleviate "firebase syndrome." One would have also thought that *Lam Son 719* would have called attention to the manner and difficulty in which ARVN conducted retrograde operations back from Laos into South Vietnam, but it doesn't appear that this "Lesson Learned" was even contemplated. Worse, the FRAC commander stated that the 56th had only spent three weeks deployed along the DMZ, instead of the few months it really had—apparently, he was unsure of what was occurring some 85 miles away.[11]

Dolvin, (his deputy) Kroesen, Dickinson, and Hollingsworth were *all* armor officers, as were Abrams, Potts, Battreal, and Sutherland. Abrams was known to have had a special affinity for the 11th Armored Cavalry. "The list of those [armor officers] who commanded it during his tenure as COMUSMACV is also an interesting one: Patton, Leach, Starry, Gerrity and Nutting."[12]

When the 324B came in, "Everyone else waited for the 304th and 308th NVA Divisions to follow." Did you think they were going to conduct VC (vs. NVA) operations then? Why wouldn't this have caused everyone to think "conventional?" Assuming the 304th and 308 would follow the 324B into SVN, the preoccupation with Hue shows again. Also, no mention of the Ho Chi Minh Trail in Laos, nor the NVA road buildup *through the DMZ* in South Vietnam.[13]

BG Haig said about firebases in his three-day trip memo, "The firebase concept is no longer tenable when the enemy has massive artillery" (p.2, Haig trip memo). Kroesen replied "… the outpost system had accomplished the classic mission of delaying and forcing the deployment of his forces into battle formation." Withdrawals were "carried out in good order …. Only at C1 and C2 were tactical errors made"[14] Yet forcing the NVA into battle formation is exactly what the NVA did in the Easter Offensive.

Some found comfort by quoting a well-known anti-war activist, as General Lam Quang Thi wrote:

> Frances FitzGerald, the noted American journalist in Viet Nam, offered an interesting explanation of the American colonialist attitude in Viet Nam which, in my opinion, was reflected in the concept of the Fire Support Base. Covered with righteous platitudes, she wrote, "theirs [the American view] was an essentially colonialist vision, born out of the same insecurity and desire for domination that had motivated many of the French. When their counterparts did not take their instructions, these advisors treated the Vietnamese like bad pupils, accusing them of corruption and laziness, and attempted to impose authority over them. And when the attempt at coercion failed, they retreated from the Vietnamese entirely, barricading themselves behind American weapons and American PX goods, behind the assumption of American superiority and the assumption that the Vietnamese were not quite human like themselves."

The ARVN general must have agreed as he continued:

> The concept of the Fire Support Base adopted by U.S. troops in Viet Nam undoubtedly mirrored this colonialist attitude, the "Fort Apache mentality," which considered any people outside the Fire Support Base as expendable because they were "not quite human" like the Americans, who barricaded themselves behind barbed wire and Claymore mines.[15]

A MACV briefer stated on April 2, 1972, that, "A crescent of fire support bases were abandoned (the troops withdrawn)"[16] on March 31, 1972. Notice it was not what really occurred—most were abandoned by fleeing ARVN troops who manned them.

On April 11, 1972, Abrams visited Kroesen in Da Nang. Of course, I wasn't invited, but my boss, MAJ Fisher, and our detachment commander, LTC McIver, attended this briefing. Without being specifically told, I had the distinct feeling that we were shoved to the side and either instructed to keep quiet, or at least it was suggested that they do so. I do remember being told that the briefing for Abrams had nothing we didn't have, but there was a distinct implication that the briefing was overly classified. There was no indication of what was briefed, though we were still publishing our INTSUM, by then, twice-a-day and MG Kroesen was receiving them, his own statement regarding the lack of intelligence coming out of his HQ notwithstanding.

A fortunate coincidence and perhaps the 571st's information/INTSUM brought CAPT Ripley and MAJ Smock to the bridge at Dong Ha with the USS *Buchanan* on the gunline off the DMZ. Their action undoubtedly had more of an effect than just preventing NVA units from crossing the bridge and redirecting enemy forces westward. It ensured that the NVA's plan to quickly capture Quang Tri was delayed, allowing ARVN and VNMC reinforcement, thereby changing the tide of battle in favor of the South Vietnamese forces.

Consider the following.

The 304th NVA Division and the 203rd Armored Regiment's entry into South Vietnam from the western DMZ and Laos went without any apparent problems. The 308th NVA Division and the 202nd Armored Regiment were prevented from crossing the Mieu Giang/Cua Viet River via the Dong Ha Bridge and apparently also by fording. The 308th and the 202nd were forced then to go miles westward to the Cam Lo Bridge, where other units were undoubtedly crossing, too. This movement was seen and reacted to by the only artillery available in the eastern area of the DMZ, the 5in guns of the USS *Buchanan* (and afterwards, other destroyers).

The 304th and the 203rd were able to begin and conduct their part of the planned blitzkrieg with their envelopment of the ARVN defensive line in the west and continued their operations (usually as regiments) against the firebases, including Camp Carroll. While some strategists may point out that there was an absence of tactical airpower necessary in a blitzkrieg, bad weather effectively nixed this requirement (especially since allied tactical airpower faced the same difficulty). Was this weather part of the North Vietnam's strategic calculations (as in the Allied invasion in Normandy in World War II) or was it coincidence? A German-style blitz was not seriously taken into consideration. In the Special Intelligence Update on December 22, 1971, Abrams is quoted as saying, "They don't believe in the blitz. That's not the way they go. It's not in the book."[17]

The 308/202 delay was costly. These units had to cross at Cam Lo (using the bridge that wasn't blown for over a week more, for some unexplained reason), ford the river in their APCs, or (as only mentioned in the FRAC *Command History* for 1972–1973) by *sampan*. When the weather began to clear, US tactical aircraft that had already returned to Vietnam pounced on NVA targets, as more the ground situation became clear. The 571st's reporting was finally accepted as factual intelligence, proving the baseline for NVA movements and locations.

One can easily surmise that if Dong Ha Bridge hadn't been brought down by Ripley and Smock and if the USS *Buchanan* hadn't been providing gunfire support, Quang Tri city would have quickly fallen as 3rd ARVN's troops and leadership proved to be no match against the NVA. With the 324B NVA Division and two independent NVA regiments tying up the 1st ARVN Division in Hue, they might have been able to have rapidly assaulted the Imperial City from the north, as well.

It is estimated that the NVA lost 100,000 troops and half its tanks and artillery pieces. during the Easter Offensive. This was enough to have GEN Giap replaced by General Van Tien Dung, who served under Giap as a division commander at Dien Bien Phu. Writing about Operation *Uphold Democracy* in Haiti in 1994–95, Lieutenant General Michael Flynn noted, "I learned just how poorly the U.S. intelligence community was set up to support war fighting. We got very little from 'national intelligence,' something that I would see years later in a place called Iraq."[18] We never saw anything at our level in Vietnam from national levels. "Among the things that I brought to the intelligence system for the joint force, and to those commanders rotating through Fort Polk's elite training center [Joint Readiness Training Center] was a rarely used approach that turned out to be crucial for the next two decades of war fighting. It was simply called 'Pattern Analysis'"[19]—just as DIA did in 1971 (COL Armstrong) about the Ho Chi Minh Trail.

"One thing more on this assignment to the Joint Readiness Training Center at Fort Polk: I learned how ineffective our human intelligence and interrogation operations were. They were essentially nonexistent, poorly executed (if at all), and had to be scripted into the live training that we did. I resolved to fix it, but such intelligence wasn't taken seriously until we got to Iraq—and mad serious errors in judgment at a place called Abu Ghraib that still impact us today—and started losing."[20] "Wasn't taken seriously …" sounds like the Easter Offensive of 1972 retold. LTG Flynn continued, "There can be no winks, no nods, there must be brutal truth telling. Those intelligence personnel who give in to their own personal weaknesses and who are overly cautious because they fear an ass-chewing or worse, are being beyond irresponsible. In combat, their weakness results in loss of life and national defeat."[21]

When I had something timely (HUMINT was usually not very time sensitive) I'd call the local S-2/G-2 or advisory team up or insure our information got to them quickly. I ignored how I was supposed to do it, but my immediate chain was always supportive, and it worked well. But between the missing page from the 525 MI Group SDO log, INTSUMs, IIRs missing or destroyed, and a classified written citation of my mostly unreadable Bronze Star medal write-up, one could get a sense of a conspiracy taking place. It is also an indication that many of the documents of the era don't seem to be protected against the ravages of time and will be lost forever unless some form of action is taken.

"For both the North and the South, the time between spring of 1972 and early 1973 was the cruelest phase of the war." Quite possibly so, especially after *Lam Son 719* the year before. However, "twelve North Vietnamese army divisions" didn't cross "the DMZ for the purpose of 'liberating' at least two-thirds of the South." The NVA did not "encircle" Hue, either.[22] The NVA was ultimately not successful in the field because:

- Lack of experience in coordinating tank and artillery support for infantry attacks.
- They kept repeating assaults at the same points, and their numerical advantage weakened as a result of losing soldiers in each attack.

- The strength of US fire support from the sea and air.
- Supply lines were more vulnerable as they lengthened, with some notable exceptions.

Yet the 1972 offensive had left communist units much closer to the major cities than ever before. For the first time, the NVA were primed near the plains instead of far back in the mountains. It apparently doesn't matter that a US president promised that we would respond if the North resumed hostilities. "You have my assurance," Nixon had written in January 1973, "that we will respond with full force should the settlement be violated by North Vietnam."[23] The way that Gerald Ford and Congress forsook an entire country is a national disgrace. The 185,000 who died in communist reeducation camps and the 250,000 "boat people" who died at sea as a result are equally national disgraces.

Wrote Stephen Young, "I lay primary blame on the Foreign Service and the Department of State. It was their job to come to terms with the political culture of Vietnam. They contented themselves with the official business of counterpart relations and after-the-fact analysis. Of course, American academics never took the time or trouble to come to grips with Vietnamese nationalism. But they have the luxury of an irresponsible existence. Unlike the Foreign Service, lives and fortunes do not turn on their mistakes."[24]

More on traitors and spies

" ... American analysts would have been still more discouraged had they known that General Nguyen Huu Hanh, the deputy commander of II Corps, was a communist sympathizer, intent of doing 'nothing to harm the revolution.'"[25]

By September 1974, a copy of Major General John E. Murray's briefing in Saigon of June 1974 was in the hands of the NVA's Deputy Chief of Staff in Hanoi. "Warrior H3," a sergeant in the office of the head of all South Vietnamese forces, General Cao Van Vien, was thought to be the spy. Further, the North Vietnamese spy Dinh Van De, who was a lower House deputy (and chairman of the Defense Committee), and others met with President Ford in March of 1975 in the White House.[26] If it was true that everyone from the White House down was looking for some scapegoats to blame for being caught in the Easter Offensive of 1972, one doesn't have to look very far.

The entire 525th MI Group, including the 571st, received a Meritorious Unit Commendation that encompassed the time period of the Easter Offensive. One wonders if fewer people would have died and the value of what we tried to do would have been more appreciated if the "high and mighty" had acted on our information.

CHAPTER 23

Last Days and Further Assignments

As MACV and the other intelligence organizations played catch-up during the first weeks of April 1972, the weather started to slowly clear as the Air Force returned in force to Vietnam, Thailand, and Guam. In Operation *Bullet Shot* SAC sent 29 B-52Ds to Andersen AFB in Guam and 10 KC-135s to Kadena AB in Okinawa. Initially thought to be a temporary deployment, it ended up becoming the first of six such B-52 transfers. As Air Force recce began, near real-time reaction by aircraft were able to inhibit the NVA advances, although not before Quang Tri eventually capitulated on May 2, 1972, to the two NVA infantry divisions and two tank regiments surrounding the city.

Even FRAC seemed a little revitalized, albeit accepting our INTSUMs with their usual distain. They were probably able to get more staffing for the G-2 and G-3 shops and were likely paying far more attention to the SIGINT traffic and the advisor reports than they had before.

> (4) Operations: In conjunction with the Lunar New Year (Tet) (1973) celebration and the departure of US personnel, MSS (Military Security Service) and ARVN Detachment 65 sponsored a dinner party in honor of the 571st Military Intelligence Detachment. Taking advantage of this opportunity, members of these organizations expressed their gratitude with the intelligence effort in MR I. They also offered their assurance that Detachment 65 was now well prepared to continue with the collection program as established and developed by the 571st Military Intelligence Detachment. After a final farewell on X+8, the bilateral operation of the 571st Military Intelligence Detachment was officially terminated.[1]

Towards the end of April, our prime agent net was being taken over by "others" who thought they knew everything there was to know about intelligence. After giving the visiting officers a briefing on the current situation and answering direct questions concerning the situation and the agent net, a lieutenant, in what appeared to be very new combat fatigues and boots, made some condescending remarks adding something like, "You analysts are all alike." After "vigorously" challenging his arrogance (yes, somehow a few choice words just spilled out of my mouth), MAJ Fisher, who was present throughout the briefing, asked the lieutenant to accompany him to another room. No sooner had the door closed when I heard the major launch into to the

"Saigon warrior." When the door opened, the lieutenant came to me and apologized, though I didn't believe him for a moment. Though these folks could easily have been CIA (the arrogance usually gave them away), I suspect they might have also come from Detachment K of the 500th MI Group in Thailand. This was probably their first in-country visit and, I learned later, they were taking over some of our "assets." Detachment K did take control of our agents, some of our equipment, and our files when the 571st and the 525th MI Group a few days before the group officially left country in early 1973.

We knew we were going to lose our best agents at some point. Not surprisingly, we lost contact with them (at least temporarily) during the latter part of April. The NVA were busy elsewhere in I Corps, but the main battle area remained in the northern two provinces, rather than the other lower three.

President Nixon's "drops" were having a dramatic effect everywhere, as USARV complied with his mandate of having the largest increment of troops, 70,000, leave Vietnam by May 1. MACV would be reduced by 42 percent from February levels by dropping 3,123 personnel. US withdrawals, which would see all American troops out of Vietnam in less than a year, had never stopped. If someone had arrived in Vietnam before a certain date, they were eligible to leave Vietnam. Two of my friends were also able to leave. Both were area specialists and we were all branch-controlled, meaning that there was a specific detailer handling our particular MOSs. They had an idea to call the Military Intelligence Branch in Virginia for our next assignment stateside, so the three of us took note of the time difference and began the call.

Using a field phone, we cranked the little wheel on the side and we reached the Saigon operator, who patched us through to Guam, onto San Francisco, St. Louis, and into Virginia. It was amazing to us all that it worked the first time! Since there was no telling how long the connection would last, they both spoke to their detailer and were happy with their results. Their detailer patched me over to mine, whom I told that I was eligible for the forthcoming drop. I asked what locations in the United States were available for my return home. I had lived in a couple of them and the others I knew I didn't want to be assigned to, so I mentioned Ft. Bliss, Texas, where my father was stationed. The detailer hemmed and hawed until he heard a noise from my end. Asking what it was, I casually told him that the airbase was getting rocketed again (after all, this was Rocket City). Amazingly, that seemed to seal the deal, though he only said something "might" be opening up there, meaning I would probably get my wish.

The next day, I told the major I worked for that I was going home. He had no idea that I was eligible for the drop nor that I had taken the initiative to find an assignment stateside. He understood my decision, but I still felt as if I had let him down. He had always treated me honestly and fairly, and we had traveled across I Corps by helicopter and jeep (he *always* drove) together.

I knew, by the types of intelligence sources that had returned to South Vietnam, and intelligence platforms that became committed to the Easter Offensive, that things were going to change very soon, even more than they had already. Our agent nets would be reorganized again and taken over by others. I literally ran into Dave Anderson in the same post I was assigned to in Germany. He told me that the 571st had vacated its small location for the nearby MACV compound a short while after I left, and that things turned out the way I imagined they would.

As the time of my departure grew nearer, the S-3 NCOIC (an agent and my friend, Dave Anderson) and MAJ Fisher decided to have a presentation ceremony of the "BFM." The "Big Fucking Medal" was made from a C-ration lid of crackers, covered with multi-color paper with "BFM" in large letters on the front. A hastily made-up, profanity-laced citation was read and I understood how close we all had become, despite the differences in age and rank. We all then had a beer together, swapped tales, and talked about what was going to happen to the 571st. It was an incredibly sad day.

The day I left the 571st the major asked me to deliver a sealed, written message to a specific officer in Saigon, which I pocketed. All of our MI personnel processed in and out of the 525th MI Group in Saigon. I said goodbye to literally everyone who remained in the 571st, then I was delivered to Da Nang airfield where I had to wait for an hour or so. After checking-in, I wandered around outside near the taxiway and it seemed that the ARVN and a few VNMC were everywhere, waiting for a flight to somewhere. I knew there were some leaving the action and I was glad that I had chosen to leave, even if it was on a C-123 again.

Arriving in Saigon later in the afternoon, I checked in at the group HQ and used the driver, with permission, to search for the officer to whom the envelope was addressed. After two unsuccessful tries, we found him in the bowling alley. I was a little more than upset—I told him that I was glad he had the leisure time to spend in a f*****g bowling alley while people were dying in I Corps. Handing the envelope to him, I turned around and left; it was a scene I have never forgotten.

Leaving the shooting war, I took an ARVN flight to Saigon over areas where there once was fighting earlier in the day and now there was a bowling alley. It all represented the weird contrast of what US forces were doing in Vietnam. The impression was again hammered home later in the evening, when I met up with one of the very few remaining friends from Intel School who still remained in-country. We went to the movies at a regular Army movie theater. Of course, it seemed that something else was bound to happen and it did. As we were walking out of the theater, we passed a 1st lieutenant who "locked me up" (put me at attention) for not saluting him. "Really?" I asked. I was about to express a few choice words, but my friend jumped to the rescue and explained that I was from out of town. Not to let it drop, of course, this Saigon warrior commanded, "Don't let it happen again."

Being "put in your place" didn't sit well with me as I bit my tongue and waited until he was out of earshot, "What'll you do? Send me to Vietnam, you stupid S.O.B.?"

We returned to the barracks area where I had a wonderful idea. I had a few pocket flares and I knew that these people kept their M16s locked up in an armory nearby. So ... it was great firing all of them and having a few guys come running out wondering aloud if the VC or NVA might not be attacking soon. I do admit thinking that this was a positive sort of payback for a day that reinforced my decision to leave. I was also hoping that one of these soldiers might be the one so concerned about saluting.

Arriving where it had all begun at Long Binh to process out, I noticed the sign was gone that had warned of a 2nd lieutenant's life expectancy. Once inside the compound and off the bus, we were all "cattle" again. Go here, go there, get a haircut, empty everything, get another haircut (seriously, this was true), and then the infamous urine analysis test for drugs in your system, aka the "piss test," the results of which would determine how long you stayed in that rat-infested stink hole. I can't help but think that Army careers were severely influenced in how we were all treated at this hell hole, among other things. Being put in your place by the Army was not quite concluded, as I soon found out.

Arriving at Ton Son Nhut AB, our planeload of Army troops waited for hours (as in, "hurry up and wait") before we boarded the plane. One last indignity was to be played out when a few Military Police (MP) dog-handlers and their drug-sniffing dogs entered the boarding area. As the dogs sniffed all the carry-on baggage, the MPs also had marijuana wrapped in clear plastic to put in the baggage to test their dog's sniffing capability. Without asking, of course, an MP chose my bag to hide the marijuana package. Going down the line, the dog reacted by spilling out the contents of my bag onto the floor. There was no apology and no assistance in restoring the contents to my bag, of course.

After the applause when we finally became airborne, most people just slept, perhaps more soundly than they had in quite some time. Arriving in Travis AFB, California, the customs people and military checked our bags once more and a bus waited to take most of us to San Francisco International.

Though I have read that many who returned from Vietnam through San Francisco International had similar stories, my experience short and sweet. I had only minutes to get to a plane and it was in a remote part of the terminal (of course), so I was literally running to the gate when two males and a female (all early to mid-20s) called out to me about being a baby-killer and other "welcoming" words. Without breaking stride, I "flipped" them off. I wouldn't have minded a "conversation" with the trio, but I had more important things to do at that time. In retrospect, I believe that these groups of hippies or protesters simply took turns harassing servicemen returning from Vietnam. Perhaps they felt it was their duty or something. Either way, there were too many of us with similar stories to dismiss these occurrences readily. Vietnam would not leave the collective consciousnesses of many of us for some time. Individually, it never quite left at all.

Fort Bliss, Texas, at the time, was the home of Army Air Defense. There wasn't much US air defense necessary in Vietnam, consequently most of the "aero-defenders" never went to Vietnam, unlike the few Army intelligence types who were stationed there—all had gone. However, I am convinced that the best thing the Army can do for a soldier is to make sure he stays a least a year in uniform after returning from a country where people are trying to kill you. Most guys had a "chip on their shoulder" after they returned from Vietnam. I was no different.

I don't remember the exact circumstance for being called in front of the battery commander (in air defense and artillery organizations, a battery is the equivalent of a company), a captain, but as I stood at attention I wasn't listening very well until I heard him say, "If you ever get in combat …." I looked at his ribbons (only a National Defense and an Army Commendation Medal) and his right shoulder (where a combat patch would be)—nothing there. I remember a little voice warning me not to fly off the handle, but I then remembered my father's advice and asked, "Permission to speak freely, sir?"

"Granted," the captain responded, and I was off to the races. I pointed to my right shoulder and the combat patch and then launched into an obscenity-laced response about his academic ability, parentage, and poor eyesight. Amazingly, asking permission worked—there was some modicum of justice in the military after all! I was dismissed without further comment and I never remember seeing him again, outside of mandatory formations.

Another time involved a brigadier general, the deputy commander of the Air Defense Center and School. The major I worked for in Vietnam had recommended me for a Bronze Star Medal and it had been approved. The ceremony took place in his office because the citation came with a classified write-up that couldn't be read in front of anyone not cleared. It was great to have my father present in uniform to watch.

After the presentation, the general asked me to remain and have coffee with him, alone. Things started well enough until he asked what I thought about the war in general. After saying something like, "If they won't let us fight, why the hell are we there? My unit had the NVA dead-to-rights and no one listened." I must have looked like I was embarrassed for using the word "hell" or something because the general told me to go ahead and speak my mind. I told him about such things as how the invasion began in I Corps and the absence of commanders who were present. He did seem genuinely interested. After five minutes or so with a variety of obscenities, I knew I had taken too much for granted and apologized. The general was gracious enough to tell me it was all right and we finished about 5–10 minutes later.

A point that I should have mentioned earlier: it seems quite common for soldiers to have returned using the "F" word as virtually every part of speech without thinking about it, but it was the one word not ever allowed in my mother's house. After about a week at home, my father took me aside and told me I was using it just like everyone did in Vietnam and my mother asked him to speak to me about it. Funny, you never think about it until someone says something.

The Yom Kippur War between Israel and its Arab neighbors in 1973 allowed me to "watch" units fight once again. Though they were aero defenders (i.e., US Army Air Defense soldiers), they had a desire to watch units move and engage, too. Information from various US intelligence agencies initially arrived at a "Secret" level and I began the process of putting maps together and locating units, once again. After a week or so, information came at a much higher level and I had to pass off these duties to a captain. Little did I know that I would watch Israel perform in combat once again a few years later.

My father retired, I married, and I set off to West Germany for two tours; I was there for a total of seven years. The unit I was assigned to was joint service and was called the European Defense Analysis Center (EUDAC). For three years, I was part of a 24-hour watch of the forward area (four days on, four days off) as a ground analyst. I watched Warsaw Pact military units move and exercise alone and with aircraft every day. For another year, I was the naval analyst of the Baltic Sea, though the personnel at the United States Navy, Europe (USNAVEUR) Headquarters in London did not like an Army NCO working the Navy desk nor did a certain USN three-star admiral, who was the J-3 of US European Commant (USEUCOM). During a regularly scheduled Saturday morning briefing (when all the "J-staff" 4-star and below generals and admirals attended), the admiral tried, unsuccessfully, to put my naval knowledge to task about the Baltic and the Soviet, Polish, and East German ships found there. Knowing how the Navy operates (given our own unit's naval personnel), it was likely that he did not care for an Army analyst giving a briefing on a naval subject, much less one who wasn't an officer. The J-2, an Air Force major general, was evidently pleased with my performance as I caught sight of him gently poking the admiral in his side with his elbow as I left the briefing area.

For the last four years in West Germany, I was an all-source Electronic Order of Battle analyst (and substitute watch analyst when someone went on leave or was sick), responsible for the eastern littoral of Africa, Syria, and Lebanon for a year. I moved over to the Iraqi desk during the Iran–Iraq War (1980–88); it was also during this time that Israeli aircraft struck the Iraqi nuclear plant at Osirak. We always kept everything up to date, so it was strange to be called in on a Saturday just to make sure there was nothing undone. The Israelis struck the next day, June 7, 1981. I then moved over to Poland during the Crisis where it looked like the Soviets might invade.

During my time in Germany, I began and finished my bachelor's degree, was awarded the Joint Service Commendation Medal and Defense Meritorious Service

Medal, and was recommended in separate efficiency reports for a direct commission, Officer Candidate School (OCS), and warrant officer.

After relying almost solely on HUMINT in Vietnam, it was obvious that it was not an equal pillar, nor held in the same regard as other types of intelligence. In Germany, I always read what HUMINT we received and didn't hesitate to chastise other analysts who did not value it very much. I am forever grateful for having experienced the value of HUMINT in Vietnam. Sometime later, however, I discovered that the intelligence field had forsaken its roots.

Quite unexpectedly, I was talking with another intel analyst from somewhere else when I mentioned The Barn. The blank look I received compelled me to ask him about his intel background. I discovered that intel wasn't his primary MOS until recently, when the Army mandated having at least two MOSs. I was soon going to experience the impact of this again at Ft. Monmouth, New Jersey.

The MI branch had changed, as well. As I was due for reassignment, I was chosen to go to the DIA. Though I knew it was going to be expensive to live in the greater Washington area I was looking forward to it, especially since the job I was currently holding also reported to the DIA. A few weeks later, I was given another assignment, instead. Calling branch, I was told that I needed a "tactical" assignment, to which I replied, "What, Vietnam wasn't enough?" The detailer hemmed and hawed and it became obvious, after a little probing, that he had changed things to benefit a friend.

More discoveries were made when I reported to this new duty assignment at Ft. Monmouth, New Jersey as a senior NCO (SFC/E-7). The commander, a colonel, of this brand-new MI unit looked at my record and my test scores (mine had always reflected the maximum score possible) and he told me that almost all of the senior NCOs had failed their tests and one of my additional duties was to make sure these, primarily former infantry senior NCOs, passed their next test. A classic case of teaching to the test, for these soldiers would never have made the grade when I first entered the field of intelligence. How far things had fallen!

These events, and the fact that a major defense company was actively headhunting me, made it easier for me to leave the service. Since I finished my bachelor's degree in Germany, I was recommended for a direct commission on Army annual evaluations, but nothing happened. Another evaluation suggested OCS, but I was told I would be too old upon graduation. I then applied for warrant officer before I left Germany, which was endorsed by my commander in Germany, a USAF colonel, which was then endorsed by the J-2, a USAF major general, and the USEUCOM Chief of Staff, an Army lieutenant general. A welcome packet for Warrant Officer School in Alabama arrived some nine months *after* I left the Army.

The first of three articles I wrote on the Easter Offensive of 1972 was published in 1997. This general time period saw numerous Vietnam articles and books, though not as much then (or even today) as about Tet 1968. I had written to the Center of Military History in 1985 explaining the Easter Offensive and the 571st's role in it. This was before, however, they published *Advice and Support: The Final Years*; there was no mention of my unit, nor any of the information I supplied the historian. Luckily however, the correspondence can be found at the Vietnam Center and Archive at Texas Tech.[2]

A number of things didn't occur after the Vietnam war that should have, particularly in terms of lessons learned and histories captured.

> After the end of each conflict, regardless of its size, there exists a need for some mechanism to capture the oral histories of those who performed where "the rubber meets the road," so to speak. None of this happened at the end of the Vietnam War. The post-1975 period, at least for intelligence, was one of discarding many of the wartime archives from Southeast Asia that spelled out what worked, what did not work, and why, placing the surviving operational files in corners somewhere, that with the passage of time have become forgotten. As we move forward on a new relationship with Vietnam, Laos, and Cambodia, some of these files my yet prove to be of value so that we do not, once again, repeat the mistakes of the past.[3]

Most often today, Vietnam has become a portion of Cold War History and not a separate course. The most commonly used modern textbooks (with varying degrees of Howard Zinn's influence) and histories often repeat the errors of previous authors, because that's how they were taught. The same historians are not inclined to confer with Vietnam veterans, often implicitly mocking them by questioning their memory.

"Even as the Army was disintegrating, officers were rewarding themselves more. Close to half the generals who served in Vietnam received an award for valor. In 1968, a year in which 14,592 Americans were killed in action in Vietnam, some 416,693 awards were bestowed. In 1970, when only 3,946 men were killed, some 522,905 awards were given. Once again, the Army seemed to be putting the interests of its officer corps first."[4]

The intelligence field hasn't seemed to change much from when I left the Army. LTG Flynn wrote, "We were overwhelmingly focused on big tank battles and still trying to get past the Soviet Union, seeking an enemy that would fight us on the plains of somewhere. Our Army found it hard to change and the intelligence system was no different. We were planning and training for big land battles as in World War II, even though we'd been badly beaten up in Vietnam by a well-organized network. There were many late-night discussions at Polk about how to fight against guerrilla forces, breaking the connectors that made them an effective network, and then destroying them piece by piece."[5]

The Army deliberately sought to forget its role in Vietnam. Like it or not, developing countries experiencing insurgencies do not normally fight pitched battles. These countries and those who might assist them must take the fight to them and fight as their opponents do.

Vietnam wasn't the only war where HUMINT was ignored by senior military and civilian commanders; I have heard and read of similar examples that others have written about Iraq and Afghanistan and, of course, the Battle of the Bulge.

Some people reading this book might think that I disliked ARVN and the South Vietnamese people. On the contrary, I have great respect for the South Vietnamese people. It was obvious to many that ARVN were not for the most part, trained very well (as the VNMC were) and were only then developing a sense of country, in large part due to the success of pacification. Vietnamization was being rushed and should have started much earlier. Our advisory positions were being drastically cut, and South Vietnam politics still reigned supreme. Many ARVN felt we were abandoning them, which we *were* due to American politics.

I have been asked why I bothered to "rock the boat." I have always replied that what we did or didn't do in the intelligence arena might cost lives, therefore there was no option. Also, having a degree of knowledge not available to some, I knew how the VC and, to a lesser degree, the NVA had treated not only Americans, but their own brethren. I found the VC to be more like sadomasochists (some NVA could be, as well). Communism was a cloak that gave cover to their actions, a fate no one should have to bear or contemplate.

Selected Weaponry Used by the NVA during the Easter Offensive of 1972

Armor

T-54/55 Medium Tanks (USSR)
Type 58 Medium Tanks (PRC)
Type 59 Medium Tanks (PRC)
Type 62 Light Tanks (PRC)
Type 63 Light Amphibious Tanks (PRC)
PT-76 Light Amphibious Tanks (USSR)
SU-76 Assault Gun (USSR)
ZSU-57-2 SP Gun (USSR)
Model 67 APC (PRC)
Two types of unidentified AA SP guns (PRC)

Artillery

M46 130mm Field Guns (USSR)
D74 122mm Field Guns (USSR)
M38 122mm Howitzer (USSR)
A-19 122mm Corps Gun (USSR)
M44 100mm Field Gun (USSR)
D44 85mm Field Gun (USSR)
Z153 76mm Field Gun (USSR)

Surface-to-Air Missile Systems

SA-2/Guideline (USSR)
SA-7/Grail (USSR)

Easter Offensive of 1972: A Prelude to Vengeance Achieved

Bob Baker

Published in the *Small Wars Journal*, October 19, 2018

The Easter Offensive of 1972, coming at the end of the Vietnam War, is usually an afterthought in most histories of the conflict, primarily because most U.S. troops had already left the country. This does a great disservice to the American and South Vietnamese militaries who remained, particularly to those killed or wounded in-action. Even beyond that, the people of South Vietnam themselves were to experience the cruelty and savagery of the North Vietnamese Army and their terrorist cohorts—the Viet Cong (VC)—for almost a year after the offensive began.

A December 1971 COSVN (Central Office for South Vietnam) resolution concludes with, "… if hit hard enough, the allies will either collapse or be forced to withdraw, *enabling the revolution to regain access to the population*" (my emphasis). If the communists had to "regain access," then they admitted to not having it. Without specifically stating it, the effects of pacification (gaining the support of the rural population for the South Vietnamese government) were obviously working.

Consider that pacification of the rural areas had shown steady positive results since 1968, to the point in late 1971 that almost 90% were considered pacified. The Popular and Regional Forces (PF/RF) had come far in protecting their local areas from the Viet Cong (VC), in many areas these terrorist units were filled-out by North Vietnamese Army (NVA) troops.

As part of my adopted daily routine with the 571st Military Intelligence (MI) Detachment, 525th MI Group in South Vietnam in 1971–1972, I kept track of all NVA and VC forces in I Corps (which became the First Regional Assistance Command—FRAC).

Two years before I arrived, Col. Andrew R. Finlayson, USMC (Ret.) remembered, "Although the local VC never stopped committing atrocities in southern Quang Nam Province … they outdid themselves in early March [1969] with a particularly vicious and egregious example of the kind of terror they were capable of inflicting on civilians. In a refugee camp 10 miles south of An Hoa, the VC came into the camp after dark, taking advantage of the South Vietnamese forces who would normally have provided security for the camp. The VC burned down thirty-one houses and murdered nine adults and twenty-two children. As they left, they warned the refugees that unless they returned to their farms in VC-controlled areas, they would return and kill all of them. Such acts, while not always on the same scale, were routine in areas where the local VC held sway in the province and provoked a profound fear among the population." (Finlayson, 2014: 77–78). Of course, a much more formatted report would have found its way into the large files I kept on each unit and/or province, but notice Finlayson wrote "the local VC never stopped committing atrocities." Multiply this statement a few times daily for every province and you can imagine how large these files became in a relatively short time. This does not include any of the VC's unreported acts of violence throughout the provinces of I Corps, especially in areas that the Saigon government did not control.

The 571st MI Detachment was fortunate on a number of occasions to be able to provide timely and accurate information which led to the destruction of Surface-to-Air Missile sites, arms caches, and the infiltration of NVA and VC units. One example while I was there was the recurring sightings of a so-called "Salt and Pepper" VC Armed Propaganda Team—a pair of presumed U.S. soldiers (one white, one black) carrying AK-47s. These two apparent military turncoats (though some has suggested they might have been French) were always reported west of Chu Lai and were of such high priority that U.S. Special Forces would conduct an immediate search after I notified them. Despite the 3–4 reports I received about them, they were never caught.

A major problem in trying to confirm or refute the Rockpile massacre of 1,500-1,800 ARVN troops of the 56th Regiment/3rd ARVN Division by the NVA in early April 1972 is the fact that a communist government is now in place in Vietnam. The Vietnamese government continues to deny anything that puts them in a bad light and has still never given a full accounting of the Hue and Dak Son massacres, nor have they indicated that anyone was tried for these atrocities.

Another bloodlust was conducted by at least one NVA battalion a few miles away from the Rockpile. However, this wanton disregard for human life was witnessed by numerous press and other eyewitness reports that were published in newspapers (albeit tucked well inside them). These NVA troops were part of a blocking force south of Quang Tri that reportedly killed between 1,000 and 2,000 soldiers, old men, women, and children escaping southward along QL-1 (the national north–south highway) during late April and early May. The commander of the battalion told his troops that anyone coming south were the enemy and they were to kill them all.

Throughout South Vietnam, VC execution squads quickly roamed the country where areas recently occupied by NVA troops dominated, finding people who could identify any VC and those who would likely take over or resume their South Vietnamese government positions if there were to be a ceasefire.

These are a few examples of specific instances of what occurred in the first few months of the offensive.

- In Quang Ngai, Local Force VC Sappers burned down 15 villages, adding to the 30,000 people made homeless in May.
- A "People's Court" in Binh Dinh executed 45 people, after they dug their own graves sometime in the summer of 1972. The VC also engaged in bayonet practice of at least three men, as well. In another instance in what has been called the "Binh Dinh Massacre," between 250–500 people were tried and executed from among 6,000–7,000 collected and executed or impressed into servitude by VC/NVA forces in the An Lao and An Hue areas.
- Forty-five people were buried alive in the Tam Quan District, as a local politician was beheaded in Bon Son village.

As of May 8, 1972, 700,000 people had fled the communist onslaught, mostly from Quang Tri and Thua Thien Provinces, which created a massive refugee problem. Also in this first month, it was estimated that 20,000 civilians were killed.

The terror campaign against civilians didn't stop after the first few months of the offensive. In early September, a VC demolition squad attacked the largest refugee camp in Vietnam northwest of Da Nang. The camp held some 50,000 civilians and this attack killed 20 and wounded almost a 100.

Though there are many reasons given as to why North Vietnam didn't simply wait until all U.S. forces were out of South Vietnam before making their assault against the South, one reason that has never been put forward is *vengeance.* A ruthless vengeance against the people of the South who hadn't yet been beaten or enslaved, people who were trying to construct a viable democracy, and a people who had asked the greatest democracy on Earth for assistance and we answered the call. It was a vengeance that was consummated two years later when 185,000 people died in re-education camps, 65,000 were executed outside of those camps, and 250,000 died in the ocean trying to escape the horrors imposed on their country.

There has been no clamor for justice, no United Nations condemnations, no war trials—the sound of silence is deafening.

References

Andrew Finlayson (2014). *Rice Paddy Recon: A Marine Officer's Second Tour in Vietnam, 1968–1970.* Jefferson, NC: McFarland & Company, Inc.

Historically and Factually Accurate?

Bob Baker

Published in *Small Wars Journal*, February 8, 2019

With the exception of the very few, most Vietnam veterans are proud of their service (~91%) and most of these seem to be "revisionist" versus "orthodox," as the distinction seems to be currently drawn.

I'm surprised that primary sources (i.e., those who were in Vietnam) don't seem to be as important as secondary ones are for historians today. Just a brief survey of what is now being taught in colleges about Vietnam, including (surprisingly) military ones, and you'll find it is now a seldom-offered course by itself and it seems consigned to being only a chapter in history books. Unfortunately, not all of these books are totally accurate and, more importantly, they repeat the errors found in the sources they quote and then in the books or articles they then publish. The old proverb "tell a lie often enough" is beginning to spread.

Most Vietnam veterans believe that there were *many* reasons, not just one, why the Vietnam War ended so miserably. Here are some of the reasons, in no particular order. All quotes are from former NVA Colonel Bui Tin[1] who served on their general staff and received the unconditional surrender of South Vietnam on April 30, 1975.

1. We didn't blockade Haiphong at the onset (where even British vessels could be found).
2. We didn't knock out the railroad lines between China and North Vietnam.
3. US ground forces were not allowed to interdict the Ho Chi Minh Trail. If they had, "Hanoi could never have won the war."
   a. Though North Vietnam clearly violated Cambodian and Laotian sovereignty (though a signatory of the 1962 UN Agreement – see Appendices), U.S. forces were not allowed to continue chasing (hot pursuit) the NVA/VC when they retreated back across these same borders.
4. The anti-war movement "was essential to our strategy." The senior leadership followed the anti-war movement in the US and "were elated" when Jane Fonda, Ramsey Clark and others visited. "America lost because of its democracy; through dissent and protest it lost the ability to mobilize a will to win."
5. South Vietnam's generals were "inept" and political.

6. The bombing of North Vietnam, if it had been concentrated (as in the Christmas bombing), "would have hurt our efforts." Piecemeal bombing gave the North time to reshuffle and rebuild.

7. The NLF (National Liberation Front) was controlled by Hanoi—it was never independent (it was always run by a Communist Party commissar), despite efforts to convince the American public and politicians otherwise.

8. Regional and Popular Forces (Ruff/Puff) were in control of 90% of the populace countryside by 1972. The often-forgotten Peoples Self-Defense Force (PSDF) were there in the rural hamlets, too.

9. Fighting in 1968 had decimated communist forces in the South. Years of rebuilding compelled them to use NVA troops to fill out the VC ranks. "If American forces had not begun to withdraw under Nixon in 1969, they could have punished us severely."

10. When President Ford failed to respond to the attack of Phuoc Long in January 1975, the North knew that their overall victory was at hand.

11. "We had the impression that American commanders had their hands tied by political factors. Your generals could never deploy a maximum force for greatest military effort."

12. The North only had to win over the American media in order to eventually be victorious because they swayed politicians (who love to be loved and, of course, reelected) and the feeble-minded university professors who love to pontificate and sell their books. Because fewer people read books today, let's not forget the pseudo-documentarians and Hollywood-types who insist on stating or insinuating how bad the military was in Vietnam and how the communists forces were the good guys or merely misunderstood.

This same type of thing also seems to occur in fictional accounts of wartime events. If they are especially outrageous, they are almost surely to be "visual humanities" and promoted as if the events actually happened. In these cases, the historian seems to be the director and the movie studio (in typical Hollywood fashion) is more concerned with making a profit. Taking a slap at the military is almost always good for business when it comes to Vietnam, though.

It is a depressing curiosity why there is still a proclivity to demean our efforts in Vietnam (while now acknowledging veterans) by the US Government and some state sites, especially educational ones, on the internet. Or is it?

A Christmas Eve, Watching

Bob Baker

Published in *The Remnant*, December 26, 2014

It didn't do any good to complain and it wasn't as if there was much else to do. Though I'd been in-country for almost four months, I still had less time there than most, so the job was mine—I had complete charge of our small compound for Christmas Eve, 1971 in Da Nang, Republic of Vietnam.

I knew what was going to happen—all of us, so far from home and homesick, everyone would drink a little (!) too much. I also knew if the Viet Cong decided to hit the wire on this night, there would be few who could be counted on to offer any kind of serious resistance. I didn't think it might happen, but the enemy's "word" could never be counted on or trusted, even though they had agreed to a 24-hour Christmas ceasefire. I always wondered about this: How does one contact a terrorist organization and agree to something like a ceasefire? How do they, in turn, tell their units across the country, by radio or phone call? Seems very odd, doesn't it?

I caught the deuce-and-a-half for chow—the MACV and CIA compounds weren't too far away. If the Viet Cong did, in fact, do something, help would come from MACV, not the CIA. CIA never even responded to communications checks for their own safety. You would never know if they really existed but for their silver Huey helicopter, their Bushmaster aircraft on Da Nang airfield and the locals who would readily tell you where their compound was located, if asked.

After chow, I returned and took over "official" control of our little installation of 4–5 very small buildings—typing the first official entry onto the log sheet.

It was then time to make the rounds. We had two Vietnamese guards—one at the only entryway into the "complex" and one on the roof, next to our water tower. Neither seemed to speak English well, but no one knew for sure. I knew they both had a couple of clips for their M1 Carbines. So between their carbines and my M16 and a bandolier of ammo, we could probably hold off a regiment or division or so. If you believe that, I have a bridge to sell cheap.

It was fairly quiet, though I knew it wouldn't be long before it was likely to become noisier; the usual game of "combat basketball" had already begun. I just hoped that no one would be seriously hurt—not due for any great humanitarian reason, but because there were no rules in this game. Punching someone jumping to make a shot was normal. The real reason for my concern was if someone was really hurt, then it was paperwork and finding someone to make the trip to the 95th EVAC, across the river, and back. It would be nearly impossible to find someone sober enough to drive a jeep soon.

Virtually every night there was a movie and this night was no exception. Only about half of the guys were in attendance—everyone else was at the meeting/recreation room—a room with a few chairs, tables and a very small bar.

Overhearing talk of home, girlfriends, wives and kids, it didn't take long to figure out how this night was going to be. This would certainly confirm the expression, "Crying in your beer." It was time to move on.

Moving through the area, I eventually stopped at the roof. Acknowledging my presence, the guard nodded and I did the same. This was always the procedure with both guards—few words were ever mentioned.

The view was at least better than nothing—if you craned your head over one way, you could just make out the water of the Han River. A little to the left was the QC (Vietnamese Military Police) compound, which you couldn't see into. In every other direction were ramshackled houses, made of wood scrounged from who knows where and corrugated tin roofs.

After a few weeks of being in-country, you didn't notice the mosquitoes and the distinct smells that are Viet Nam. When I first arrived and began exiting the airplane's stairs to the tarmac, as I reached the plane's door, the smell made me stop immediately and by the time I reached the pavement, I thought every mosquito in the world had bitten me, bite-upon-bite!

None of this was noticed now, after almost four months, little seemed to change except for the degree of fear at any given time and that usually depended on where you were and what you were doing, but not always. Most times, it was the sound of someone firing a weapon, whether a M16 or an AK-47. Reaction was immediate if your trained ear determined it was close. If the distance was more than local, you kept note of it, especially if you were headed in that direction. You became wary of everyone but Americans. Even kids were almost feared because of the instances where they were used to deliver grenades and babies were booby trapped. Sometimes it felt like you were always coiled up, ready to spring at a second's notice for your own safety and the safety of your guys.

It was peaceful on the roof. I sat and just looked around and thought of nothing. Odd as it may seem, just "clicking" your brain into neutral can be very beneficial and relaxing. After a few minutes, it was time to go. A quick nod to the guard, slinging my ever-present M16 behind a shoulder and back down I went.

One more stop—our CONEX container, which contained the teletype, all the crypto gear and its army operator. As the CONEX was air-conditioned due to the equipment, you rarely saw whoever was inside unless you had the duty. A quick knock on the door and a blast of air-conditioned comfort hit you in the face and sent a chill throughout your body. This was really only a courtesy call, so whoever had the duty inside the CONEX would know who had the duty for everything else. A brief exchange of pleasantries and complaints and the door closed once again.

Back to where it had all began. The typewriter beckoned: the second entry became, "All posts checked. All secure." And the time led off the entry in the log. A quick look at the radio next to the desk to see if the correct frequency was dialed-in and a flip of the switch to make sure it had power and then it was switched off until it was time for the communication (comm) checks in a few hours.

I decided to try to read the book I had been trying to get through. I was able to read for a half-hour or so, stopping every now and then to hear a somewhat louder bunch of guys as darkness fell, halting the basketball game. This small group made its way to the movie or the bar, adding a perceptible change in the overall volume.

All of this generally repeated itself over the next few hours, changed only by the movie ending and almost everyone now in the bar. I discovered in making a later, hourly round that the bar area was jammed, as I tactfully declined a drink from many of the guys.

Completing my rounds, I returned to my office, typed in the log, checked the radio and was about to re-start my book when one of the guys poked his head in and asked if I intended to go to Midnight Mass. I explained that I had the duty, but he replied that, if I was interested, he'd find someone to fill in for an hour or so. I said sure, but it can't be a drunk though. He understood.

There was about an hour and a half before it would be time to go, enough for a quick round in an hour. Varying times was standard procedure anyway. I then made a comm check. Having had the duty a few times before, I knew what was going to happen—nothing. Trying to contact our HQ in Saigon and the CIA compound down the street had always been unsuccessful for everyone.

About 20 minutes before Mass was to begin, my friend returned and had the 1st sergeant in tow. My surprise was obvious, as the top kick told me to return ASAP. We jumped in the jeep, both of us armed with our M16s, waited for the compound gate guard to open things up and then I flew down the road as fast as I could. As it was almost midnight and we were virtually alone on the street, we stuck out like a sore thumb as a target for anyone. (The first time I was fired on was driving a jeep after being in-country for three days—by now Parnelli Jones and Jackie Stewart had nothing on me.)

Arriving at the MACV compound and surprising the guard, who obviously wasn't expecting visitors, we were let in. A quick right and the small, little chapel was in front of us. There was a rifle rack for weapons just before you entered and a bunch of plastic rosaries just inside the entryway.

The Mass started exactly on-time—Latin hadn't yet surrendered to English. The chapel, being small, captured the incense and retained it as almost a fog that lingered in the air. The words majestic, their emphasis succinct and clear. Both of the soldier altar servers seemed to be as one with each other and the priest, the responses and every note of music. It was awe-inspiring and one I shall never forget.

The time seemed to slip by and then it was done. Not over, just done, for it remained vividly imprinted in memory and in what was soon to come.

Returning in the same way and in the same manner in which we had come, the top kick seemed irked and before he could speak, I gave him my thanks for allowing us to attend Mass. At this, there was a softening in his expression and a look of understanding, to which he merely wished us Merry Christmas and moved off to his rack. I suspected he was probably Catholic, which I later found out to be true. My friend bade me goodnight and I did the same, adding my appreciation to his having set up a replacement to be able to go the Mass.

Looking at the log, there was nothing entered, so I walked my rounds once again. Things were still rowdy, but not as much as I thought it might be. I suspected the 1st sergeant had laid down a few "suggestions" to the rowdier ones. There was no one who could have passed a breathalyzer test and it was obvious something had to be done, so I turned away and yelled "Last call" in the best 1st sergeant voice I could.

It seemed to work as the majority seemed headed for the door. It looked like my job would be easy—after most went staggering away and a few stopping to be sick, there only remained a handful of older soldiers who waved to me as if to say they'd be leaving soon. Waving back, I had to help a few guys into their racks and the snoring could already be heard. It would soon become outrageously loud. It couldn't be helped—they'd all have a huge headache in the morning.

I continued to make what had become a long walk around. I had heard some weapon rounds go off in the distance on the way back from Mass and sporadically since. On top of the roof, I heard some again and could see tracers in the distance, too. The tracers arched up from the ground, so there was still some celebrating going on somewhere.

In noticing the guard was awake, I wished him a Merry Christmas. Expecting no response, he seemed to know what I said as he greeted me in the same way, in Vietnamese. I reached over and shook his hand and left to finish my rounds that had taken almost an hour to complete.

The last comm check made—this time wishing them a Merry Christmas, too—with not a peep in return. The log typed, I sat back and wondered at all that had happened in the past few hours. The sadness of those far from home, expressed itself it drinking so they could forget home and all it represented. No one I ever encountered desired to be there then or ever said they wanted to return after the war was over.

By now, it was after 0300 and the stillness of the night was fully laden on all things. "Sleep, perchance to dream," I remember thinking. There would be many across the world that were still abed while I was here awake. Funny but I wasn't tired, not yet at least. So another round I went. No changes from the last time, though quieter. Every once in a while now, an explosive device could be heard far away—probably a flare just to make sure the Viet Cong weren't sleep walking up to the wire somewhere.

Making the roof, acknowledging the guard, I sat for a while, thinking about nothing. Putting my hand in my shirt pocket, I felt the rosary I had taken while at Mass. Fingering it, I began whispering the Rosary. As I did so, my voice must have grown louder as the guard, who I had wished Merry Christmas to, began to recite the Rosary in Vietnamese. I became aware of it and started reciting it normally, but slower so the guard (about 20 feet away) and I could stay in sync with each other.

As we neared the end of a decade of the Rosary, a flare lit the sky many miles away and I couldn't help but think of the heavenly star the Three Wise Men followed to see the "babe in swaddling clothes."

I sat for another few minutes thinking of all that had happened, wondering about God's plans for this warring country, the conflict occurring in the streets of the United States, my friends fast asleep and myself. I said a prayer for all of these that all things would be healed and that all would find the peace we all wanted and desperately needed.

Military Science-ROTC to Induct Four Silver Star Recipients into Hall of Heroes

As mentioned previously, we (the 571st MI Detachment) took advantage of what time we had our assigned 358th Detachment Huey. Having flown as a door gunner a half-dozen times also afforded me a kind of kinship with the crew. This is why I take pride in knowing how the crew distinguished itself, epitomized by its pilot, Arthur B. Cook, Jr., and his induction into his alma mater for what he and his crew accomplished in April 1972.

The Hall of Heroes annually honors ROTC alumni who have distinguished themselves through valor and service. The Silver Star is the third highest military decoration that can be awarded to a member of the United States Armed Forces and is awarded for gallantry in action against an enemy of the United States:

> Cook is from Caruthersville, Mo. He graduated from Arkansas State in 1970 with a bachelor of science degree in Business Administration and a ROTC commission as a second lieutenant in the United States Army. His period of service lasted from 1970 to 1973. During that time, he completed Army Helicopter Aviation School and served a tour in Vietnam from 1971 to 1972. Lieutenant Cook's awards and honors include the Silver Star, the Bronze Star, the Air Medal, National Defense Service Medal, Vietnam Service Medal, and Army Aviation Badge. He received an honorable discharge from the Army in 1973. He is presently a right-of-way supervisor for Doyle Land Services, Inc. on a gas transport line.
>
> On April 28, 1972, First Lieutenant Cook distinguished himself while serving as pilot of a rescue helicopter with the 358th Aviation Detachment, 525th Military Intelligence Group. Lieutenant Cook accepted a rescue mission to extract American advisors from Quang Tri City. During the mission, he flew over enemy-held territory occupied by a regimental-sized North Vietnamese Army force equipped with anti-aircraft weapons.
>
> As he maneuvered to recover the Americans, his aircraft became the target of intense hostile fire, and Lieutenant Cook repeatedly placed accurate fire on the enemy. Cook completed the extraction of six Americans and three Vietnamese civilians from Quang Tri City.

USS *Buchanan* (DDG-14) in 1972

Five months after the bridge at Dong Ha was destroyed, then Major John Ripley, USMC, wrote to the commander of the USS *Buchanan* (DDG-14) describing his view of the splendid naval gunfire support the ship contributed to the bridge's destruction. Ripley describes the NVA movement before and after the bridge was destroyed, the NVA tanks the *Buchanan* destroyed, and his personal thanks in providing the aid this mission needed in delaying the NVA from continuing their southward advance.

8 September 1972
Commander William J. Thearle, USN
Commanding Officer
USS *BUCHANAN* (DDG-14)
FPO San Francisco *96601*

Dear Commander Thearle:

We have not met. My first introduction to your ship was somewhat indirect, in fact at the time I had no way of identifying the ship with which I was working. Our relationship was established of operational combat necessity, and in very short order was proven to be one of the most successful and rewarding relationships from the standpoint of combat effectiveness in the war—specifically during the continuing enemy Easter Offensive of 1972.

My purpose in writing is to relate to you some background relative to the invasion, the part my battalion played, and the part played by the USS *BUCHANAN*, during the first few days of the invasion. Hopefully it will provide a clearer picture to you and your crew of the vital role of NGF as a supporting arm to ground combat forces, and in particular the superlative effectiveness of the *BUCHANAN* in this role.

The Intelligence information disclosed that the enemy Easter Offensive began 30 March 1972. On that day the northern and western DMZ firebases began receiving heavy indirect fire from enemy artillery along both firebase lines. The fact that the enemy was able to take almost all of these firebases under fire either simultaneously or in rapid succession should have been sufficiently significant to indicate that this was more than just a diversion. He was using more than one tube, more than a battery, and he was firing from multiple positions. We now know that he was employing in excess of a regiment of artillery from fixed, prepared positions with two additional regiments in reserve. All of his ordnance had been stockpiled and in such quantities that his rate of fire/target coverage in virtually every attack was staggering. Rarely was any attack by fire less than 1000 rounds.

Enemy ground forces began their attacks by probing the firebases. Within two days of these indirect attacks they initiated standard infantry assaults against these firebases, always heavily supported by their artillery and other crew served weapons. The western firebases, all in heavy jungle and mountainous terrain did not experience any attacks by armor, however, these same terrain limitations removed any hope of resupply to, or evacuation from the firebases. On the other hand, the northern firebases lay along the coastal plain from A-2 (Gio Linh) to A-4 (Con Tien) and the majority of this terrain lent itself to vehicular movement, either limited wheeled vehicular movement or general use of tracked vehicles. Taking advantage of this terrain the enemy attacks along the northern base line, immediately below the DMZ, were characterized by an almost exclusive use of armor. Having generally overrun each of the bases with tanks, the enemy infantry would then come along for the consolidation, or "mopup," of what little resistance remained.

With the foregoing as background I will now turn to the events centering around the battalion I advised, the 3rd Vietnamese Infantry Battalion. We were positioned at Dong Ha as Division Reserve for the 3d ARVN Division. When the enemy attack reached us on Easter Sunday morning April 2nd, we were the last unit lying astride the enemy's route of advance, National Route #1 (QL-1). There was still one more Marine battalion south of us at Quang Tri Combat Base (Ai Tu Base), which was the 6th battalion. Their mission was the defense of the entire base including the remaining elements of the 3d ARVN Division and that portion of Route #1 which ran through the base. It would have been virtually impossible for them to successfully defend the road at this point because of their necessarily excessively thin defense and the fact that there was no natural barrier at that point. There were units south of us but they were "disorganized" to the point that they were ineffective. The headquarters of the 3d ARVN Division had moved to Quang Tri City so officially there was a Division Command Post behind us. However, the regiments of this Division were either heavily engaged, had disappeared altogether, or as in the case of the 56th Regiment, were on the point of surrender. The closest organized force was another 30 to 40 miles away to the west of Hue. Here the bulk of the ARVN 1st Division was defending FBs Bastogne and Birmingham. There was so little of the 1st Division remaining other than what was necessary for the defense of those hills that it could not spare as much as one battalion for the defense of Hue.

It is seen then that the hopes of a nation rested on the shoulders of that battalion of Marines along with their support. I trust this is not too strong a wording of a situation which had quite rapidly gone from grim to hopeless. The enemy firepower and massive use of armor had blitzed the strong points he had thus far encountered and had taken him to the north bank of Mieu Giang/Cua Viet River at Dong Ha. Three full mechanized divisions were in the attack, and one was attacking due south along Route #1. These divisions consisted of approximately, the following figures:

8,000–10,000 infantry
150 tanks (Russian T54, T55, and PT76)
50–75 tracked, mobile antiaircraft vehicles
one artillery regiment—approximately 47 130mm guns
anti-aircraft missile units (SAMs)

Then there were the various other special units which make up a division, i.e., engineers, heavy weapons, etc. A conservative figure of the total strength of this division would be 15,000 men with related equipment. The preponderance of force is staggering when one considers that the Marine Battalion defending Dong Ha numbered just 700 men and at the time of the enemy's attack that morning only half of the battalion, two rifle companies, were actually in Dong Ha. When the enemy arrived on the north bank, these two companies defended the village along the river alone. One company went into position along the highway bridge and the other just off of Route #9 near the partially destroyed railroad bridge which was already in enemy hands. These two companies defended the village against a furious attack by the enemy to cross at both places. The enemy actually did get across at the railroad bridge site establishing a foothold there, but was contained by the Marines. It was at this point that I employed my first Naval Gunfire mission. I requested a continuous NGF mission in the vicinity of the railroad bridge, 300 meters to the right and left of the bridge, and 200 meters deep (north) as interdiction to the enemy forces attempting to cross. My request was sent directly to the senior advisor with the VN Marine Brigade then located at Quang Tri Combat Base. There was an ANGLICO team co-located with the Brigade advisory staff which forwarded my request to your ship. This was to be my primary and most effective method of requesting and employing NGF during our defense of Dong Ha. Occasionally a spotter aircraft with NGF capability was used, but never as effectively or with as rapid a response as the ANGLICO teams. This same advisory team with the Brigade worked up a number of defensive fire boxes (targets) north of the river in the general vicinity of the highway and began firing indiscriminate unobserved fire. None of us could see the impact of the rounds, but as most were landing in this area where the concentration of the enemy forces was the greatest the effect of this varied and continuous mission in disorganizing the enemy must have been superb. It forced him to go to ground or to suffer casualties, thus definitely limiting his ability to mass for attack. Still the enemy had many tanks and these were generally unaffected by NGF except for a direct hit, although the infantry normally accompanying the tanks were seriously limited in providing any protection to them.

This was the situation when the enemy finally arrived at the highway bridge around 1015 that morning. Naval Gunfire had been in continuous use for at least an hour interdicting the approaches to both bridges. I was personally too busy to adjust the fire and had requested that it be fired in boxes approximately 2000 × 1000 meters with the linear axis generally east to vest and that these fires be shifted from bridge to bridge, as well as north of the bridges, randomly. In accordance with a fire plan worked up by the Brigade advisory staff and the ANGLICO team. It was a simple, efficient system, very effective primarily because of its simplicity. It was only necessary for me to say "give me more fire at the bridge" or, "I can hear tanks on the north bank about 200 meters up the road" and in less than a minute the NGF would come rolling, in. No fire commands, no lengthy map checks, or adjustments, nothing but "give me some fire here" and in it came. Furthermore it stayed coming until I wanted it turned off, a very helpful factor. It was the perfect example of the flexibility of our system. I needed fire support and needed it badly; I had no direct communication link with you; I didn't even know if you were out there, or even if I was within range; and for your part, you couldn't have known very much about friendly locations. None of us did. It almost seems like a compilation of the worst possible factors regarding fire support except one: you had the support and I needed it. This fact was abundantly clear to us all and you lost no time in getting it to me.

It is unfortunate that a battlefield assessment could not be made to determine just how much damage NGF did. Nevertheless, one fact is obvious; it contributed greatly to the overall success of our defense and without it, I have serious doubts that this letter would have been possible. On the many, many occasions that I used it, it was totally responsive and accurate. Furthermore, it impressed the South Vietnamese and inspired confidence in them when their need for confidence was the greatest. We were watching from a vantage point when the four PT76 tanks were destroyed by your ship on the beach just south of Cua Viet. We could see them burning clearly.

My counterpart, the Marine Battalion CO, and the tank Battalion CO were both observing this superb display of Naval Gunfire. When the tanks were hit and burning they were both surprised and elated in seeing the potential of NGF. I was to receive many requests for NGF by the Vietnamese after this attack.

Another celebrated incident occurred the night of the 2nd after the bridge had been blown. We could hear tanks moving on the north bank then soon could see approximately 20 of them moving westerly along what appeared to be route TL-8B. They were apparently making a dash for the Cam Lo area where they hoped to be able to cross the river. NGF was requested to interdict the road along its entirety to the maximum range limit which was approximately half way to Cam Lo. The mission was worked up right away and very shortly thereafter we could both see and hear the effects of the mission. One tank was actually hit and remained on the road burning, thus illuminating the other tanks as they passed close by. We were able to take the other tank under fire more easily while they were illuminated by the burning one. This tank kill was credited to NGF but I don't know if you ever received it. None of the tanks ever reached the Cam Lo area either so the interdiction mission must be considered a success. Our own forces were firing on the tanks that night also, but NGF was first to engage and apparently scored the first kill.

Another area where NGF was used to a very good effect was in the rescue attempts of downed pilots and other aviation personnel. We knew the general location of one pilot just across the river and approximately 2000 meters west of us. He was unable to move and completely surrounded as he described his situation to us. I fired NGF close enough to his position to remove most of the immediate enemy threat and permit him to move somewhat. This same type mission was fired on other indiscriminate targets nearby so as to avoid pointing out his location to the enemy. In two days' time he walked into friendly lines. I think that the contribution of NGF to the success of this joint operation is more than obvious.

When I went to work at the bridge, I had to leave my radio and operator back south of the bridge in a covered position. Thus I was out of communication for the hour or so that I was under the bridge. I had previously requested that the NGF fires then in effect be continued and shifted on the north bank opposite me. This was done by the advisory staff at Brigade with the ANGLICO team. Your fire support and the classic defense of the bridge by the Vietnamese Marines permitted me to get on with my task and successfully complete it.

My battalion was replaced at Dong Ha by an ARVN Army unit a week later and we returned to Quang Tri Combat Base. Our operations continued in this area although we were generally out of range of NGF and therefore saw very little use of it.

Leaving the field just prior to my return to the United States, I reported to my commanding officer in Hue. It was here that I learned that during our week in Dong Ha, I had used over 10,000 rounds of NGF. I was interviewed by the press a number of times and carefully pointed out on each occasion the role of NGF in the successful defense of Dong Ha. I also emphasized this role to my Commandant and to the Secretary of the Navy in my discussions with them. Of course they were quite aware of the vital necessity of NGF, but at that time neither had talked with someone who had recently been on the receiving end of this outstanding support.

Summarizing the events which took place that week at Dong Ha the following becomes apparent:

Because of the almost complete loss of artillery assets the only all-weather indirect fire supporting arm available was Naval Gunfire.

Naval Gunfire was capable of firing all standard fire-support missions. e.g., destruct, interdiction, etc., as well as special purpose missions (protection of downed pilots), limited only by the initiative of the ship and the observer.

Naval Gunfire was responsive to fire requests in every case and was the only supporting arm which could respond with a volume of fire approaching that of the enemy's.

The interdiction of enemy armor was found to be a valid use of NGF. The destruction of enemy armor by NGF was considered effective, but normally only when the ship could observe its target.

For other missions Naval Gunfire remained very effective, even when it could not be directly observed or controlled by the observer.

An intermediate agency apart from the observer (ANGLICO team or Advisory team) could control the fires with reasonable effectiveness once the fire mission had been established.

The use of air was severely limited as close air support (CAS) for two reasons: first, the preponderance of enemy anti-aircraft fire was of such an extent that any ground support mission was considered unacceptably hazardous by the VNAF and secondly, the scale of the enemy attack throughout the country was so large that the availability of friendly air was limited, due to other priorities. These factors combined to make Naval Gunfire the primary supporting arm from the standpoint of availability. *BUCHANAN* exemplified the flexibility and responsiveness of Naval Gunfire in the support of ground forces. The South Vietnamese were impressed with the continuous availability of Naval Gunfire. Almost in every case their first reaction to an enemy threat was to request NGF. There have been many times in history, of course, when NGF was called on, to provide fire support to ground forces. I feel that the performance of *BUCHANAN* at Dong Ha represents one of the finest examples of this support in recent history. The professional and aggressive fire support delivered by your ship was made more noteworthy because of the urgency of our needs during this defense.

Please pass to all hands of *BUCHANAN* my deepest appreciation, and on behalf of my counterpart, the Battalion Commander, and the 200 Marines who left Dong Ha a week later, our sincere praise for the exemplary support given us.

Kindest regards,
JOHN W. RIPLEY
MAJ USMC
Letter provided by Dean M. Myer.

NVA Order of Battle, Easter Offensive

North Vietnamese Army (NVA) Divisions and Regiments in I Corps at the Onset of the Easter Offensive

304th Infantry Division/B5 Front
9th Infantry Regiment
24th Infantry Regiment
66th Infantry Regiment
38th Composite Artillery Regiment (assigned)
203rd Armored Regiment/B5 Front (assigned)
241st Anti-Aircraft Regiment(attached)

308th Infantry Division/B5 Front
36th Infantry Regiment
88th Infantry Regiment
102nd Infantry Regiment
164th Composite Artillery Regiment (assigned)
202nd Armored Regiment/B5 Front (assigned)

B-5 Front/Attached Elements
246th Independent Infantry Regiment/B-5 Front
270th Independent Infantry Regiment/B5 Front
27th Independent Infantry Regiment/B5 Front
31st Independent Infantry Regiment/B5 Front
65th Composite Artillery Regiment/B5 Front
84th Composite Artillery Regiment/B5 Front
365th Air Defense Division
126th Water Sapper Regiment (North Viet. Navy)

324B Infantry Division/MRTTH
29th Infantry Regiment (*Pride of Ho Chi Minh*)
803rd Infantry Regiment
812th Infantry Regiment
5th Independent Infantry Regiment/MRTTH (attached)
6th Independent Infantry Regiment/MRTTH (attached)

711th Infantry Division/MR5
31st Infantry Regiment
38th Infantry Regiment
270th Independent Infantry Regiment/B5 Front

(The 270th Independent Infantry Regiment/B5 Front came across the DMZ, engaged ARVN forces for a short while, proceeded westerly to the Ho Chi Minh Trail in Laos, reentered southern I Corps, and transferred to the 711th NVA Division in June/July 1972.)

The commander of the Tri-Thien campaign was Major General Le Trong Tan, Deputy Chief of the General Staff.

A Composite Artillery Regiment was permanently assigned to the 304th and 308th Infantry Divisions.

38th Composite Artillery Regiment/304th NVA Division (aka, "Cotton Mop")
130mm (M-46) field guns
122mm (D-30) field guns
85mm (probably D-44) field guns
140mm Multiple Rocket Launcher System (BM-14)
160mm mortars

164th Composite Artillery Regiment/308th NVA Division was configured the same as the 38th Composite Artillery Regiment.

Artillery divisions were a Soviet Army concept usually tasked with providing concentrated firepower support to higher combined-arms formations, such as corps and fronts. Artillery divisions were used by the NVA from 1971 as a means to concentrate overwhelming firepower in a small geographical area to achieve a strategic penetration of the enemy's defenses. The 65th, 84th, and 365th Composite Artillery Regiments were subordinate to the B5 Front and were interspersed on the battlefield between the 38th and 164th Composite Artillery Regiments.

The 246th and 270th Independent Infantry Regiments/B5 Front began the Easter Offensive coming through the eastern DMZ.

The 246th IIR was active around FSB Fuller in January 1972.

The 84th Arty, 31st IIR, and 270th IIR conducted ops generally east of FSB A-4 on January 29, 1972.

Prisoner from 126th Naval Sapper Regiment captured near Hue, which indicates how far south this regiment had penetrated.

North Vietnamese Army (NVA) Divisions and Regiments in I Corps/FRAC During the Easter Offensive

304th Infantry Division/B5 Front
9th Infantry Regiment
24th Infantry Regiment
66th Infantry Regiment
38th Composite Artillery Regiment
203rd Armored Regiment/B5 Front (assigned)
241st Anti-Aircraft Regiment

308th Infantry Division/B5 Front[1]
36th Infantry Regiment
88th Infantry Regiment
102nd Infantry Regiment
164th Composite Artillery Regiment
202nd Armored Regiment/B5 Front (assigned)

320B Infantry Division
48B Infantry Regiment (April)
64B Infantry Regiment (late-May)

325th Infantry Division/B5 Front
18th Infantry Regiment (May)
95th Infantry Regiment (July)
101st Infantry Regiment (July)

312th Infantry Division (mid-August)
141st Infantry Regiment
165th Infantry Regiment
209th Infantry Regiment

324B Infantry Division/MRTTH
29th Infantry Regiment
803rd Infantry Regiment

812th Infantry Regiment
5th Independent Infantry Regiment/MRTTH (assigned)
6th Independent Infantry Regiment/MRTTH (assigned)

711th Infantry Division/MR5
31st Infantry Regiment
38th Infantry Regiment
270th Independent Infantry Regiment

Non-Divisional Units
246th Independent Infantry Regiment/B5 Front
270th Independent Infantry Regiment/B5 Front[2]
27th Independent Infantry Regiment/B5 Front
31st Independent Infantry Regiment/B5 Front
65th Composite Artillery Regiment/B5 Front
84th Composite Artillery Regiment/B5 Front
365th Composite Artillery Division[3]
126th Water Sapper Regiment (North Viet. Navy)

525th MI Group Staff Duty Logs, 1972

DAILY STAFF JOURNAL OR DUTY OFFICER'S LOG For use of this form, see AR 220-15; the proponent agency is Office of Deputy Chief of Staff for Military Operations.				PAGE NO. 1		NO. OF PAGES 4	

ORGANIZATION OR INSTALLATION	LOCATION	PERIOD COVERED				
525th MI Group	Bldg 616 Tan Son Nhut AFB	FROM		TO		
		HOUR 1700	DATE 31 Mar 72	HOUR 0800	DATE 1 Apr 72	

ITEM NO.	TIME IN	TIME OUT	INCIDENTS, MESSAGES, ORDERS, ETC.	ACTION TAKEN	INI- TIALS
1	1700		Journal opened		LT
2	1710		Received telephone call from SP/4 SHELDON, HHC, 525 MI Group, that he was informed by Emergency Operational Center(EOC), MACV, that security condition is GREY, effective immediately.	Informed Asst Adjutant	LT
3	1745		Telephoned MACV Operations Center(923-4564) and was informed by SP4 Collins that alert condition as of 1745 hrs 31 Mar 72 is WHITE.	Telephoned UTAH, 519th Bn, 504th, HHC and McKarrick compound. Orally informed CPT COX, LTC HAMEL	LT
4	1800		Telephoned 571st MID. Status: Reported information on Quang Tri Combat Base.	Informed Asst S3, Opns	LT
5	1830		Commo check w/519th via Motorola	Loud/Clear	LT
6	1900		Negative contact with 571st MID. Receiving busy signal via telephone.	Keep trying	LT
7	1930		Commo check w/519th, Utah & Polyhouse.	Loud/Clear	LT
8	1955		Received call from LT WALKER,573 MID, that they will be in Alert Condition YELLOW from 2200 hrs to 0600 hrs 31 Mar-1 Apr 72.	Informed S3 & CPT GREEN	LT
9	2000		Contacted 571st, SGT BAKER. Was informed that elec msg priority OO on wires but was unable to raise 504th. BAKER passed info to	Informed 504th thru courier to have operator	LT

TYPED NAME AND GRADE OF OFFICER OR OFFICIAL ON DUTY LEWIS M. TALMADGE, CW2, USA	SIGNATURE

DA FORM 1594 1 NOV 62   PREVIOUS EDITION OF THIS FORM IS OBSOLETE.   ☆ U.S. GOVERNMENT PRINTING OFFICE. 1670- -379-741

			DAILY STAFF JOURNAL OR DUTY OFFICER'S LOG For use of this form, see AR 220-15; the proponent agency is Office of Deputy Chief of Staff for Military Operations.		PAGE NO. 2	NO. OF PAGES 2

ORGANIZATION OR INSTALLATION	LOCATION	PERIOD COVERED			
525th MI Group	Bldg 616 Tan Son Nhut AFB	FROM		TO	
		HOUR 1700	DATE 31 Mar 72	HOUR 0800	DATE 1 Apr 72

ITEM NO.	TIME IN	TIME OUT	INCIDENTS, MESSAGES, ORDERS, ETC.	ACTION TAKEN	INITIALS
9			Cont'd. SDO.	stand by to receive 571st. Related to MAJ GREIFE context of telephone con w/BAKER.	LT
10	2030		Commo check w/UTAH, 519th and Poly House	Loud and clear	LT
11	2100		Negative contact with 571st via telephone. Busy signal.	Keep trying.	LT
12	2130		Commo check w/519th, Utah & Polyhouse	Loud/Clear	LT
13	2200		Attempted to contact LTC OKYEN re item 8, with negative results.	Will attempt at 2230 hrs.	LT
14	2230		Commo check w/UTAH, Poly House, 519th	Loud and clear	LT
15	2250		Received radio msg from 519th that their RTT rig site at XUAN LOC is receiving incoming rounds. Follow-up report will be submitted.	Notified LTC HAMEL. Unable to contact Command House	LT
16	2253		Received telephone call from LT WALKER, 573d that they are are RED ALERT as of 2253 hrs. Alert notification came from 3d Brig, 1st Cav TOC.	Notified LTC HAMEL. Unable to reach Command house. LTC HAMEL advised SDO to obtain additional info from 573d.	LT
17	2303		Contacted MAJ RICHARDS, 573d MID and was advised that YELLOW ALERT was from 573d area		LT

TYPED NAME AND GRADE OF OFFICER OR OFFICIAL ON DUTY	SIGNATURE
LEWIS N. TALMADGE, CW2, USA	

DA FORM 1594
1 NOV 62

PREVIOUS EDITION OF THIS FORM IS OBSOLETE.

☆ U.S. GOVERNMENT PRINTING OFFICE: 1970 -370-740

DAILY STAFF JOURNAL OR DUTY OFFICER'S LOG For use of this form, see AR 220-15; the proponent agency is Office of Deputy Chief of Staff for Military Operations.				PAGE NO. 1		NO. OF PAGES	

ORGANIZATION OR INSTALLATION	LOCATION	PERIOD COVERED					
52 th MI Group	Bldg 616 Tan Son Nhut AFB	FROM			TO		
		HOUR 1630	DATE 3 Apr 72		HOUR 0.00	DATE 4 Apr 72	

ITEM NO.	TIME IN	TIME OUT	INCIDENTS, MESSAGES, ORDERS, ETC.	ACTION TAKEN	INI-TIALS
1.	1630		Journal opened		JDG
2.	1800		504th Courier deleivered 3 IIR'S to LTC Hamel and 6 IIR'S from MACV		JDG
3.	1830		Commo check with 519th	L/C	JDG
4.	1850		SP Wickline, SAB, departed bldg		JDG
5.	1900		Cpt Scott, 519th Telephone Check, SP4 Bishop, runner		JDG
6.	1915		Security check conducted SDNCO, discrepancies were noted in the following areas: S-3 Air: One CONFIDENTIAL folder was located in the desk of SP Wessen, also one FOUO folder. S-1 Admin: Filing cabint contained numerious CONFIDENTIAL documents, Bookcase contained numerous classified reference publication. Necessary action should be taken to place all classified documents in approved storage containers.		JDG
7.	1925		504th Courier deleivered one MACV message		JDG
8.	1930		Commo check with 519th, Utah BOQ, and POLY	L/C	JDG
9.	1954		Maj Greife entered Bldg		JDG
10.	2010		Cpt Green entered Bldg		JDG
11.	2025		Cpt Green departed Bldg		JDG
12.	2030		Commo check with 519th, Utah BOQ, and Poly	L/C	JDG
13.	2100		LTC Treadwell entered Bldg to make phone call		JDG
14.	2125		504th Courier deleivered 7 IIRS		JDG
15.	2135		Commo check with 519th, Utah BOQ, and POLY	L/C	JDG
16.	2140		Command Section was notified concerning MR I tactical suition.	LTC Okyen notified	JDG
17.	2142		Maj Greife departed Bldg with copy of message 0.07000 April concerning tactical suition in MR I		JDG

TYPED NAME AND GRADE OF OFFICER OR OFFICIAL ON DUTY	SIGNATURE
JAMES D. GRANDSTAFF, CPT	

DA FORM 1594 1 NOV 62   PREVIOUS EDITION OF THIS FORM IS OBSOLETE   ☆ U.S. GOVERNMENT PRINTING OFFICE: 1970—675-780

DAILY STAFF JOURNAL OR DUTY OFFICER'S LOG For use of this form, see AR 220-15; the proponent agency is Office of Deputy Chief of Staff for Military Operations.				PAGE NO. 1		NO. OF PAGES 3	

ORGANIZATION OR INSTALLATION	LOCATION	PERIOD COVERED					
		FROM		TO			
525th MI Group	Bldg 616 Tan Son Nhut AFB	HOUR 1700	DATE 05 Apr 72	HOUR 0800	DATE 09 Apr 72		

ITEM NO.	TIME IN	TIME OUT	INCIDENTS, MESSAGES, ORDERS, ETC.	ACTION TAKEN	INI-TIALS
1	1700		Journal opened.		
2	1830		Commo check w/519th - L/C.		
3	1835		SDNCO conducted security check; light, south rear corner, is out.		
4	1845		MAJ Halloran called to tell LTC Brown to contact Deputy J2, COL CREGO at MACV. Contacted LTC Brown at 1847 and passed on message to him.		
5	1900		504th courier arrived w/msg traffic; picked-up 525th msg's DTG 081045Z & 081050Z; dpt.		
6	1930		Commo check w/519th, Poly and Utah - L/C.		
7	1941		LTC Hamel arrived.		
8	1947		LT Stewart, SDO 3rd MID called; at 1900 hrs "both teams' classified material (all) was returned to HQ 3rd MID by CPT Rice, 1st CAV supplied transportation."		
9	1957		CPT Dickson, USA Mortuary, needs combination changed on safe; told him to contact DAME in morning.		
10	1958		CPT Kirby dpt w/duty driver to MACV "tank" w/ISUM (part II) fm 571st MID.		
11	2000		CPT Nimitz arrived.		
12	2020		LTC Hamel, MAJ Greife, CPT Nimitz, SFC Benson departed.		
13	2030		Commo check w/519th, Poly and Utah - L/C.		
14	2031		504th courier arrived w/msg traffic - dpt.		
15	2055		MAJ Richards to CPT Kirby: follow up on action at Nui Ba Din, Tay Ninh; US casualties: 7 WIA, 1 MIA, 2 KIA (one off and one enlist) (assasinated - hands tied behind backs and shot). All US except MIA and KIA evacuated fm Nui Ba Din to MACV Comp East, Tay Ninh. 2 US and unk # of ARVN still on mountain as of 082030H (local).		
16	2125		SDO, 3rd MID, called; couldn'd raise 504th for commo check.		
17	2130		Commo check w/519th, Poly and Utah -L/C.		

TYPED NAME AND GRADE OF OFFICER OR OFFICIAL ON DUTY
PETER J. FINCH, 1LT, SDO

SIGNATURE

DA FORM 1594   PREVIOUS EDITION OF THIS FORM IS OBSOLETE.   ☆ GPO: 1969 O—343-753/563

\multicolumn{9}{l}{**DAILY STAFF JOURNAL OR DUTY OFFICER'S LOG**}

DAILY STAFF JOURNAL OR DUTY OFFICER'S LOG
For use of this form, see AR 220-15; the proponent agency is Office of Deputy Chief of Staff for Military Operations.

PAGE NO. 3
NO. OF PAGES

ORGANIZATION OR INSTALLATION	LOCATION	PERIOD COVERED			
		FROM		TO	
		HOUR	DATE	HOUR	DATE
HQS, 525 CI GP	TSN AFB, RVN		16 Apr 72		17 Apr 72

ITEM NO.	TIME IN	TIME OUT	INCIDENTS, MESSAGES, ORDERS, ETC.	ACTION TAKEN	INI-TIALS
			STOYLEMYER stated that they would give the 573 MID another call.		
18	2250		Made call back to 573 MID and relayed message to CPT Karebach that the 504th will be giving them another commo check.		
19	2130		Made commo check w/519th, Polyhouse & Utah	Loud/Clear	
20	0030		504th Courier arrived w/6 Messages.		
21	0140		504th Courier arrived with a INSUM from 573 MID.	Sent two cys to the Tank, 1 cy for DISUM & 1 cy for S3	
22	0415		504th Courier arrived w/INSUM from 571 MID	Same as above	
23	0515		Dispatched Duty Driver for DISUM Ifficer		
24	0530		WO CHAPMAN entered building.		
25	0620		504th Courier arrived w/6 messages and one INSUM from 571 MID	Sent two cys to the Tank	
26	0621		Duty Driver took WO CHAPMAN to MACV Annex.		
27	0700		Made contact w/TSN Information, they will send someone down to pick up photos (Item # 16)		
28	0800		The duty driver was dispatched 4 times, no discrepancies in the security check and the commander was not called.		
29			JOURNAL CLOSED		

TYPED NAME AND GRADE OF OFFICER OR OFFICIAL ON DUTY
T. R. RUTENBERGER, CW2, USA

SIGNATURE

DA FORM 1594
1 NOV 62

PREVIOUS EDITION OF THIS FORM IS OBSOLETE.

☆ GPO: 1969 O—343-783/365

\multicolumn{3}{c}{DAILY STAFF JOURNAL OR DUTY OFFICER'S LOG}				PAGE NO. 1	NO. OF PAGES

For use of this form, see AR 220-15; the proponent agency is Office of Deputy Chief of Staff for Military Operations.

ORGANIZATION OR INSTALLATION	LOCATION	\multicolumn{4}{c}{PERIOD COVERED}

		\multicolumn{2}{c}{FROM}	\multicolumn{2}{c}{TO}
52th MI Group	Bldg 616 Tan Son Nhut AFB	HOUR 1630	DATE 3 Apr 72	HOUR 0.00	DATE 4 Apr 72

ITEM NO.	TIME IN	TIME OUT	INCIDENTS, MESSAGES, ORDERS, ETC.	ACTION TAKEN	INITIALS
1.	1630		Journal opened		JDy
2.	1800		504th Courier deleivered 3 IIR'S to LTC Hamel and 6 IIR'S from MACV		JDy
3.	1830		Commo check with 519th	L/C	Jy
4.	1850		SP Wickline, SAB, departed bldg		JDy
5.	1900		Cpt Scott, 519th Telephone Check, SP4 Bishop, runner		JDy
6.	1915		Security check conducted SDNCO, discrepancies were noted in the following areas: S-3 Air: One CONFIDENTIAL folder was located in the desk of SP Wessen, also one FOUO folder S-1 Admin: Filing cabint contained numerious CONFIDENTIAL documents, Bookcase contained numerious classified reference publication. Necessary action should be taken to place all classified documents in approved storage containers.		JDy
7.	1925		504th Courier deleivered one MACV message		JDy
8.	1930		Commo check with 519th, Utah BOQ, and POLY	L/C	JDy
9.	1954		Maj Greife entered Bldg		JDy
10.	2010		Cpt Green entered Bldg		JDy
11.	2025		Cpt Green departed Bldg		JDy
12.	2030		Commo check with 519th, Utah BOQ, and Poly	L/C	JDy
13.	2100		LTC Treadwell entered Bldg to make phone call		JDy
14.	2125		504th Courier deleivered 7 IIRS		JDy
15.	2135		Commo check with 519th, Utah BOQ, and POLY	L/C	JDy
16.	2140		Command Section was notified concerning MR I tactical suition.	LTC Okyen notified	JDy
17.	2142		Maj Greife departed Bldg with copy of message 0.07000 April concerning tactical suition in MR I		JDy

\multicolumn{2}{l}{TYPED NAME AND GRADE OF OFFICER OR OFFICIAL ON DUTY}	SIGNATURE
JAMES D. GRANDSTAFF, CPT	

DA FORM 1594 1 NOV 62   PREVIOUS EDITION OF THIS FORM IS OBSOLETE   ☆ U.S. GOVERNMENT PRINTING OFFICE: 1970—879-780

CIA Countrywide Listing of All NVA Forces, September 1971–August 1972

SECRET (b)(3)

Table 2

Organic Units That Deployed
from North Vietnam to the War Zone
During the Period September 1971
Through August 1972

Military Region 1

304th Infantry Division
9th Infantry Regiment
24th Infantry Regiment
66th Infantry Regiment
68th Artillery Regiment

308th Infantry Division
36th Infantry Regiment
88th Infantry Regiment
102nd Infantry Regiment

312th Infantry Division
141st Infantry Regiment
165th Infantry Regiment
209th Infantry Regiment

320B Training Division
48B Infantry Regiment
64B Infantry Regiment

324B Infantry Division
29th Infantry Regiment
803rd Infantry Regiment
812th Infantry Regiment

325th Infantry Division
18th Infantry Regiment
95th Infantry Regiment
101st Infantry Regiment

270th Regiment/711th Infantry Division

202nd Armor Regiment
203rd Armor Regiment
38th Independent Artillery Regiment
45th Independent Artillery Regiment
58th Independent Artillery Regiment
84th Independent Artillery Regiment
164th Independent Artillery Regiment
166th Independent Artillery Regiment

Military Region 2

320th Infantry Division
48th Infantry Regiment
52nd Infantry Regiment
64th Infantry Regiment
Two battalions of the former
54th Artillery Regiment
Two battalions of the 203rd
Armor Regiment

Military Region 3

271st Infantry Regiment
18th Infantry Regiment[a] [b]
Three battalions of the 203rd
Armor Regiment

Military Region 4

Z-17 Infantry Regiment (deployed
as the 95th Regiment)[b]

Z-18 Infantry Regiment (deployed
as the 101st Regiment)[b]

a. Appears to have been broken down and used as fillers for VC/NVA units in MR 3.
b. Generated and trained in North Vietnam by the 325th Division sometime prior
to the current offensive.

7

SECRET (b)(3)

Hanoi's Manpower Commitment to the Southern War Zones; CIA Estimates September 1971–August 1972

SECRET (b)(3)

Table 1

Hanoi's Manpower Commitment to the Southern War Zones

Destination	Regular Infiltration Cycle (Sep 1971 - Jun 1972)	Wet Season (Jul-Aug 1972)	Total
GVN MRs 1 and 2	82,000	36,000	118,000
VC MR TTH	35,000	35,000	70,000
VC MR 5	17,000	0	17,000
VC B-3 Front	30,000	1,000	31,000
GVN MRs 3 and 4/Cambodia	38,000	0	38,000
Southern Laos/northeast Cambodia	16,000	7,000	23,000
Subtotal	136,000	43,000	179,000
Unit deployment outside the infiltration system[a]	55,000	14,000	69,000
Total	191,000	57,000	248,000

a. All organic unit deployments outside regular infiltration channels went to VC Military Region Tri-Thien-Hue (TTH).

BARREL ROLL Routine

In an effort to protect friendly units from North Vietnamese units and material from using the "back door" in to South Vietnam, a joint program involving USAF and USN aircraft was instituted. While STEEL TIGER focused on the SAM and AAA environment in northern Laos, BARREL ROLL missions concentrated on HCM Trail traffic in southern Laos.

The 388th Tactical Fighter Wing, based at Korat AB, was one such element that utilized Fast-Mover FACs. Bullwhip RF4D (flown out of Udorn AB, 432nd Tac Recce Wing, in northern Thailand) imagery was processed overnight before the next day's bombing missions. The film was couriered to Korat and exploited overnight by TIGER FAC photo interpreters for the FAC's next-day missions, which usually lasted about five hrs. These were unusually long missions, requiring three trips to the tanker. Typical F4 bombing missions would normally only be 1½ hours in duration. Those fragged to Korat would be Tiger FAC supported. Once the target was confirmed by the TIGER FACs, they would mark the target with white phosphorus for the F4s to drop their 500- or 1,000-pound bombs onto the target.

Operational Report on Lessons Learned, 525th Military Intelligence Group, Period Ending April 30, 1972, RCS CSFOR-65 (R3) (U), dated May 18, 1972, p.17.

2. <u>Lessons Learned</u>: Commander's observations, Evaluations, and Recommendations.

  g. Communications

    (2) Dedicated Communications System

      (a) <u>Observation:</u> With the onset of the enemy offensive in Quang Tri Province, reporting on the tactical situation was not reaching Saigon in an expeditious manner.

      (b) <u>Evaluation:</u> The 525th MI Group Detachments with trained intelligence officers had the capability to gather and prepare INTSUM messages and transmit those messages over our dedicated communications network thereby filling a serious time lag. This service was previously provided by the tactical units and the large advisory teams in each of the major Corps areas, however, with the drawdown that capability no longer exists.

      (c) <u>Recommendation:</u> That any intelligence group with a mission similar to the 525th MI Group be provided a dedicated communications system. That any intelligence group with a mission similar to the 525th MI Group be prepared to gather and disseminate tactical information and information received from preliminary PW reports and liaison with other information gathering agencies. That the requirement for the collection of information from all sources to enable the highest level of command to receive this information by the most expeditious means be officially levied on the 525th MI Group.

      (d) <u>Command Action:</u> Detachments of the 525th MI Group have been given the task of providing INTSUMs twice a day.

Memoranda from Al Haig to Henry Kissinger, March–April 1972

March 30, 1972

MEMORANDUM FOR: HENRY A. KISSINGER

FROM: AL HAIG

SUBJECT: Situation in I Corps Area

General Abrams has just flashed to Admiral Moorer the following situation report:

--   Three ARVN fire support bases in I Corps are under ground attack.

--   Eight additional fire support bases are under a heavy and persistent attack by fire.

General Abrams stated that the situation is not critical but is developing. He notes that General Lam, the ARVN Corps Commander, is reacting well and will, of course, need heavy U.S. air and gunship support. The usual complication exists. Weather is bad and visual bombing conditions are precluded due to the weather. A further complication is that the North Vietnamese SAM fan has been extended well into Northern I Corps, making helicopter gunship support and C-130 gunship support very risky. General Abrams will report regularly as the situation develops and Admiral Moorer will keep us fully informed.

MEMORANDUM

THE WHITE HOUSE
WASHINGTON

TOP SECRET/SENSITIVE   April 19, 1972

MEMORANDUM FOR: HENRY A. KISSINGER

FROM: AL HAIG

SUBJECT: Southeast Asia Trip Report

Although in Vietnam for just three days, the trip team was impressed by the strength and the vitality of allied efforts. The current NVA offensive, probably their major effort of the war, has stalled and is behind schedule. I believe that GVN supported by us now has a rare opportunity to achieve a major military and political victory over a vulnerable over-extended NVN. This assessment is based both upon the apparent nature of enemy intentions and the solid response of the South Vietnamese.

The enemy probably intended this to be a prolonged campaign to seize and hold three major areas -- Northern MR-1 (Quang Tri/Hue), central MR-2 (Kontum, Dak To), and northern MR-3 (Loc Ninh - An Loc). Evidence suggests that NVN intended initially to launch the attacks in MR-2 in February but were preempted by U.S. air power and ARVN readiness. President Thieu believes that the enemy's strategic aim is to re-establish "Leopard Spot" situations by rebuilding the infrastructure in the country side with the support of psychologically significant base areas from which flags could be shown. Success would have created an impression of stalemate as in 1968 leading to a resurgence of U.S. domestic opposition and a new U.S. Administration which would subsequently accept a ceasefire and settlement favorable to Hanoi's political objective in GVN. Thieu believes NVN planned a six- to 12-month campaign which would result in a new U.S. President and culminate in a settlement which favored further political advances in the South.

It is now evident that the enemy has thus far failed to achieve initial objectives even if these objectives may be more limited than Thieu suggests. The enemy is foundering in costly attacks on ARVN outposts largely away from population centers. However, he still has

TOP SECRET/SENSITIVE   - 2 -

unused capabilities: the infrastructure has not been activated in all
areas and he continues to have the military ability to engage in
sensational but limited value attacks on population centers. Our
response in the North may indeed provoke such efforts -- which
would be wholly consistent with the "go for broke" character of the
offensive. But Hanoi's forces have obviously been unable to match
intentions with solid, successful actions.

Several factors emerge from our brief survey:

    -- U.S. air support has been an essential aspect of success
achieved thus far. It has blunted the effect of Hanoi's introduction
of sophisticated equipment in conventional ground attacks and its
presence in both North and South has been the psychological core of
the ARVN's performance in most areas.

    -- Yet ARVN has successfully held on their own in MR-1
with minimum air support.

    -- A second element of U.S. support has also been essential.
U.S. logistic airlift permitted RVN to responsively move reinforcements -- the 21st Division and the RVNAF reserves (Marines, Airborne
and Rangers). Reliance on more limited organic transport might have
been fatal.

    -- There have been instances of poor ARVN performance --
3rd, 5th, 22nd and 25th Divisions -- but the average performance
is encouraging thus far.

    -- RF/PF have fought well -- not only defending their own
areas but in many cases in neighboring provinces.

    -- The fire base concept is no longer tenable when the enemy
has massive artillery. Further, the inadequacies of Vietnamese
helicopter assets require ARVN to deploy combat assets to secure
the routes of supply to units in combat with the enemy. Thus, we
should restudy SVN helicopter needs and the possible reorganization
of selected RF/PF units into battalion structures to permit their
employment as route security.

    -- The country has clearly pulled together in response to
the invasion and an air of calm and confidence prevails. The U.S.
bombing of the Haiphong and Hanoi areas was an electrifying shot
in the arm of military and civilian morale.

TOP SECRET/SENSITIVE   - 3 -

-- Thieu remains politically strong with opportunities to further improve his position as a successful national leader.

-- No major economic problems are expected -- U.S. aid for CY-72 should remain sufficient unless there are major new destabilizing developments.

-- Our estimate is quite optimistic at this juncture but we are not out of the woods. It will be a long summer of military tests -- some of which may involve such spectacular events as investiture of additional province capitals, cutting of major national routes or the shelling of major population centers. Vietnamese and U.S. public opinion have rude shocks ahead.

-- U.S. air and naval reinforcements should be maintained in Southeast Asia throughout the campaign. The effect will be not just to demonstrate what U.S. assurances represent but to enable the GVN to decisively defeat the North Vietnamese. In exploiting initial success, we should:

-- 1. Hold U.S. troop levels at about 49,000 effective July 1 through September. This approximate level is needed to secure essential command and control including that required for augmentation units, sustain the advisory effort and permit an acceptable logistic wrap-up.

2. Be alert to prevent the erosion of U.S. support for U.S. and ARVN forces through declining sortie rates, ammunition expenditures and other funding constraints.

3. Current air assets except in cases of rare tactical emergency in the South will permit a regular allocation of both fighter bomber and B-52 sorties to an air campaign in the north. Targets below the 18° parallel are limited at this point and favor a steady route recon effort designed to interdict logistics flow.

4. In the weeks ahead, the character of combat air operations in the South will shift from emphasis on massive

TOP SECRET/SENSITIVE   - 4 -

close support air operations to a campaign which should
place increasing emphasis on enemy logistics targets
as enemy forces break contact and seek to regroup,
resupply and prepare for a second offensive surge.

Camper and Brown's After Action Report, April 13, 1972

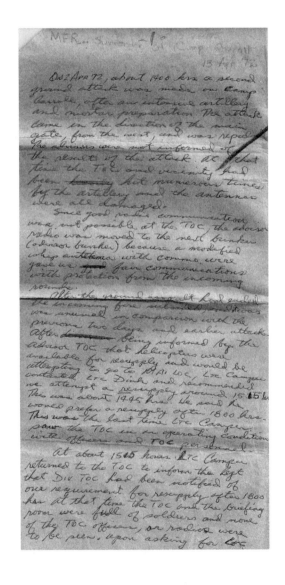

- 2 -

Dinh, the reply in Vietnamese was not understood and the Col could not be found. He noticed more troops arriving at the TOC and starting to fill the inner perimeter by the flag pole. Many of them did not have weapons. Also observed were some radio men with radios on back packs. LTC Camper went to the Regt C.O. Bunker and found many of the officers in there having a meeting. Col Dinh was also said to be there. As we had no fights it was fairly dark. LTC Camper decided to wait until the C.O. had finished his meeting to talk to him. MAJ Brown became suspicious of the Regt activities at this point so we prepared one radio for backpack and plans for evacuation with the Regt should that be their plan.

About 1530 LTC Dinh, the Regt C.O. came to the advisor Bunker. He was crying and his voice was very broken. He tried twice to speak saying "I don't know how to tell you this" before he was understandable. He stated that the men had refused to fight anymore and they wanted to surrender. He continued that he had personally shot two of them but they still refused to return to their battle positions. He said he thought that he would kill himself and wondered if we would not want to do the same rather than become prisoners. LTC Camper answered with MAJ Brown okay that we did not intend to commit suicide or surrender. LTC Dinh continued that the plan was for the troops to march unarmed to the gate and surrender. He further added that maybe we (he and advisors)

-3-

could hid among the mass of troops and after passing the gate, drop out of the crowd and escape in the grass. This offer was rejected as it was daylight and the U.S. advisor could hardly go unnoticed thru the gate. LTC Camper asked LTC Dinh if he could not rally enough soldiers to fight our way out, after all there was one tank, APC's, and dusters and Quad 50's still intact. He replied that was now not possible.

LTC Dinh was told by both advisors that we would call MACV for help and E&E thru the wire rather than surrender. He asked if we would tell Gen Giai of this in our radio conversation and we assured him that our call was only to U.S. personnel for our own assistance. LTC Camper informed LTC Dinh, because of the circumstances he (Dinh) should no longer feel responsible for us, we would take care of ourselves, and wished him luck in whatever he did. That was the last time either of the advisors saw LTC Dinh.

LTC Camper called MACV TOC on the radio while Maj Brown prepared the equipment and our two ARVN (driver EP, generator man FOY) for our E&E. Maj Brown then provided security for the bunker as the classified materials and the bunker was destroyed by incendiary grenades. When burning had begun we departed the bunker.

As we left the bunker, there were more men arriving, filling the TOC outside area and taking off their equipment and placing their weapons on the ground. As we passed thru the crowd LTC Camper spotted a

4

Chieu uy. ~~Ngu~~ NHAN, who worked
in the S3 and spoke English. He
called to him and said "Where is your
weapon C/O ?". ~~The~~ ~~to reply if~~
~~him~~ "Are you a traitor?" The C/O
replied "I don't know what is going
on, but I was told to get rid of
my weapon". As we left the C/O
~~followed~~ us. The road between the
TOC and the VIP Pad was lined
with weapons and equipment.

As we approached the perimeter
wire we noticed the 11th Cav
people ~~were~~ still armed, probably
had not been notified by the Regt
of the decision to surrender. Some
of them followed us ~~this~~ in our
attempt to find our way thru
the wire. There was no artillery
or small arms fire at all, very
~~quiet~~ ~~and~~ strangely quiet.

MACV TOC called on the radio
in answer to our message that the
Regt was surrendering and we were
going to try E&E. The call stated
there was a resupply helicopter in
~~the~~ vicinity of Mai Loc and gave
a frequency which we could speak
to it (005 was calling). ~~the~~
We switched frequency and CH47
replied it would be there in 5
minutes. As the CH47 came into
view so did the enemy troops
moving on the camp. The gunship
fired keeping the enemy down and
the "hook" landed and picked us
up. About 30 ARVN also ran and
jumped on the chopper before it
got into the air. C/O NHAN was one
also the 2 ARVN, EP and FOX who

-5-

originally decided to escape with us. The stock took us to the Pad at Lac Vang - When we arrived at the 3d Div Toc, the above incident was reported to Gen Bowden, Gen Giai, and Col Metcalf on 2 Apr 72.

William C. Campbell
LTC, INF
ADV TM 155

Joseph Brown, Jr
MAJ Infantry
Adv Tm 155

Select Bibliography

Books

Adkins, Bennie G., and Jackson, Katie Lamar, *A Tiger Among Us*, New York, NY: Da Capo Press, 2018.

Albracht, William, and Worf, Marvin, *Abandoned in Hell*, New York, NY: NAL Caliber, 2016.

Allen, Colonel Robert S., *Lucky Forward*, New York, NY: Manor Books, 1965.

Andrade, Dale, *America's Last Vietnam Battle,* Lawrence, KS: University Press of Kansas, 2001.

Andrade, Dale, *Trial by Fire,* New York, NY: Hippocrene Books, 1995.

Anthony, Victor B. and Sexton, Richard R., *The War in Northern Laos, 1954–1973*, Washington, DC: Center for Air Force History, 1993.

Appy, Christian G., *Patriots: The Vietnam War Remembered from All Sides*, New York, NY: Penguin Books, 2004.

Baker, Bob, "Warning Intelligence: The Battle of the Bulge and the NVN Easter Offensive," *American Intelligence Journal 17*, no. 3/4 (1997).

Botkin, Richard, *Ride the Thunder*, Los Angeles, CA: WND Books, 2009.

Canfield, Dr. Roger B., "Vietnam 1972: Is the End Near?" in *Indochina in the Year of the Rat—1972*, Houston, TX: Radix Press, 2019.

Chandler, Lieutenant Colonel Stedman and Robb, Colonel Robert W., *Front-Line Intelligence*, Washington, DC: Infantry Journal Press, 1946.

Collins, Jr., James Lawton, *The Development and Training of the South Vietnamese Army*, Washington, DC: Department of the Army, 1975.

Davidson, Philip B., *Vietnam at War: The History 1946–1975*, Novato, CA: Presidio Press, 1988.

Flynn, LTG Michael T., *The Field of Fight*, New York, NY: St. Martin's Press, 2016.

Ha, Mai Viet, *Steel and Blood: South Vietnamese Armor and the War for Southeast Asia*, Annapolis, MD: Naval Institute Press, 2008.

Hammond, William M., *Reporting Vietnam: Media and Military At War*, Lawrence, KS: University Press of Kansas, 1998.

Hastings, Max, *Vietnam, An Epic Tragedy, 1945–1975*, New York, NY: HarperCollins Publishers, 2018.

Hersh, Seymour M., *The Price of Power: Kissinger in the Nixon White House*, Summit Books, NYC, NY, 1983.

Howard, John D., *First In, Last Out: An American Paratrooper in Vietnam with the 101st and Vietnamese Airborne*, Guilford, CT: Stackpole Books, 2017.

Karnow, Stanley, *Vietnam: A History*, New York, NY: Penguin Book, 1997.

Kissinger, Henry, *Ending the Vietnam War*, New York, NY: Simon and Schuster, 2003.

Koch, Brig. Gen. Oscar W. with Hays, Robert G., *G-2 Intelligence for Patton*, Atglen, PA: Schiffer Military History, 1999.

Kort, Michael G., *The Vietnam War Reexamined*, New York, NY: Cambridge University Press, 2018.

Lam Quang Thi, *The Twenty-Five Year Century: a South Vietnamese General Remembers the Indochina War to the Fall of Saigon,* Denton, TX: University of North Texas Press, 2001.

Lomperis, Timothy J., *The Vietnam War from the Rear Echelon*, Lawrence, KS: University Press of Kansas, 2011.

Long, Lonnie M. and Blackburn, Gary B., *Unlikely Warriors: The Army Security Agency's Secret War in Vietnam 1961–1973*, Bloomington, IN: iUniverse LLC, 2013.

Lanning, Michael Lee (LTC, Ret), *Senseless Secrets: The Failure of U.S. Military Intelligence from George Washington to the Present*, New York, NY: Barnes & Noble Books, 1996.

Lanning, Michael Lee and Cragg, Dan, *Inside the VC and the NVA*, College Station, TX: Texas A&M University Press, 2008.

McKenna, Thomas P., *Kontum: The Battle to Save South Vietnam*, Lexington, KY: The University Press of Kentucky, 2011.

Miller, John Grider, *The Bridge at Dong Ha*, Annapolis, MD: Naval Institute Press, 1989.

Moore, Lt. General H. G., and Galloway, Joseph L., *We Were Soldiers Once … and Young*, New York, NY: Random House Publishing Group, 1992.

Nelson, Charles D. (Major USMC) and Curtis G. Arnold (Lieutenant Colonel, USMC), *U.S. Marines in Vietnam The War That Would Not End 1971–1973*, Washington, DC: Headquarters, U.S. Marine Corps, 1991.

Nguyen, Lien-Hang T., *Hanoi's War*, Chapel Hill, NC: The University of North Carolina Press, 2012.

Palmer, Bruce, *The 25-Year War*, Lexington, KY: University Press of Kentucky, 1984.

Palmer, Dave Richard, *Summons of the Trumpet U.S. – Vietnam in Perspective*, San Rafael, CA: Presidio Press, 1978.

Palmer, Jr. General Bruce, "US Intelligence and Vietnam," CIA Studies in Intelligence, Langley, VA, 1984.

Perret, Geoffrey, *There's a War to be Won*, New York, NY: Random House 1991.

Pike, Douglas, *People's Army of Vietnam*, Novato, CA: Presidio Press, 1986.

Plaster, John L., *SOG: The Secret Wars of America's Commandos in Vietnam*, New York, NY: Dutton Caliber, 1997.

Prados, John, *The Hidden History of the Vietnam War*, Chicago, IL: Elephant Paperback, 1998.

Radvanyi, Janos, *Delusion and Reality: Gambits, Hoaxes, & Diplomatic One-Upmanship in Vietnam*, South Bend, IN: Gateway Editions, Limited, 1978.

Randolph, Stephen R., *Powerful and Brutal Weapons: Nixon, Kissinger, and the Easter Offensive*, Cambridge, MA: Harvard University Press, 2007.

Ricks, Thomas E., *The Generals: American Military Command from World War II to Today*, New York, NY: Penguin Press, 2013.

Ryan, Cornelius, *A Bridge Too Far*, New York, NY: Popular Library, 1974.

Sherman, Stephen (ed), *Indochina in the Year of the Rat—1972*, Houston, TX: RADIX Press, 2019.

Sorley, Lewis, *A Better War*, New York, NY: Harcourt Brace & Company, 1999.

Sorley, Lewis, ed., *The Vietnam War: An Assessment by South Vietnam's Generals*, Lubbock, TX: Texas Tech

Sorley, Lewis, *Thunderbolt*, Bloomington, IN: Indiana University Press, 2008.

Sorley, Lewis, *Vietnam Chronicles: The Abrams Tapes 1968–1972*, Lubbock, TX: Texas Tech University Press, 2004.

Starry, General Donn A., *Armored Combat in Vietnam*, Indianapolis, IN: Arno Press, 1980.

Stearman, William Lloyd, *An American Adventure*, Annapolis, MD: Naval Institute Press, 2012.

Summers, Jr., Harry G., *Historical Atlas of the Vietnam War*, Boston, MA: Houghton Mifflin Company, 1995.

Summers, Jr., Harry G., *On Strategy*, New York, NY: Presidio Press, 1995.

The Military Institute of Vietnam (Merle L. Pribbenow, translator), *Victory in Vietnam*, Lawrence, KS: University of Kansas Press, 2002.

Turley, Col. G. H.,USMC, Ret, *The Easter Offensive*, Novato, CA: Presidio Press, 1985.

Veith, George J., *Black April: The Fall of South Vietnam 1973–1975*, New York, NY: Encounter Books, 2013.

Webb, Willard J. and Poole, Walter S. ed, *The Joint Chiefs of Staff and the War in Vietnam, 1971–1973*, Office of Joint History, Washington, D.C. 2007.

Whitcomb, Darrel D., *The Rescue of BAT 21*, Annapolis, MD: Naval Institute Press, 1998.

Wiest, Andrew, *Vietnam's Forgotten Army*, New York, NY: New York University Press, 2008.

Willbanks, James H., *Abandoning Vietnam*, Lawrence, KS: University Press of Kansas, 2008.

Willbanks, James H., *The Battle of An Loc*, Bloomington, IN: Indiana University Press, 2005.

Young, Stephen, Thompson, W. Scott, and Frizzell, Donaldson D., ed, *The Lessons of Vietnam*, Crane, Russak & Company, Inc., New York, NY: 1977.

Articles

Armstrong, Peter F. C., (Col. USMC, ret), "Capabilities and Intentions," in *Marine Corps Gazette*, September 1986.

Busboom, USAF, Lieutenant Colonel Stanley L., "BAT-21: A Case Study," US Army War College, Carlisle Barracks, PA, 1990.

CIA Intelligence Memorandum, "NVA Infiltration and Unit Deployments Since September 1971," ER IM 72-159, November 1972 (declassified and approved for release on 2016/05/10, C02897838, at author's request).

Correll, John T., "The HCM Trail," *Air Force Magazine*, November 2005.

Glenn, Tom, "Was the Tet Offensive Really a Surprise?" *New York Times*, November 3, 2017.

Gourley, USAR, Captain Scott R., "The Asian Artillery Threat," *Field Artillery Journal*, January–February 1987, Ft. Sill, OK: US Army

Palmer, Jr. Bruce, "How Bright, How Shining? Sheehan's Portrait of Vann and Vietnam," Carlisle Barracks, PA: Parameters, June 1989.

Smith, Richard, "The War That Won't Go Away," *Newsweek*, April 17, 1972.

Smock, Major James E., "0-52-0," *Armor magazine,* September–October 1974, Ft. Knox, KY.

Stars and Stripes, "ARVN Leader in North Vows to Hold Quang Tri (UPI)," April 6, 1972.

Stars and Stripes, "Reds Push Deeper South (AP)," April 4, 1972.

Stars and Stripes, "The Quang Tri Campaign – Sign of Horrors to Come?" April 5, 1972.

The People's Army Newspaper Online (PANO), "1972 Tri Thien Victory changes complexion of battlefield," Sunday, December 28, 2014.

Tourison, Sedgwick, "Military Intelligence in Southeast Asia, 1970–1975," Vietnam Center and Archive, Texas Tech University, presented on April 18, 1996.

Online Sources

FRAC, "Vietnam Helicopter History," www.angelfire.com/ga2/vnhistory/FRAC.html, accessed January 5, 2020.

Howard, John D., "Ragged Edge of Vietnamization," April 10, 2017, https://www.historynet.com/ragged-edge-vietnamization.htm, retrieved February 28, 2021 (also published in June 2016 in *Vietnam magazine*).

Naval Special Warfare Group, Vietnam, "Subject: SEAL Intelligence Support": www.scribd.com/doc/59867803/CIA-Navy-Trade-Craft, accessed September 9, 2019.

People's Army Newspaper, "Bong Lau's Firestorm Forced a Puppet Regiment to Surrender," *People's Army Newspaper Online*, retrieved June 11, 2015.

Shaw, Ian, History of U.S. Drones, https://understandingempire.wordpress.com/2-0-a-brief-history-of-u-s-drones/, accessed June 30, 2015 and August 27, 2019.

Springston, Chuck, "Colin Powell's Vietnam and the Making of an American Statesman," https://www.historynet.com/colin-powell-vietnam-making-american-statesmen.htm, retrieved January 22, 2020 (also published in August 2016 in Vietnam magazine).

Willbanks, James H., "Lam Son 719: South Vietnam invades Laos 1971", April 13, 2017, https://www.historynet.com/south-vietnam-invades-laos-1971.htm, accessed April 4, 2019.

Pamphlets and Studies

304 Division, Volume II, Peoples' Army Publishing House, Hanoi, 1990.

CHECO, "Combat Skyspot," HQ, PACAF, August 9, 1967.

CNA Study 1035, "Defense of Hue and Quang Tri City: The 1972 Invasion of MR-1" Alexandria, VA, 1974. (Copyright © 1974 CNA, www.cna.org. "All Rights Reserved. Reproduction by persons or organizations other than Mr. Baker or for purposes other than as stated, requires CNA's express permission."

Combined Document Exploitation Center (CDEC), "Study of Military Information on the 5th Battalion, 203rd Armored Regiment, NVA Armor Command, on the An Loc Battlefield" CDEC, Republic of Vietnam, July 27, 1972.

MACDI Study 73-01, "The Nguyen-Hue Offensive", Saigon, RVN: US MACV, January 12, 1973.

National Security Agency (NSA), American Cryptology during the Cold War, 1945–1989, CCH-E32-95-03 TCS 54649-54649-95, 1995.

Documents

Directorate of Intelligence, "The Communist Winter–Spring Offensive in South Vietnam, Intelligence Memorandum," (declassified and approved for release on May 11, 2016, C03006503, at author's request). Langley, VA: Central Intelligence Agency, February 7, 1972

First Regional Assistance Command (FRAC) Command History 1972–1973, US Army, Da Nang, RVN, March 28, 1973

General Cao Van Vien, "The U.S. Advisor," Indochina Monographs.

History Branch, Office of the Secretary, Joint Staff, MACV Command History, United States Military Assistance Command Vietnam Jan 1972–March 1973 Volume I.

History Branch, Office of the Secretary, Joint Staff, MACV Command History, United States Military Assistance Command Vietnam Jan 1972–March 1972 Volume II.

Hoang Ngoc Lung, COL, ARVN, ACSI, JGS, 31 Oct 76, "Indochina Refugee Authored Monograph Program," OAD-CR-155.

Hoang Ngoc Lung, Indochina Refugee Authored Monograph Program, OAD-CR-155, October 1976.

Kroesen, Major General Frederick J., "Quang Tri: The Lost Province: An Identification of the Factors Which Culminated in the Loss of a Major Campaign to the Forces of North Vietnam in the Spring of 1972," U.S. Army War College Paper, 16 January 1974.

Lee, Thomas H., "Military Intelligence Operations and the Easter Offensive," USA Center of Military History document in the Virtual Vietnam Archive, Texas Tech University, TX: September 1990.

Metcalf, Colonel Donald J. "Why Did The Defense of Quang Tri Province, SVN Collapse?" Student Essay, Carlisle Barracks, PA: US Army War College, 1972.

Operational Report on Lesson Learned, 525th Military Intelligence Group, Period Ending 30 April 1972, RCS CSFOR-65 (R3) (U), dated May 18, 1972.

OPORD 215, After Action Report COUNTDOWN, Vol. I, June 4, 1973.

Wright, Joe, "Hanoi Week—Ending 4 April," 2. FCO 15/1647, National Archives, Kew, U.K.

Endnotes

Introduction

1   Geoffrey Perret, *There's a War to be Won*, Random House, 1991, p.399.

Chapter 4

1   Lewis Sorley, editor and concluding essays, *The Vietnam War: An Assessment by South Vietnam's Generals*, Lubbock, TX: Texas Tech University Press, 2010, p.343 (hereafter cited as Sorley, *The Vietnam War*).

2   Roy Perez Benavidez and John R. Craig, *Medal of Honor: One Man's Journey from Poverty and Prejudice*, Lincoln, NB: Potomac Press, 1999, p.77.

3   Andrew R. Finlayson, *Rice Paddy Recon: A Marine Officer's Second Tour in Vietnam, 1968–1970*, Jefferson, NC: MacFarland & Company, 2014, p.37.

4   Bennie G. Adkins, *A Tiger Among Us: A Story of Valor in Vietnam's A Shau Valley*, NYC, NY: De Capo Press, 2018, p.166 (hereafter cited as Adkins and Jackson, *A Tiger Among Us*).

5   Eric Smith, *Not By The Book*, New York, NY: Ivy Books, 1993, p.100.

6   Lewis Sorley, *Vietnam Chronicles: The Abrams Tapes 1968–1972*, Lubbock, TX: Texas Tech University Press, 2004, p.801 (hereafter cited as Sorley, *The Abrams Tapes*).

7   Phil Tompkins, *Ruff Puff*, 2010, Chapter 17.

Chapter 5

1   Lewis Sorley, *A Better War*, New York, NY: Harcourt Brace & Company, 1999, p.230 (hereafter cited as Sorley, *A Better War*).

2   Max Hastings, *Vietnam: An Epic Tragedy, 1945–1975*, New York, NY: HarperCollins Publishers, 2018, p.574.

3   *Ibid.*, p.582.

4   Seymour M. Hersh, *The Price of Power: Kissinger in the Nixon White House*, New York, NY: Summit Books, 1983, p.307 (hereafter cited as Hersh, *The Price of Power*).

5   *Ibid.*, p.308.

6   Lam Quang Thi, *The Twenty-Five Year Century: A South Vietnamese General Remembers the Indochina War to the Fall of Saigon*, Denton, TX: University of North Texas Press, 2001, p.264 (hereafter cited as Thi, *The Twenty-Five Year Century*).

7   Nguyen Duy Hinh, *Indochina Monographs, Lam Son 719*, ADA324683, pdf, Washington, DC: US Army Center of Military History, 1979, p.168.

8   Stephen R. Randolph, *Powerful and Brutal Weapons: Nixon, Kissinger, and the Easter Offensive*, Cambridge, MA: Harvard University Press, 2007, pp.49–50 (hereafter cited as Randolph, *Powerful and Brutal Weapons*).

9   The Military Institute of Vietnam (Merle L. Pribbenow, translator), *Victory in Vietnam*, Lawrence, KS: University of Kansas Press, 2002, p.264 (hereafter cited as Pribbenow, *Victory in Vietnam*).

10 Bernard C. Nalty, *The War Against Trucks: Aerial Interdiction in Southern Laos, 1968–1972*, ADA476352, pdf, Washington, DC: Air Force History and Museums Program, 2005, p.174.

11 William M. Hammond, *Reporting Vietnam: Media and Military At War*, Lawrence, KS: University Press of Kansas, 1998, p.249 (hereafter cited as Hammond, *Reporting Vietnam*).

12 *Ibid.*, p.245.

13 James H. Willbanks, *Abandoning Vietnam*, Lawrence, KS: University Press of Kansas, 2008, pp.114–15 (hereafter cited as Willbanks, *Abandoning Vietnam*).

14 Sorley, *The Abrams Tapes*, p.570

15 James H. Willbanks, "*Lam Son 719*: South Vietnam invades Laos 1971," April 13, 2017, HistoryNet, May 2014: https://www.historynet.com/south-vietnam-invades-laos-1971.htm, accessed April 4, 2019.

16 Sorley, *The Vietnam War*, p.609.

17 *Ibid.*

18 Victor B. Anthony and Richard R. Sexton, *The War in Northern Laos, 1954–1973*, Washington, DC: Center for Air Force History, 1993, p.353.

19 Pribbenow, *Victory in Vietnam*, p.287.

20 Dr. Roger B. Canfield, "Vietnam 1972: Is the End Near?" in Stephen Sherman, *Indochina in the Year of the Rat—1972*, Houston, TX: Radix Press, 2019, p.131.

Chapter 6

1   Douglas Pike, *People's Army of Vietnam*, Novato, CA: Presidio Press, 1986, p.229 (hereafter cited as Pike, *People's Army of Vietnam*).

2   Lien-Hang T. Nguyen, *Hanoi's War*, Chapel Hill, NC: The University of North Carolina Press, 2012, p.234.

3   Pike, *People's Army of Vietnam*, pp.239–240.

4   Randolph, *Powerful and Brutal Weapons*, p.22.

5   Sorley, *A Better War*, p.231.

6   Michael Lee Lanning and Dan Cragg, *Inside the VC and the NVA*, College Station, TX: Texas A&M University Press, 2008, p.201.

7   *Ibid.*, 197.

8   Harry G. Summers, *On Strategy*, New York: Presidio Press, 1995, p.134 (hereafter cited as Summers, *On Strategy*).

9   *Ibid.*, p.135.

10 Email with G. Duane Whitman and author, April 12, 2015.

11 William Albracht and Marvin Worf, *Abandoned in Hell*, New York: NAL Caliber, 2016, p.221 (hereafter cited as Albracht and Worf, *Abandoned in Hell*).

12 CNA Study 1035, "Defense of Hue and Quang Tri City: The 1972 Invasion of MR-1" Alexandria, VA, 1974 (Copyright © 1974 CNA, www.cna.org. All Rights Reserved. Reproduction by persons or organizations other than Mr. Baker or for purposes other than as stated, requires CNA's express permission.) (hereafter cited as CNA Study 1035).

13 CNA Study 1035, p.40.

14 Albracht and Worf, *Abandoned in Hell*, p.207.

15 Sorley, *The Abrams Tapes*, pp.769–70.

16 *Ibid.*, pp.767–68.

17 Philip B. Davidson, *Vietnam at War: The History 1946–1975*, Novato, CA: Presidio Press, 1988, p.675 (hereafter cited as Davidson, *Vietnam at War*).

18   Pribbenow, *Victory in Vietnam*, p.283.

19   Randolph, *Powerful and Brutal Weapons*, p.31.

20   Colonel Peter F. C. Armstrong (USMC, ret.), "Capabilities and Intentions," in *Marine Corps Gazette*, September 1986, pp.45–46 (hereafter cited as Armstrong, "Capabilities and Intentions").

21   *Ibid.*, p.46.

22   *Ibid.*

23   Pribbenow, *Victory in Vietnam,* p.290.

24   Major Charles D. Nelson (USMC) and Lieutenant Colonel Curtis G. Arnold (USMC), *US Marines in Vietnam: The War That Would Not End 1971–1973*, Washington, DC: Headquarters, US Marine Corps, 1991, p.33 (hereafter cited as Nelson and Arnold, *US Marines in Vietnam, 1971–1973*).

25   Sorley, *The Abrams Tapes*, p.812.

26   Pribbenow, *Victory in Vietnam*, p.289.

27   Sorley, *The Abrams Tapes*, pp.628–29.

28   *Ibid.*, p.808.

29   Colonel G. H. Turley (USMC, Ret.), *The Easter Offensive*, Novato, CA: Presidio Press, 1985, p.49 (hereafter cited as Turley, *The Easter Offensive*).

30   Pribbenow, *Victory in Vietnam*, p.265.

31   Captain Scott R. Gourley, USAR, "The Asian Artillery Threat," *Field Artillery Journal*, January–February 1987, Ft. Sill, OK: US Army Field Artillery School, p.14 (hereafter cited as Gourley, "The Asian Artillery Threat").

32   Sorley, *The Abrams Tapes*, p.756.

33   Pribbenow, *Victory in Vietnam*, p.290.

34   Bruce Palmer, *The 25-Year War*, Lexington, KY: University Press of Kentucky, 1984, p.120 (hereafter cited as Palmer, *The 25-Year War*).

35   Henry Kissinger, *Ending the Vietnam War*, New York: Simon and Schuster, 2003, pp.233–34.

36   Dave Richard Palmer, *Summons of the Trumpet: US–Vietnam in Perspective*, San Rafael, CA: Presidio Press, 1978, p.249.

37   Richard Smith, "The War That Won't Go Away," in *Newsweek*, April 17, 1972, pp.16–21 (hereafter cited as Smith, "The War That Won't Go Away").

38   First Regional Assistance Command (FRAC) *Command History* 1972–1973, US Army, Da Nang, RVN, March 28, 1973, p.5 (hereafter cited as FRAC *Command History* 1972–1973).

39   Hammond, *Reporting Vietnam*, p.256.

40   Thi, *The Twenty-Five Year Century*, p.255.

Chapter 7

1   Nelson and Arnold, *US Marines in Vietnam, 1971–1973*, p.38.

2   Major General Frederick J. Kroesen, "Quang Tri, The Lost Province," Student Essay, Carlisle Barracks, PA: US Army War College, 1974, p.5 (hereafter cited as Kroesen, "Quang Tri, The Lost Province").

3   Sorley, *The Vietnam War*, p.359

4   CNA Study 1035, p.6.

5   Palmer, *The 25-Year War*, p.125.

6   Colonel Donald J. Metcalf, "Why Did the Defense of Quang Tri Province, SVN Collapse?" Student Essay, Carlisle Barracks, PA: US Army War College, 1972, pp.2–3 (hereafter cited as Metcalf, "Why Did The Defense of Quang Tri Province, SVN Collapse").

7   Thomas H. Lee, "Military Intelligence Operations and the Easter Offensive," USA Center of Military History document in the Virtual Vietnam Archive, Texas Tech University, TX: September 1990, pp.30–31 (hereafter cited as Lee, "MI Operations and the Easter Offensive").

8   Kroesen, "Quang Tri, The Lost Province," p.2.

9   Thomas P. McKenna, *Kontum: The Battle to Save South Vietnam*, Lexington, KY: The University Press of Kentucky, 2011, p.63 (hereafter cited as McKenna, *Kontum*).

10 Major James E. Smock, "0-52-0," *Armor magazine*, September–October 1974, Ft. Knox, KY, p.32.

11 Ha, Mai Viet, *Steel and Blood: South Vietnamese Armor and the War for Southeast Asia*, Annapolis, MD: Naval Institute Press, 2008, p.120 (hereafter cited as Ha, *Steel and Blood*).

12 Pribbenow, *Victory in Vietnam*, p.290.

13 Sorley, *A Better War*, pp.283–84.

14 Sorley, *The Abrams Tapes*, p.636.

15 *Ibid.*, p.517.

16 Sorley, *The Vietnam War*, p.613.

17 *Ibid.*, 806.

18 Nelson and Arnold, *US Marines in Vietnam*, p.58.

19 Turley, *The Easter Offensive*, pp.87–89.

20 Hersh, The Price of Power, p.506.

Chapter 8

1   Directorate of Intelligence, "The Communist Winter–Spring Offensive in South Vietnam, Intelligence Memorandum," (declassified and approved for release on May 11, 2016, C03006503, at author's request). Langley, VA: Central Intelligence Agency, February 7, 1972, p.7 (hereafter referred to as CIA, "The Communist Winter–Spring Offensive").

2   *Ibid.*, p.798.

3   Hoang Ngoc Lung, Indochina Refugee Authored Monograph Program, *OAD-CR-155*, October 1976, p.157. (Colonel Lung was an ARVN JGS Assistance J-2.)

4   Smith, "The War That Won't Go Away," p.20.

5   Kroesen, "Quang Tri: The Lost Province," p.5.

6   Bob Baker, "Warning Intelligence: The Battle of the Bulge and the NVN Easter Offensive," *American Intelligence Journal*, 17, no. 3/4 (1997).

7   Lee, "MI Operations and the Easter Offensive," pp.30–31.

8   Tom Glenn, "Was the Tet Offensive Really a Surprise?" *New York Times*, November 3, 2017.

9   Lewis Sorley, *Thunderbolt*, Bloomington, IN: Indiana University Press, 2008, pp.266–67.

10 Email with Timothy Lomperis and author, September 7, 2017.

11 Email from Robert Destatte to author, August 25, 2019.

12 CIA, "The Communist Winter–Spring Offensive," pp.6–7

13 Vern Dreiger, phone interview with author, November 8, 2018.

14 Sorley, *The Abrams Tapes*, pp.788–89.

15 General Donn A. Starry, *Armored Combat in Vietnam*, Indianapolis, IN: Arno Press, 1980, p.201 (hereafter cited as Starry, *Armored Combat in Vietnam*).

16 Sorley, *The Abrams Tapes*, p.589.

17 Pribbenow, *Victory in Vietnam*, p.289.

18 *The People's Army Newspaper Online* (PANO), "1972 Tri Thien Victory changes complexion of battlefield," Sunday, December 28, 2014.

19 Turley, *The Easter Offensive*, pp.69–70.

20 Sorley, *The Vietnam War*, p.359.

21 Nelson and Arnold, *US Marines in Vietnam, 1971–1973*, p.34.

22 LTC (Ret) Michael Lee Lanning, *Senseless Secrets: The Failure of U.S. Military Intelligence from George Washington to the Present*, New York, NY: Barnes & Noble Books, 1996, p.266.

23 Colonel Robert S. Allen, *Lucky Forward*, New York, NY: Manor Books, 1965, p.157.

24 Nelson and Arnold, *US Marines in Vietnam*, p.48.

25 Randolph, *Powerful and Brutal Weapons*, p.64. (The reference is on p.354 of the book, reference #4, "FRAC 311215Z Mar 72, 'Quang Tri Situation,' CMH/Abrams Messages.")

26 Kroesen, "Quang Tri: The Lost Province," p.7.

27 Randolph, *Powerful and Brutal Weapons*, pp.64–65.

28 CNA Study 1035, p.49.

29 Randolph, *Powerful and Brutal Weapons*, p.65. (The reference cited is on p. 354 of the book, reference #6, COMUSMACV 011400ZApr 72, "COMUSMACV Personal Appraisal of the Enemy and Friendly Situation.")

Chapter 9

1 Sorley, *The Abrams Tapes*, pp.618–19.

2 Hammond, *Reporting Vietnam*, p.254.

3 *Ibid.* (Quoted from MFR, sub: Briefing of March 22, 1971, Kissinger Briefing Notes.)

4 History Branch, Office of the Secretary, Joint Staff, MACV, *Command History, United States Military Assistance Command Vietnam Jan 1972–March 1973 Volume I*, C-28 (hereafter cited as Jan 1972–Mar 1973 *MACV Command History I*).

5 Willard J. Webb and Walter S. Poole, eds., *The Joint Chiefs of Staff and the War in Vietnam, 1971–1973*, Office of Joint History, Washington, DC, 2007, p.140 (hereafter cited as Webb and Poole, *JCS*).

6 *Ibid.*, p.141.

7 *Ibid.*, p.365.

8 *Ibid.*, p.140.

9 Hammond, *Reporting Vietnam*, p.273.

10 *Ibid.*, p.254.

11 John D. Howard, "Ragged Edge of Vietnamization," April 10, 2017, https://www.historynet.com/ragged-edge-vietnamization.htm, retrieved June 17, 2019 (also published in June 2016 in *Vietnam* magazine).

12 Webb and Poole, *JCS*, p.365.

13 *Ibid.*

14 Turley, *The Easter Offensive*, p.60.

15 Andrew Wiest, *Vietnam's Forgotten Army*, New York, NY: New York University Press, 2008, p.249 (hereafter cited as Wiest, *Vietnam's Forgotten Army*).

16 Jan 1972–Mar 1973 *MACV Command History I*.

17 Pike, *People's Army of Vietnam*, p.244.

18 Nelson and Arnold, *US Marines in Vietnam, 1971–1973*, p.66.

19 John L. Plaster, *SOG: The Secret Wars of America's Commandos in Vietnam*, New York, NY: Dutton Caliber, 1997, p.304 (hereafter cited as Plaster, *SOG: The Secret Wars*).

20 McKenna, *Kontum*, p.104.

21 *Ibid.*, p.xii.

22 Hammond, *Reporting Vietnam*, p.273.

23 Timothy J. Lomperis, *The Vietnam War from the Rear Echelon*, Lawrence, KS: University Press of Kansas, 2011, p.59 (hereafter cited as Lomperis, *The Vietnam War from the Rear Echelon*).

24 *Ibid.*

25 Sorley, *The Vietnam War*, p.360.

26 Dale Andrade, *America's Last Vietnam Battle*, Lawrence, KS: University Press of Kansas, 2001, 351 (hereafter cited as Andrade, *America's Last Vietnam Battle*).

27 James H. Willbanks, *The Battle of An Loc*, Bloomington, IN: Indiana University Press, 2005, p.94 (hereafter cited as Willbanks, *An Loc*).

28 *Ibid.*, p.156.

29 *Ibid.*

30 *Ibid.*

31 Lieutenant General H. G. Moore and Joseph L. Galloway, *We Were Soldiers Once . . . and Young*, New York, NY: Random House Publishing Group, 1992, p.171.

32 Sorley, *The Abrams Tapes*, p.789.

33 Thi, *The Twenty-Five Year Century*, p.257.

34 Harry G. Summers, Jr., *Historical Atlas of the Vietnam War*, Boston, MA: Houghton Mifflin Company, 1995, p.168.

35 Adkins and Jackson, *A Tiger Among Us*, p.2.

36 *Ibid.*, p.28.

37 *Ibid.*

38 *Ibid.*, p.101.

39 *Ibid.*, p.104.

40 *Ibid.*, pp.76–79.

41 *Ibid.*, pp.80–83.

42 *Ibid.*

Chapter 10

1   Lee, "MI Operations and the Easter Offensive," p.6.

2   Pribbenow, *Victory in Vietnam*, p.290.

3   *Ibid.*, pp.265–66.

4   *Ibid.*, pp.286–87.

5   Ha, *Steel and Blood*, p.119.

6   *Ibid.*, p.393, endnote #6.

7   CIA, "The Communist Winter–Spring Offensive," p.7.

8   *Ibid.*, pp.359–360.

9   CIA Intelligence Memorandum, "NVA Infiltration and Unit Deployments Since September 1971," ER IM 72-159, November 1972 (declassified and approved for release on May 10, 2016, C02897838, at author's request), November 1972, 11.

10 Lomperis, *The Vietnam War from the Rear Echelon*, p.59.

11 Gourley, "The Asian Artillery Threat," p.14.

12 Sorley, *The Vietnam War*, p.655.

13 Combined Document Exploitation Center (CDEC), "Study of Military Information on the 5th Battalion, 203rd Armored Regiment, NVA Armor Command, on the An Loc Battlefield" CDEC, Republic of Vietnam, July 27, 1972.

14 Van Kiet was decorated with the USN's Navy Cross in assisting USN SEAL Lieutenant Tom Norris in rescuing USAF Lieutenant Colonel Icel Hambelton and Lieutenant Mark Clark, who had been separately shot down.

Chapter 11

1   Wiest, *Vietnam's Forgotten Army*, p.234.
2   Stephen Young, W. Scott Thompson, and Donaldson D. Frizzell, ed, *The Lessons of Vietnam*, Crane, Russak & Company, Inc., New York, NY: 1977, 227 (hereafter cited as Thompson and Frizzell, *The Lessons of Vietnam*).
3   Palmer, *The 25-Year War*, p.120.
4   Wiest, *Vietnam's Forgotten Army*, pp.237, 238, 241.
5   Thi, *The Twenty-Five Year Century*, p.266.
6   Wiest (interview of Team 155's commander), *Vietnam's Forgotten Army*, p.237.
7   Kroesen, "Quang Tri: The Lost Province," p.2.
8   James Lawton Collins, Jr., *The Development and Training of the South Vietnamese Army*, Washington, DC: Department of the Army, 1975, pp.90–91.
9   Willard J. Web and Walter S. Poole, *The Joint Chiefs of Staff and the War in Vietnam 1971-1973*, Washington, DC: Office of Joint History, 2007, p.212.
10 Wiest, *Vietnam's Forgotten Army*, p.235.
11 Hammond, *Reporting Vietnam*, p.266.
12 Kroesen, "Quang Tri, The Lost Province," p.5.
13 John D. Howard, *First In, Last Out: An American Paratrooper in Vietnam with the 101st and Vietnamese Airborne*, Guilford, CT: Stackpole Books, 2017, p.127 (hereafter cited as Howard, *First In, Last Out*).
14 *Ibid.*, p.128.
15 Palmer, *The 25-Year War*, pp.118–19.
16 Email between General Boomer (USMC, ret) and author on May 2, 2021.
17 Turley, *The Easter Offensive*, p.188.

Chapter 12

1   Wiest, *Vietnam's Forgotten Army*, p.254.
2   "Bong Lau's Firestorm Forced a Puppet Regiment to Surrender," *People's Army Newspaper Online*, retrieved, June 11, 2015.
3   Wiest, *Vietnam's Forgotten Army*, p.259.
4   Wiest, *Vietnam's Forgotten Army*, p.254.
5   Wiest, *Vietnam's Forgotten Army*, p.238 (Giai taped interview).
6   Wiest, *Vietnam's Forgotten Army*, p.252.
7   Andrade, *America's Last Vietnam Battle*, p.89.
8   Sorley, *The Abrams Tapes*, pp.806–07.
9   Palmer, *The 25-Year War*, p.119.
10 Haig memo, p.2.
11 McKenna, *Kontum*, p.54.
12 *Ibid.*, p.147.
13 Starry, *Armored Combat in Vietnam*, p.208 (footnote).
14 Sorley, *The Abrams Tapes*, p.814.
15 FRAC *Command History* 1972–1973, p.13.
16 Kroesen, "Quang Tri, The Lost Province," p.8.
17 *Ibid.*, 9.
18 McKenna, *Kontum*, p.xii.
19 *Ibid.*, p.66.
20 Willbanks, *An Loc*, p.156.

21 "ARVN Leader in North Vows to Hold Quang Tri (UPI)," *Stars and Stripes*, April 6, 1972, p.1.

22 "Reds Push Deeper South (AP), *Stars and Stripes*, April 4, 1972, pp.1 and 24.

23 Thi, *The Twenty-Five Year Century*, pp.266–67.

24 Wiest, *Vietnam's Forgotten Army*, p.245.

25 Nelson and Arnold, *US Marines in Vietnam*, p.38.

26 CHECO/Corona, "The 1972 Invasion of Military Region I: Fall of Quang Tri and Defense of Hue," HQ, PACAF, March 15, 1973, p.11.

27 Nelson and Arnold, *US Marines in Vietnam*, p.32.

28 Sorley, *The Abrams Tapes*, p.804.

29 Randolph, *Powerful and Brutal Weapons*, p.66.

30 Ha, *Steel and Blood*, p.122.

31 www.angelfire.com/ga2/vnhistory/FRAC.html, accessed January 5, 2020. "That afternoon, LTC Camper and Major Brown were flown to 3rd Division headquarters. Camper reported to Brigadier General Giai and told him about LTC Dinh. General Giai did not believe the advisor. He and the Colonel Dinh had been personal friends. Instead, he accused Camper of cowardice and desertion in the face of the enemy. (22) The next day, Radio Hanoi broadcast an appeal from Dinh for all ARVN soldiers to lay down their arms and rally to the North Vietnamese. (23) When General Giai heard this, he personally went to LTC Camper and apologized. (24) Dave Brookbank also heard the broadcast. He was later told by ARVN officers that most of the captured soldiers of the 56th Regiment were marched northwest to a place called the "Rockpile" and executed. (25)"

32 Turley, *The Easter Offensive*, pp.311–12.

33 Howard, *First In, Last Out*, p.190.

34 Davidson, *Vietnam at War*, p.681.

35 Sorley, *The Vietnam War*, pp.613–14.

36 McKenna, *Kontum*, 124.

37 Sorley, *The Abrams Tapes*, p.812.

38 Sorley, *A Better War*, p.339.

Chapter 13

1 Andrade, *America's Last Vietnam Battle*, p.64.

2 Nelson and Arnold, *US Marines in Vietnam, 1971–1973*, p.60 footnote.

3 FRAC *Command History* 1972–1973, p.13.

4 John Grider Miller, *The Bridge at Dong Ha*, Annapolis, MD: Naval Institute Press, 1989, p.75 (hereafter cited as Miller, *The Bridge at Dong Ha*).

5 Starry, *Armored Combat in Vietnam*, p.208.

6 Ha, *Steel and Blood*, p.135.

7 Nelson and Arnold, *US Marines in Vietnam*, p.65.

8 Dale Andrade, *Trial by Fire*, New York, NY: Hippocrene Books, 1995, p.93.

9 Miller, *The Bridge at Dong Ha*, p.49.

10 Sorley, *The Vietnam War*, p.619.

11 Andrade, *America's Last Vietnam Battle*, p.75.

12 *Ibid.*, p.505 (citation #25).

13 http://www.angelfire.com/ga2/vnhistory/FRAC.html, accessed August 19, 2019. Citation references: 28. Message/DTG 021400Z From I-DASC Da Nang to 7AF Subj: BDA (Bomb Damage Assessment) Report of 0600H-2000H, April 2, 1972. The strike coordinates were YD 24136108, exactly on the north end of the bridge. National Archives, Suitland, Maryland and 29. 3rd Division TOC Log, April 2, 1972, items 54 and 55.

14 CHECO, "Combat Skyspot," HQ, PACAF, August 9, 1967, p.23 (hereafter cited as "Combat Skyspot").

15 History Branch, Office of the Secretary, Joint Staff, *MACV Command History, United States Military Assistance Command Vietnam Jan 1972–March 1972 Volume II, L-13* (hereafter cited as *Jan 1972–Mar 1973 MACV Command History II*).

16 http://www.angelfire.com/ga2/vnhistory/FRAC.html, accessed August 19, 2019. Chapter 3, citation reference Number 30. Fulghum, Maitland, p.139. See also Miller, John G., *The Bridge at Dong Ha*, Naval Institute Press, Annapolis, MD, 1989, which well describes this operation for which CAPT Ripley received the Navy Cross.

17 Nelson and Arnold, *US Marines in Vietnam*, p.61.

18 Richard Botkin, *Ride the Thunder*, Los Angeles, CA: WND Books, 2009, p.263.

19 Randolph, *Powerful and Brutal Weapons*, p.65.

20 Hansen, *USS Buchanan*, email August 6, 2018.

21 *Ibid.*, email March 15, 2016.

22 Sorley, *The Abrams Tapes*, p.807.

23 *Ibid.*, p.117.

24 *Ibid.*, p.117.

25 *Ibid.*, p.115.

26 Randolph, *Powerful and Brutal Weapons*, p.69.

27 *Ibid.*, p.71.

28 Kroesen, "Quang Tri, The Lost Province," p.8.

29 FRAC *Command History* 1972–73, p.14.

30 CNA Study 1035, p.21.

31 *Ibid.*, p.22.

32 Randolph, *Powerful and Brutal Weapons*, p.69.

Chapter 14

1 Lieutenant Colonel Stanley L. Busboom, USAF, "BAT-21: A Case Study," US Army War College, Carlisle Barracks, PA, 10 (hereafter cited as Busboom, "BAT-21").

2 *Ibid.*, p.13.

3 *Ibid.*, p.15.

4 *Ibid.*

5 Randolph, *Powerful and Brutal Weapons*, p.67.

6 *Ibid.*, p.68.

7 Plaster, *SOG: The Secret Wars,* p.255.

8 Darrel D. Whitcomb, *The Rescue of BAT 21*, Annapolis, MD: Naval Institute Press, 1998, p.43.

Chapter 15

1 MACDI Study 73-01, "The Nguyen-Hue Offensive," Saigon, RVN: US MACV, January 12, 1973.

2 Sorley, *The Abrams Tapes*, p.811.

3 Sorley, *A Better War*, p.323. (The referenced footnote states "that Luat had previously been a problem as commander of the 17th Armored Squadron during *Lam Son 719*.)

Chapter 16

1   Armstrong, "Capabilities and Intentions," p.43.
2   CNA Study 1035, p.6.
3   Andrade, *America's Last Vietnam Battle*, pp.8–9.
4   Directorate of Intelligence, "Communist Winter–Spring Offensive."
5   *Ibid.*, p.1.
6   *Ibid.*, p.3.
7   *Ibid.*, p.4.
8   Lewis Sorley, *The Abrams Tapes* p.801.
9   Andrade, *America's Last Vietnam Battle*, p.6.
10 Armstrong, "Capabilities and Intentions," p.44.
11 *Ibid.*, p.45.
12 *Ibid.*, p.46.
13 Hersh, *The Price of Power*, p.503.
14 Armstrong, "Capabilities and Intentions," p.47.
15 *Ibid.*
16 *Ibid.*, p.40.
17 *Ibid.*, p.42.
18 Davidson, *Vietnam at War*, p.675.
19 *Ibid.*
20 Army Signals Intelligence in Vietnam, James L. Gilbert, US INSCOM, 2003, p.102: https://babel.hathitrust.org/cgi/pt?id=uiug.30112064013359;view=1up;seq=3The Most Secret War,
21 National Security Agency (NSA), *American Cryptology during the Cold War, 1945-1989*, CCH-E32-95-03 TCS 54649-54649-95, 1995, p.583 (hereafter cited as NSA, *American Cryptology during the Cold War*).
22 John Prados, *The Hidden History of the Vietnam War*, Chicago, IL: Elephant Paperback, 1998, p.203 (hereafter cited as Prados, *Hidden History*).
23 Lonnie M. Long and Gary B. Blackburn, *Unlikely Warriors: The Army Security Agency's Secret War in Vietnam 1961-1973*, Bloomington, IN: iUniverse LLC, 2013, 425 (hereafter cited as Long and Blackburn, *Unlikely Warriors*).
24 Ibid, 417.
25 Sorley, *The Abrams Tapes*, p.749.
26 Ian Shaw, "History of U.S. Drones," https://understandingempire.wordpress.com/2-0-a-brief-history-of-u-s-drones/, accessed June 30, 2015 and August 27, 2019.
27 John T. Correll, "The HCM Trail," *Air Force Magazine*, November 2005, p.67.
28 NSA, *American Cryptology during the Cold War*, pp.111–116, p.583.
29 Joe Wright, "Hanoi Week-Ending 4 April," 2. FCO 15/1647, National Archives, Kew, UK.

Chapter 17

1   Sorley, *The Abrams Tapes*, pp.798–99.
2   Sorley, *The Abrams Tapes*, p.817.
3   *Ibid.*, p.814.
4   Pacific *Stars and Stripes*, "The Quang Tri Campaign—Sign of Horrors to Come?" April 5, 1972, p.7.
5   Lee, "MI Operations and the Easter Offensive," p.6.
6   *Ibid.*, p.5.

7   Memo from John Oseth to Jeff Clarke, "Assessment of Screenplay Easter Offensive": https://www.vietnam.ttu.edu/ Number: 24992117006, accessed September 2, 2019, 6 (hereafter cited as, Oseth, "Assessment").

8   Sorley, *The Abrams Tapes,* p.249.

9   Lieutenant Colonel Stedman Chandler and Colonel Robert W. Robb, *Front-Line Intelligence,* Washington, DC: Infantry Journal Press, 1946, p.15.

10 Lomperis, *The Vietnam War from the Rear Echelon,* p.76.

11 *Ibid.,* p.70.

12 *Ibid.,* p.72.

13 *Ibid.,* p.75.

14 Sorley, *A Better War,* p.340.

15 Oseth, "Assessment," p.6.

16 Sorley, *The Abrams Tapes,* p.803.

17 Naval Special Warfare Group, Vietnam, "Subject: SEAL Intelligence Support": www.scribd.com/doc/59867803/CIA-Navy-Trade-Craft, accessed September 9, 2019.

Chapter 18

1   Long and Blackburn *Unlikely Warriors,* p.329.

2   Starry, *Armored Combat in Vietnam,* p.202.

3   Wiest, *Vietnam's Forgotten Army,* p.235.

4   *304 Division, Volume II,* Peoples' Army Publishing House, Hanoi, 1990, 175.

5   Willbanks, *An Loc,* p.34.

6   Lomperis, *The Vietnam War from the Rear Echelon,* p.70.

Chapter 19

1   Armstrong, "Capabilities and Intentions," p.44.

2   Palmer, *The 25-Year War,* p.117.

3   Sorley, *The Abrams Tapes,* p.734.

4   Sorley, *The Abrams Tapes,* p.770.

5   Operational Report on Lesson Learned, 525th Military Intelligence Group, Period Ending April 30, 1972, RCS CSFOR-65 (R3) (U), dated May 18, 1972, p.3.

6   Lee, "MI Operations and the Easter Offensive," p.24.

7   Sorley, *The Abrams Tapes,* p.798.

8   Operational Report Lessons Learned, 525th MI Group, period Ending 30 April 1972, RCS CSFOR-65 (R3) (U)

9   Plaster, *SOG: The Secret Wars,* p.304.

10 *Ibid.,* 254.

11 Sorley, *The Abrams Tapes,* p.783.

12 Brigadier General Oscar W. Koch with Robert G. Hays, *G-2 Intelligence for Patton,* Atglen, PA: Schiffer Military History, 1999, p.132 (hereafter cited as Koch, *G-2 Intelligence*).

13 McKenna, *Kontum,* p.48.

14 Randolph, *Powerful and Brutal Weapons,* p.64.

15 Sorley, *The Abrams Tapes,* p.814.

16 Major Charles D. Nelson (USMC) and Lieutenant Colonel Curtis G. Arnold (USMC), *US Marines in Vietnam: The War That Would Not End 1971–1973,* Washington, DC: Headquarters,

US Marine Corps, 1991, p.48 (hereafter cited as Nelson and Arnold, *US Marines in Vietnam, 1971–1973*).

17 Lee, "MI Operations and the Easter Offensive," p.32.

18 Koch, *G-2 Intelligence*, p.113.

19 General Bruce Palmer, Jr., "Studies in Intelligence—US Intelligence and Vietnam," Endnote #37, p.120 (hereafter cited as Palmer, "Studies in Intelligence").

20 Hoang Ngoc Lung, COL, ARVN, ACSI, JGS, October 31, 1976, "Indochina Refugee Authored Monograph Program," OAD-CR-155, p.157.

21 General Cao Van Vien, "The U.S. Advisor," Indochina Monographs, p.23.

22 OPORD 215, After Action Report COUNTDOWN, Vol. I, June 4, 1973, pp.12–13.

Chapter 20

1 Lee, "MI Operations and the Easter Offensive," p.30.

2 Bob Baker, "Warning Intelligence: The Battle of the Bulge and the NVN Easter Offensive," *American Intelligence Journal*, 17, no. 3/4 (1997), pp.71–79.

3 NSA, *American Cryptology during the Cold War*, pp.111–16, 583.

4 Sorley, *The Abrams Tapes*, p.638.

5 From a letter to General Bruce Palmer, Jr., from Lieutenant General Phillip B. Davidson, Jr., dated July 18, 1973, and his response dated August 24, 1973, concerning the Assistant Secretary of Defense for Intelligence (ASDI)-convened committee to compile the intelligence lessons learned in Vietnam at the major force level.

6 General Bruce Palmer, Jr., "How Bright, How Shining? Sheehan's Portrait of Vann and Vietnam," Carlisle Barracks, PA: Parameters, June 1989, p.22 (hereafter referred to as Palmer, "How Bright....").

7 Wiest, *Vietnam's Forgotten Army*, p.211.

8 Palmer, "How Bright…," p.22.

9 Howard, *First In, Last Out*, p.28.

10 McKenna, *Kontum*, p.48.

11 Davidson, *Vietnam at War*, p.639.

12 Oseth, "Assessment," p.6.

13 Thi, *The Twenty-Five Year Century*, pp.273–74.

14 Andrade, *America's Last Vietnam Battle*, pp.64–65.

15 McKenna, *Kontum*, p.129.

16 Christian G. Appy, *Patriots: The Vietnam War Remembered from All Sides*, New York, NY: Penguin Books, 2004, pp.4–5.

17 Willbanks, *An Loc*, p.46.

18 Andrade, *America's Last Vietnam Battle*, p.6.

19 Prados, *Hidden History*, p.262.

20 Armstrong, "Capabilities and Intentions," p.47.

21 Metcalf, "Why Did The Defense of Quang Tri Province, SVN Collapse," pp.1–4.

22 Kroesen, "Quang Tri, The Lost Province," pp.3–4.

23 Sorley, *The Abrams Tapes*, pp.729–30.

24 Kroesen, "Quang Tri, The Lost Province" p.6.

25 Summers, *On Strategy*, p.138.

26 Kroesen, "Quang Tri, The Lost Province," p.2.

27 *Ibid.*, p.10.

28 *Ibid.*, p.16.

29 Sorley, *The Vietnam War*, pp.610–11.

30 Richard Botkin, *Ride the Thunder*, Los Angeles, CA: WND Books, 2009, pp.246–47.
31 Thi, *The Twenty-Five Year Century*, p.262.
32 Armstrong, "Capabilities and Intentions," p.47.
33 Sorley, *The Abrams Tapes,* p.811.
34 Andrade, *America's Last Vietnam Battle*, p.40.

Chapter 21

1   Stephen Randolph, "Foreign Policy and the Complexities of Corruption: The Case of South Vietnam," https://www.afsa.org/foreign-policy-and-complexities-corruption-case-south-vietnam, January 22, 2020.
2   Chuck Springston, "Colin Powell's Vietnam and the Making of an American Statesman," https://www.historynet.com/colin-powell-vietnam-making-american-statesmen.htm retrieved January 22, 2020 (also published in August 2016 in *Vietnam* magazine).
3   Stanley Karnow, *Vietnam, A History*, New York, NY: Penguin Books, 1997, p.655.
4   Michael G. Kort, *The Vietnam War Reexamined*, New York, NY: Cambridge University Press, 2018, p.189 (quoting from Turley, *The Second Indochina War*, p.186).
5   Palmer, "Studies in Intelligence," p.93.
6   Albracht and Worf, *Abandoned in Hell*, p.188.
7   Davidson, *Vietnam at War*, p.681.
8   Palmer, "Studies in Intelligence," p.93.
9   Pribbenow, *Victory in Vietnam*, p.264
10 Starry, *Armored Combat in Vietnam,* p.201.
11 Webb and Poole, *JCS*, pp.157–58.
12 Hammond, *Reporting Vietnam*, p.254.
13 *Ibid.*, p.256.
14 *Ibid.*, p.267.
15 *Ibid.*, p.269.
16 McKenna, *Kontum*, p.90.
17 FRAC *Command History* 1972–1973, p.16.
18 Ha, *Steel and Blood*, p.125.
19 Andrade, *America's Last Vietnam Battle*, p.102.
20 Andrade, *America's Last Vietnam Battle*, 102.
21 Nelson and Arnold, *US Marines in Vietnam, 1971–1973*, p.71.
22 Sorley, *A Better War*, pp.186–87.
23 Thi, *The Twenty-Five Year Century*, p.274.
24 Thi, *The Twenty-Five Year Century*, p.273.
25 Ha, *Steel and Blood*, p.127.
26 FRAC *Command History* 1972–1973, p.16.

Chapter 22

1   William Lloyd Stearman, *An American Adventure*, Annapolis, MD: Naval Institute Press, 2012, p.185.
2   Email with Dr. William Stearman and the author, March 25, 2019.
3   Pike, *People's Army of Vietnam*, p.229.
4   Geoffrey Perret, *There's a War to be Won*, New York: Random House 1991, pp.398–99.
5   Turley, *The Easter Offensive*, p.26.

6   Palmer, *The 25-Year War*, p.118.
7   Sorley, *The Vietnam War*, p.154.
8   Kroesen, "The Lost Province," p.2.
9   *Ibid.*, p.2.
10 Hammond, *Reporting Vietnam*, p.265–66.
11 Kroesen, "The Lost Province," p.5.
12 Lewis Sorley, *Thunderbolt*, Bloomington, IN: Indiana University Press, 2008, p.299.
13 Kroesen, "The Lost Province," p.4.
14 *Ibid.*, 7.
15 Thi, *The Twenty-Five Year Century*, pp.252–55.
16 Sorley, *The Abrams Tapes*, p.805.
17 *Ibid.*, p.729.
18 Lieutenant General Michael T. Flynn, *The Field of Fight*, New York, NY: St. Martin's Press, 2016, p.31 (hereafter cited as Flynn, *Field of Fight*).
19 *Ibid.*, p.33.
20 *Ibid.*, p.34.
21 *Ibid.*, p.45.
22 Janos Radvanyi, *Delusion and Reality: Gambits, Hoaxes, & Diplomatic One-Upmanship in Vietnam*, South Bend IN: Gateway Editions, Limited, p.251.
23 Karnow, *Vietnam: A History*, p.672.
24 Thompson and Frizzell, *The Lessons of Vietnam*, p.226.
25 Randolph, *Powerful and Brutal Weapons*, p.133.
26 George J. Veith, *Black April: The Fall of South Vietnam 1973–1975*, New York, NY: Encounter Books, 2013, pp.124–25.

Chapter 23

1   Appendix 2 to Annex H, page H-2-10, APPENDIX 5 (8th Radio Research Field Station) to Annex G to USARV/MACV SUPCOM After Action Report, 1070614001C. X-Day (Ceasefire) was on January 28, 1973 at 0800L (midnight January 27, 1973, GMT/Zulu time).
2   Vietnam Center and Archive at Texas Tech (Item Number: 1070312026, Record Number: 74157, Title: Correspondence Between Jeffrey J. Clarke and Walter R. Baker: 571st MI Detachment).
3   Sedgwick Tourison, "Military Intelligence in Southeast Asia, 1970–1975" Vietnam Center and Archive, Texas Tech University, presented on April 18, 1996.
4   Thomas E. Ricks, *The Generals: American Military Command from World War II to Today*, New York, NY: Penguin Press, 2013, p.327.
5   Flynn, *Field of Fight*, p.33.

Appendix 3

1   August 3, 1995, *The Wall Street Journal.*

Appendix 7

1   March 29, 1972 (just prior to hostilities). The 316th NVA Division remained in Laos.
2   270th IIR left via HCM Trail for 711th NVA Division.
3   In late 1972, the 365th redeployed into North Vietnam.

Index

Index